LINGUISTICS AND
LITERARY THEORY

LINGUISTICS AND LITERARY THEORY

KARL D. UITTI

W·W·NORTON & COMPANY·INC·

NEW YORK

FOREWORD

What is the purpose of humanistic scholarship? What, in fact, does the humanist scholar do?

The job of the humanist scholar is to organize our huge inheritance of culture, to make the past available to the present, to make the whole of civilization available to men who necessarily live in one small corner for one little stretch of time, and finally to judge, as a critic, the actions of the present by the experience of the past.

The humanist's task is to clear away the obstacles to our understanding of the past, to make our whole cultural heritage—primitive, pre-Columbian, African, Asian, aboriginal, Near Eastern, classical, medieval, European, American, contemporary, and all the rest—accessible to us. He must sift the whole of man's culture again and again, reassessing, reinterpreting, rediscovering, translating into a modern idiom, making available the materials and the blueprints with which his contemporaries can build their own culture, bringing to the center of the stage that which a past generation has judged irrelevant but which is now again usable, sending into storage that which has become, for the moment, too familiar and too habitual to stir our imagination, preserving it for a posterity to which it will once more seem fresh.

The humanist does all this by the exercise of exact scholarship. He must have the erudition of the historian, the critical abilities of the philosopher, the objectivity of the scientist, and the imagination of all three. The scholar who studies the history of science, for example, must combine a knowledge of languages, history, and philosophy with the knowledge of a scientist. And so on with the scholars who study music, art, religion, literature, and all the rest.

The job is, obviously, impossible for any man; and the humanist scholar, knowing he can never attain his true goal, is always tempted to run after wooden idols whose cults are less exacting and which proffer an easy bliss.

Sometimes the humanist is tempted to bypass the rigorous training of the scholar and to wrap himself in the cloak of the sophist. Then he lapses into a painful wooliness and becomes the "literary" sort of humanist whose only accomplishment is a style which achieves the appearance of sublimity at the cost of an actual inanity. His opposite number is the hardheaded humanist who reacts against empty loftiness by becoming a pedant: he devotes himself to antiquarian detail no less trivial than the banalities of some social science or the mere collecting spirit which is sometimes found in the natural sciences. "Physical science can be at least as trivial as any other form of inquiry: but this is less obvious to the outsider because the triviality is concealed in the decent obscurity of a learned language."

Given the magnitude of his task and the impossibility of total perfection, the humanist scholar must, of course, specialize and his works will often be esoteric. But the belief persists that somehow specialization must be converted to generalization if the humanist scholar is to complete his job. Humanist scholars have not solved the problems of excessive specialization and must share the blame for that catastrophe of communication which besets modern learning.

Humanist scholars have been accused of being overly genteel, contemptuous of popular culture, snobbish and antidemocratic after the fashion of their aristocratic Renaissance progenitors, backward looking, hostile to the present, fearful of the future, ignorantly petulant about science, technology, and the Industrial Revolution—"natural Luddites." "It is a sad thought indeed that our civilization has not produced a *New Vision*," a modern technologist complains, "which could guide us into the new 'Golden Age' which has now become physically possible, but only physically. . . . Who is responsible for this tragi-comedy of Man frustrated by success? . . . Who has left Mankind without a vision? The predictable part of the future may be a job for electronic predictors but the part of it which is not predictable, which is largely a matter of free human choice, is not the business of the machines, nor of scientists . . . but it ought to be, as it was in the great epochs of the past, the prerogative of the inspired humanists." (Dennis Gabor, "Inventing the Future," *Encounter,* May 1960, p. 15.)

Scholars in the humanities may modestly reject the suggestion that they can ever be the inspired prophets of a new age. But their scholarship is essential to enable us to distinguish the inspired prophets from the fanatical Pied Pipers.

In planning the Princeton Studies of Humanistic Scholarship in America, we determined from the outset to have a volume on linguistics.

Linguistics, as Professor Uitti makes clear, is an ancient subject. But its formal recognition as a distinct discipline is relatively recent; moreover, only in recent times have linguistic scholars achieved an influence and a visibility in the scholarly community comparable to that of the literary critics and the literary historians. Linguistics appears on the university horizon as one of the new subjects. And as Professor Uitti makes clear, the study of linguistics in America is one of those subjects, like art history, that benefited enormously from the influx of European refugee scholars, which began in the third decade of the present century.

In the process of becoming a scholar in his own right, the linguist divorced himself from the historians of literature and of culture and from the literary critics, and he became a specialist. As Professor Uitti says, "By definition, specialization tends to be exclusivist. . . . Exclusivism, in linguistic study, has been a matter of general assumption as well as technique. The linguistic disciplines generated a momentum of their own which, over time, contributed much to characterize the 'language' they studied." The results of this development can be seen in Professor Uitti's book. Of all the Princeton Studies, this, I think, is the one most difficult for the general reader to comprehend. And by a subtle irony, the student of language and communication has, because of the present state of his discipline, the hardest job of communicating!

But the reader who will patiently read and reread Professor Uitti will get a full sense of the exciting and basic intellectual achievements that the linguistic scholars have given us in recent decades.

RICHARD SCHLATTER
General Editor

PREFACE

Although we live in an age of intense specialization, we should not lose sight of the fact that many scholars in different fields are interested in related problems. The series of works of which the present volume and study are a part will eventually cover the range of recent humanistic scholarship in America. "Humanism" and "scholarship" are two unifying factors here; they quite properly claim the attention of numerous specialists, students, and educated men and women who represent widely differing intellectual persuasions but who share a concern for humane learning as it is practiced in this country. This series of studies is designed, one suspects, to remind us just what it is our particular disciplines share with the others represented in the series. As we proceed, we should find ourselves, not in terra incognita, but in a relatively familiar landscape with perhaps a few exotic touches here and there to add a little color. And when developments in fields other than our own seem to show some particular originality, we should be tempted to ask what this new viewpoint or method can do for us.

The following report deals with "linguistics" and "literary theory," already a hybrid subject. The problems are not presented from a specialist's point of view. The study is directed to informed and interested readers working mainly in other disciplines, although to a certain degree it is addressed as well to eventual "literary" or "linguist" readers. In conformity with the general purpose of the series, I concentrate on contemporary American research—its characteristic outlooks, successes, and weaknesses. However, a few preliminary words of explanation will be useful, since the scope of my report differs considerably from that of companion studies in this series.

The basic fact remains that, today, linguistics and literary study enjoy separate status as two independent branches of learning. This has not always been the case. Modern literature, its study, as well as the linguistic sciences are humane activities possessing deep roots in the past, and they are intensely cosmopolitan. Unless we take cognizance of certain cultural and philosophical traditions, and unless we consider the American points of view in conjunction with given European trends, we risk falsifying the issues. We should, for example, be forced to present linguistics and literary scholarship as two distinct—and even opposed—fields when the lessons of the past and when present tendencies run counter to such an appreciation. I have therefore decided to examine certain basic features of the Western concept of language in Chapter 1 of my study. Chapter 2 deals with linguistics and literary study as practiced in this country (and abroad) in recent years. In Chapter 3, I offer a number of suggestions concerning increased collaboration between the two fields.

Throughout this study the terms *linguistics* and *literature* will be defined and redefined. After some hesitation I have decided on the title *Linguistics and Literary Theory*. I wish to avoid from the start the simplistic notion that *linguistics* signifies a technique, a pure method, while *literature* means some kind of textual *corpus.* The fact is that *literature* implies a method (or a number of possible methods) too—hence my preference for *literary theory,* a fashionable nomer today— and *linguistics,* as frequently practiced over the past century-and-a-half, just as surely calls to mind a "material," an object of study. My purpose therefore cannot be merely to apply one method to a different, though related, material; that would be too easy (and wrong). Rather I shall have to examine the interaction of several methods, the classification of various materials, and the status of both methods and materials, a far more delicate job. We shall see that an impressive group of contemporary American scholars have navigated these treacherous waters with a far greater skill than many have received credit for.

Several acknowledgments are in order. Part of the time provided by the generosity of the John Simon Guggenheim Memorial Foundation in 1964 was spent in preparing this study. My thanks go to the Foundation for this opportunity. I should also like to thank a number of friends whose careful reading of certain portions of this work has been invaluable to me: Professor Enrique Tierno Galván, of Madrid and Princeton University; Professor Claudio Guillén, of the University of California (San Diego); Professor Frank Bowman, of the University of Pennsylvania; and Professor Peter F. Dembowski, of the University of Chicago.

Finally, I wish to dedicate the following pages to three colleagues, distinguished scholars and men of letters, whose teaching careers are coming to a close. Their work and their humane learning will long be remembered by students of French literature and language in this country. I wish Professor Alfred Foulet (Princeton), Professor Henri Peyre (Yale), and Professor Ira O. Wade (Princeton) a joyous and a profitable retirement.

KARL D. UITTI

CONTENTS

xv

LANGUAGE, THOUGHT, AND CULTURE

The Foundation

Since remotest antiquity Western man has been concerned in systematic ways with a general theory of language and consistently has established more or less distinct, though related, categories of "linguistic" analysis in terms of given religious, metaphysical, or cultural assumptions. Theories of language have necessarily implied theories of language study ("grammar," "linguistics"), and such theoretical speculation has consistently taken stock of cultural contingencies as well as of philosophical perspective. Specific sets or constructs of theory are thus related to matters as general and as pervasive as dominant world-view or, by the same token, to rather more specialized activities such as dramaturgy, speech-making, grammatical analysis, or syllogistic thought. It is well-known that Greco-Roman speculation on language evolved extremely nuanced, though constantly shifting and interrelated, doctrines of grammar, rhetoric, poetics, and dialectic. Both Plato and Aristotle—not to mention the pre-Socratics, numerous stoic philosophers, and the rhetorical sophists—indulged in such speculation and, though substantially unlike one another in various ways, shared a manner of stating problems that has been highly influential upon subsequent periods.

I

The diffusion of ancient linguistic speculation throughout the Mediterranean world and its reconciliation with the new world-view of Christianity have been the object of considerable historical research. The legacy of antiquity in medieval Europe is undeniable. We know that whatever of linguistic speculation and lore was preserved by Augustine and the Fathers, and what was lost—as well as the very process of transmission to the European Middle Ages—provide significant clues for the understanding of the makeup of the Western mentality. It is therefore useful to speak of this mentality in terms of a "historical structure," i.e., as a series of possibilities worked out over time by thinkers and writers. Conscious of its cultural past, the Middle Ages understood language, as manifested in literature, philosophical speculation, or scripture, in relation to various theoretical systems of permanent values and procedures transmitted from generation to generation in the form of authoritative traditions (*traditio*). Yet, in keeping with the very dynamism of this past, the Middle Ages recognized that these traditions required unending adjustments to meet the exigencies of new theoretical understanding and practical activity.

Literary history exemplifies this process of adjustment. The finite, static world-view implied in pagan thought supported rhetorical or stylistic frameworks in literature that resulted in hierarchical deployments of expressive devices. Thus, the noble or grave style was devised in order to express suitably an inherently grave subject-matter. The notion of stylistic hierarchy was retained by Augustine (*De doctrina christiana,* IV), but, in line with the Christian view of the dignity of all Creation, the high style came to be identified more closely with the effect the orator wished to produce on his audience. The ostensible subject-matter itself counted for less than previously. To cite Augustine's examples, the Christian theme of virginity could be spoken of in the moderate style and the theme of ladies' cosmetics dealt with in the high style. This change in emphasis did much to further, during the Middle Ages, the creation of a new, vernacular noble style, both like and unlike the grave style, say, of Vergil's *Æneid*. Historically, this new noble style was formed on the basis of the very lowbrow Christian *sermo humilis* (see Erich Auerbach, *Literatursprache und Publikum in der lateinischen Spätantike und im Mittelalter* [Bern, 1958] English translation, Pantheon, 1965). Thus, the Middle Ages at once preserved the static framework of ancient literary theory and created a new set of operating principles that kept up with changed metaphysical and practical conditions. In a sense Chrétien de Troyes "imitates" or "reproduces" Vergil; he certainly identifies his own France with ancient Rome and Greece.[1]

The development of medieval speculative philosophy, especially in its elaboration of logic, illustrates still another kind of adjustment. The literary culture inherited from antiquity and developed in the eleventh- and twelfth-century schools presented a number of barriers to the proper formula-

1. I refer here to the topos of *translatio studii,* as contained in a well-known passage of *Cligés* (ll. 25 ff.) in which Chrétien tells of the birth of *chevalerie* ("culture") in Greece, its removal to Rome, and final arrival in France. Alcuin, Bernard of Chartres, and others, like Chrétien, saw themselves as "moderns," i.e., as different from the ancients. Though, in their view, culture had come to dwell in France, it was nevertheless because of their knowledge of the ancients that the "moderns" could aspire to know more than the ancients had known.

3

tion of the kind of logical discourse the scholastic philosophers wished to achieve. Consequently, certain philosophers emphasized features of the ancient linguistic—or "grammatical"—tradition to the exclusion of others. "Philosophy" was thus opposed to "belles-lettres" in thirteenth-century Europe, and, as we shall see below, the grammatical tradition was subjected to severe revision.

These facts suggest that linguistics and literary theory can be approached most concretely in the framework of the "historical structure" that underlies them. The notion of theory of language, as well as the very ideas of literature and linguistic science, should be related pertinently to the possibilities contained in the continuity we call Western culture. If it is true that every systematic philosophy, or world-view, contains a theory of language, it is equally true that every theory of language implies a set of philosophical perspectives, and hence even truer that a study of linguistics and literary theory must attempt to take stock, systematically, of the *kinds* of relationships obtaining between possible world-views and theories of language.

By definition, interpretative study is somewhat arbitrary. One chooses one's perspectives in the hope that they will be fruitful. With this in mind, I have chosen to consider the very real *fact* of "Western culture" as the dimension in which these kinds of relationships best lend themselves to analysis. Loose though it may be, the continuity of this "culture" allows one to point out that both the medieval logician Petrus Hispanus and Dante owe much to Aristotle as well as to show the implications of their debt for our understanding of the nature and uses of language. The same cultural continuity provides

4

referential touchstones that permit one to differentiate between the "modern" attitudes toward the phenomena of language and the attitudes that antedate modernity. The medieval logicians are close to modern linguistic philosophers, yet they are also worlds apart. Modern poetic theory tends to conceive of language in ways highly reminiscent of Plato, but the differences are perhaps even more significant. What do the ancient grammarian Priscian and the twentieth-century linguist have in common? Where do they diverge? How do the modern "linguist" and "literary critic"—assuming there are such beings—differ and to what extent should they join in a common cause? Finally, and perhaps fundamentally, any understanding of the possibilities exploited by our predecessors that should emerge from this study will, it is hoped, contribute to our recognizing legitimate complexities that surround the problem of language and literature by dispelling certain trivialities and prejudices.

I shall discuss the modernist view of language and the various disciplinary ramifications—literary and linguistic—of this view in the second section of this introductory chapter. Preliminary study of the fundamentals of our subject-matter is essential. The present section will deal with these fundamentals.

Before examining the premodern tradition in general and, in particular, the kinds of activity related to grammatical study in antiquity and the Middle Ages, I shall discuss certain writings of Plato and Aristotle. These two systematic philosophers offer a convenient, and useful, point of departure. Neither was concerned primarily with language or literature as such. Yet both wrote on language, and, in different cultural and temporal contexts, what they stated assumes new relevance and import. Plato was the first major theorist of what may be called the symbolic view of language; Aristotle, the principal representative of the opposed—but in some senses complementary—doctrine of language as analytic instrumentality. Both these theories, as we shall see, also generated a way of looking at, or studying, linguistic phenomena. Their influence was—and remains—great.

Plato and Aristotle. Plato's *Cratylus* takes up the old debate whether names are "natural" or "conventional," whether "there is a truth or correctness in them, which is the same for Hellenes as for barbarians" (p. 323),[2] or whether, in fact, meanings are but a matter of "convention and agreement." Arguing that names are determined by usage, Hermogenes notes that "Hellenes differ from barbarians in their use of names, and the several Hellenic tribes from one another" (p.

2. The following discussion of Plato is based on the *Cratylus,* since, of his works, this dialogue treats the problem of language in the most characteristically Platonic way. Obviously, the present study cannot deal exhaustively with the question of "Plato and language." I attempt only to present certain fundamental aspects of that question. The *Cratylus* thus offers a convenient point of departure, no more. Since Plato's *manner of stating* is directly connected to what he states and, of course, since this "connection" implies a theory of language, an analysis of the *Cratylus*—its arguments, its structure, and its ironies—provides an almost graphic illustration of Plato's views. Quotations from the *Cratylus* will be taken from the translation by Benjamin Jowett, *The Dialogues of Plato, I,* 3rd edition (Oxford, 1892); indications of pagination refer to this work. The discussion of Aristotle, below, is based on the *Organon,* tr. by O. F. Owen, I–II (London, 1889); *The Art of Rhetoric,* tr. by J. H. Freese, Loeb Classics (London and Cambridge, Mass., 1926); *The Metaphysics,* tr. by Richard Hope (Ann Arbor, 1960); and *The Poetics,* tr. by S. H. Butcher, 4th ed. (London, 1922).

325). The problem of linguistic pluralism is thus faced, but only to be dismissed. Socrates holds that the "business of a name . . . is to express the nature" of the thing. Protagoras is wrong, as are those sophists and rhetoricians who argue "that man is the measure of all things, and that things are as they appear to me, and that they are to you as they appear to you" (p. 326). Socrates insists upon separating the true from the false; things possess an inherently stable nature, as do actions. Since speaking is an activity, naming must possess its own nature and norms. He reasons analogically: the name is an instrument, a means, with which we learn and distinguish things, just as a shuttle is a means with which we manufacture garments. Naming should be done by people who know how, who are capable of impressing upon the syllables of the name the essential form of the thing or action to be expressed. The judge of semantic adequacy, however, is not the legislator— the namer—but the philosopher, the *dialektikós*. The dialogue takes an etymological turn. Socrates examines the names of heroes and of gods in order to discover links between these names and the essences of the beings named. Unlike modern etymology, Platonic etymology concentrates on such links; form for form's own sake is irrelevant, since the results of etymological investigation must lead to the essential reality of the things expressed by the word.[3] Virtually two-thirds of the dialogue is given over to etymology. That fact alone suffices to show Plato's viewpoint. Yet, one is tempted to re-

3. According to Socrates, "the etymologist is not put out . . . by the change of all the letters, for this need not interfere with the meaning" (Jowett, p. 336). By and large, antiquity and the Middle Ages retained and utilized this view of etymology.

mark, etymology *proves* nothing; it merely *illustrates*. Plato designs such illustration to be a superior kind of "proof"; it *emblematizes*. As Socrates' etymological elucubrations become more and more conjectural, his interlocutor breaks in—very significantly—to note the inspired passion with which he speaks. Later, Cratylus himself is led to affirm that "a power more than human gave things their first names" (p. 386). Socrates sidesteps that remark. Yet, in centuries to follow, his notion of "truth" will be interpreted as being the result of divine power or will be correlated with other absolutes of one kind or another.[4]

A kind of critical analysis follows these statements of principle. If a thing—or word or proposition—is true, all its parts must be true too. Thus, Socrates endeavors to show truth in the elements—sounds and syllables—that make up words: *r* stands for movement, certain aspirates show intangibility, and so forth; Socrates elaborates a complex essay in sound symbolism. This is the core that expresses his notion of the symbolic character of language. Meanwhile, Cratylus declares his approval of Socrates' argument, but insists that no words may be false or even only partly true, since unless words are true they are at best non-words. Words imitate things, but how? Cratylus holds that either they do imitate things or they do not, there is no middle ground between these extremes.

At this point the dialectic involving Socrates and Cratylus becomes interesting in its own right. What Plato argues is, in

---

4. For a discussion of such absolutes in connection with the Gospel use of *Verbum* and its stoic counterparts, see E. M. Sidebottom, *The Christ of the Fourth Gospel, in the Light of First-Century Thought* (London, 1961), especially chap. iii, "The Logos and God."

fact, what the dialectic—or dialogue—presents.
sense, one suspects, may be conveniently ident
with Socrates nor with Cratylus entirely; what
way their arguments interlock.[5] A word may be i
someone, usually the namegiver himself, neglect... attributes a name whose characteristics stand for one object or action to a different object or action. Or a name may be inexact
when the imitation is too close; the perfect name would be a
copy of the object imitated. The perfect imitation of Cratylus
would be a (verbal) rival to Cratylus himself, an impossible
artifact. Therefore, Socrates cannot be so exigent as Cratylus;
he must accept the fact that in practice words are more or less
suitable, truer or more false. He seems to fall back on the rhetorical—or sophistic—doctrines of his day. Exactness of
names is a function, *in practice,* determinable by appeal to usage and homology: "How can you ever imagine, my good
friend, that you will find names resembling every individual
number, unless you allow that which you term convention
and agreement to have authority in determining the correctness of names?" (p. 382). The mockery Socrates consistently
makes of the sophists cannot allow us to take him seriously
except in the context of his discussion with Cratylus; his very
ambivalence is fruitful, since it justifies what will later become
the grammatical tradition. Now then, Cratylus holds that
words not only designate true things but also render our
search for and discovery of truth possible. To which Socrates

5. Were one in fact to list, consecutively, Socrates' arguments as
they appear in *Cratylus,* they would contradict one another. The
work's form is essentially dialogic: there is perfect continuity and
interaction of structure, language, and thought.

ounters by asking why the first man to give names to things did not discover the truth. Cratylus favors the theory that names possess divine power, that meanings were stabilized by the gods. But Socrates claims that names should hardly be so mixed up as they are if the gods had in fact stabilized them. No, the true criterion of the exactness of names must not be sought in the names themselves but rather in things. Furthermore, the search for truth must always be referred to things, not their names. Thus, Socrates rejects Heraclitus' view that all things are in a state of motion and flux: "No man of sense will like to put himself or the education of his mind in the power of names: neither will he so far trust names or the givers of names as to be confident in any knowledge which condemns himself and other existences to an unhealthy state of unreality; he will not believe that all things leak like a pot, or imagine that the world is a man who has a running at the nose" (p. 388). But Cratylus speaks his mind in rejoinder: "The result of a great deal of trouble and consideration is that I incline to Heraclitus." The dialogue ends inconclusively, as Platonic dialogues tend to do, generically, so to speak. Socrates' affirmation is met by—and crossed with—Cratylus' doubt.

Plato's position is absolutist, but his absolutism is translated into dialogic form, which makes it difficult to pin down analytically. Ultimate reality—itself definable as that which is permanent—exists outside of names, which are, of course, imitations of things. The ideal is monolithic. But underlying all of Plato's writing is the practical understanding that our grasp of the truth of the monolithic ideal depends on the ways we operate, on our discursive procedures. Socrates is Plato's mouthpiece to the extent that he translates this basic insight into the context of the dialogue's give-and-take. He mocks Hermogenes' relativism in the name of rigorous truth, but attacks Cratylus' intransigence in the name of procedure. Socrates asks: "But how would you [you or I or the next man] expect to know them [i.e., things, without names]?" In short, it is by being conscious of the historical and formal limitations of language that one may better use language in the discovery of truth. The dialogue itself illustrates Plato's doctrine; Socrates' discourse interacts with the replies of his interlocutors in a linguistic act, a speech situation, that imparts sense and relevance to the positions taken. Thus, Cratylus' espousal of Heraclitus' theory of the eternal flux of reality is shown to be what prevents him from accepting Socrates' idealistic stance and procedural technique. Truth is; there is no problem. The problem lies in our accepting truth for what it is and the implications of this acceptance. As Plato puts it in the *Republic:* "Words are more plastic than wax." On the one hand words are informed by the symbolic processes and structures that accrue to them as the representatives of things (and ideas), but on the other hand they in turn inform our discourse and can be communicatively effective when properly used by the philosopher. Words are both counters and, if one wills, the tangible side of thought processes in action.

The modern reader may be tempted to find Plato ambiguous or paradoxical. But the contradictions in the *Cratylus* are in fact resolved when one takes the trouble to render their contexts explicit. Though the ambiguities may not be easily cleared away—such a dismissal is beside the point—they lend themselves to consequential interpretation. The essential finiteness of Plato's view does not prevent his being either comprehensive or, for that matter, remarkably analytic. Without being "ideal," language fits into the scheme of Plato's idealism; his abstractions are clothed in the flesh of real situations. Plato does not speak of "language" and "literature," of true versus fictional discourse, or of linguistic structures—real or supposed—as contrasted with, say, linguistic invention. To be sure, elsewhere Plato rails against the poets who have the temerity to pit their works against the ultimate reality of the ideal. They take their compositions to be the duplicate of things, like Socrates' hypothetically "perfect" imitation of Cratylus, and since fools believe them, they must be banished from the Republic. In a sense the poets take linguistic symbolism far too seriously and, thus, are politically corrupting. By the same token Socrates rejects the sophistic rhetors who place their trust in words but who, as the dialogue *Cratylus* points out, do not back up this trust with a clear and true philosophy, i.e., a metaphysics. The "false speech" remains false, the worst form of corruption, since, though truth is not language, one must seek to serve truth *in* language.

Plato is the first and greatest exponent of the monolithic–absolutist view of language. This view posits an overriding and ineffable quality or governing principle that can be approached, in practice, by men who are aware of it and who are willing to seek out the phenomenological correlates that constitute evidence of its power. Platonic dialectic reproduces what may be called an essentially emblematic process. This process takes place because, in reality, Plato's system of knowledge ignores transcendence. It is tautological.

The monolithic–absolutist view of language leads to what we may call the creativity principle. Or, in other words, what is often called "creativity" today harks back to Plato's concern. What separates Plato from his modernist counterparts, however, is the metaphysical context that pervades and, in fact, envelops his linguistic theory. Plato's metaphysics underlies all aspects of his thought as well as his expression, whereas the metaphysical elements of a Wilhelm von Humboldt, for example, are perhaps better viewed as subordinated to a methodology. As we shall see in due course, the fundamental, qualitative difference separating modern from premodern thought concerning language lies in the importance modernity concedes to the mediating influence of the specialized discipline: the "science of language" stands between man and expression. The germ of the modern creativity principle is nevertheless fully present in the *Cratylus,* since, in reasoning on language, Plato's protagonists are in a sense reasoning "on" nothing. What they say in contradistinction to one another creates their subject-matter. Plato's tautological metaphysics causes language to be entirely historical, i.e., factual. Thus, Socrates is understandably proscriptive. He seeks to channel as well as to correct what his interlocutors state; but his own "corrections" remain in and of themselves—as well as within the framework of the dialogue—a body of statements that exemplify what language is. The ontological status of language depends therefore on the meaningfulness of statements; meanings range from false to true, and include intermediary stages. The nature of language itself—not only that of discourse—is symbolic. Over time the human mind "improves" itself; that is, it bequeathes a record of its achievements symbolized—incarnated—in the discourse that has been preserved. To the extent that poets are *truly* meaningful, their works constitute philosophy. This poetic creativity is essentially qualitative, however, as Socrates remarks to Cratylus when the latter objects that if names are not true they cannot be said to exist: "I believe that what you say may be true about numbers, which must be just what they are, or not be at all . . . but this does not apply to that which is qualitative [i.e., ποιός] or to anything which is represented under an image" (p. 378).

Already in Plato, then, one finds the unitary view according to which whatever concerns language is indissolubly linked to a wider structure of thought, a world-view that, in Plato's case, is idealistically absolute and essentially metaphysical. Specialties of discourse—speeches, poetry, or other generic distinctions—are invalid insofar as they tend to emphasize their peculiarities and not the common denominator of pure philosophy. Just as Plato's king must be a philosopher, so must his poet. Analysis—e.g., Socrates' etymologies—serves to exemplify, if I may be permitted the non sequitur, rather than to dissociate; the facts of language-in-history are utilized in order to clarify relationships that otherwise remain unclear or abstract. The mediation of Socrates in pointing out such proper relationships leads to the correction of Hermogenes' and Cratylus' positions. (The reader realizes that he must accept Heraclitus' philosophy if he wishes to indulge in Cratylus' brand of absolutism.) But perhaps most important of all—and this is a point readers have not always seen fit to make—the dialogue itself incarnates what it says. The example of the *Cratylus* shows that the structure of the discourse, the language of its protagonists, and their substantival enunciations fuse into a whole greater than the sum of these three elements, and that it is this form, or viewpoint, as represented by the whole that imparts sense and relevance to everything else. The *Cratylus* functions poetically; it is, if one prefers, a discipline in and of itself: it "generates," so to speak, what it means. The shape of the work is coequal to—and inseparable from—its content.

The *use* Plato makes of the equivalence of form and content in a theoretical exposition treating of the relationship between linguistic form and the reality that that form is designed to represent will be duplicated, in other genres, by certain poets. Here the "poeticalness" of the Platonic dialogue is reproduced, formally and functionally, in ostensibly poetic works. Mallarmé in particular justified poetry by stressing and connecting its cognitive and creative nature. The poet is God's rival. Form and content are one; the poet's knowledge, as embodied in his *œuvre,* is (or should be) truth. And for romantic theorists of language the essence of language itself lies precisely in the creative process of which all speech must partake and which all speech thereby exemplifies. Plato's metaphysics may be seriously modified or even rejected by his modern counterparts, but, along with his monolithic doctrine of language, his creative practice and its implications have survived and flourished.

Aristotle offers other perspectives. Both Plato and Aristotle speak of *logos,* but the latter refers principally to logic and certain congeners. Unlike Plato, Aristotle conceived of thought as the object of a special science. There is next to no ostensible reflection on the form of reasoning in Plato simply because, as we saw, form is situational, an integral part of the dialogic process, not something about which one could reason at all. However, for Aristotle, language (and its "expressions"

15

in discourse, e.g., tragedy, speeches, etc.) could be provisionally considered as an autonomous object, possessing definable characteristics and entering into describable relationships; language is the instrument of logic and discourse. Or, to put it another way, Aristotle preserves the Platonic notion of system but *in practice* splits it into the system (or workings) of the object studied and the system of the tools used for the study. Thus language itself—or given discourse—becomes a system worthy of analysis. In order to perform this analysis properly a sufficiently powerful analytic language—a methodological syntax—must be elaborated beforehand. Meanwhile, Plato's universalist bias is maintained, though in a different form.

If in Plato's *Cratylus* the boundaries between "discourse form" and "philosophy" are at best obscure, in Aristotle's *Organon* the markers separating language from logic are equally fuzzy. Discourse is as fundamental to Aristotle's thought as it is to Plato's—more so, in fact, if one gives sufficient weight to the problem of technique as dealt with by Aristotle. The workings of discourse are first analyzed by him and then made to fit the rational scheme of the logical syllogism or the persuasive scheme of the rhetorical enthymeme. Aristotle proceeds by defining the meanings of words (i.e., expressing their "core," or denotative value), then by going on to make distinctions involving classes of reality, and finally by making axiomatic assumptions. Like Plato, Aristotle believes in a metaphysical truth: words represent intelligible objects, actions, or ideas which may be known. Definitions apply to things, not only to names. Definitions lead to the establishment of categories—universals—which themselves permit further analysis when properly linked syntactically (*Cate-*

gories, i-ii). Alone, the categories refer to incomplex things (substance, quality, quantity, relation, etc.). "A man runs" is complex; "man" and "runs" are incomplex.

In the second chapter of the *Categories* Aristotle deals with the logical division of things and their attributes in discourse; this is essential. All things are divided into two substantival and attribute classes: universal and singular substances, and universal and singular attributes. Some things may be affirmed *of* a subject without being *in* a subject (universals are predicable of individual subjects): "man" is predicated of a subject, i.e., of "a certain man." Others are *in* a subject, like "a certain whiteness," but are not predicated of any specific subject; all predicates, by definition, must be general, not particular. Thus "a certain whiteness" must be in a body, since color cannot be independent of a body, but the subject is not predicated in this case. Other things are at once predicated *of* a subject and *in* a subject; these are universal attributes. "Science" is *in* a subject ("a certain grammar") since it is a universal. Finally, some things—individual substances—are neither *in* a subject nor predicated *of* one, e.g., "this man," "that horse." Furthermore, when a thing is attributed to its subject, then what is affirmed of the predicate must also be affirmed of the subject: "man" is attributed to "a certain man," and "animal" is attributed to "man"; consequently, "animal" must be attributed to "a certain man," since "a certain man" is at once "man" and "animal."

Language (i.e., discourse or *logos*), things, and thought are inextricably entwined, since what allows for the relationships alluded to above is mental activity channeled through, or molded by, grammatico-logical structure. This is one of the thorniest issues in the history of philosophy, and one that has led to much debate as to whether Aristotle confused the grammatical structure of Greek with logical syntax; that is, whether his ontology remains, in fact, contingent upon Greek structure. For our purposes, these questions may be considered beside the point, since only the general implications of the interrelationships of discourse, *realia,* and thought are what concern us here primarily.

Aristotle's reasoning does not require, like Plato's in the *Cratylus,* a dialogic working-out. Metaphysical truth is identified with what may be apprehended by syllogistic—or related procedures. Contemplative silence is given a value different from that attributed to it by Plato, and is achieved by other means. Essentially, the validity of the reasoning process receives a more complete theoretical treatment than that to which this process is to be applied. Words and the things they designate are subordinated to the archetypal relationships to which they may be made to fit; we saw the variety of purposes to which "man," as counter, could be put. Aristotle's common sense has often been praised; he takes things as they come, by and large as he is able to observe them, and only after observation does he submit them to his analysis, i.e., to interpretation. Thus in the book on *Interpretation* itself, Aristotle discusses the proposition, the form of the declarative sentence, as it reflects "the passions of the soul" and whatever "falsehood and truth" are involved in the syntax of composition and division. Nor, indeed, does the form of reasoning itself necessarily possess a truly absolute character in all instances or situations. Logical forms are, of course, absolute, but other probable syllogisms—e.g., the enthymemes used in persuasive rhetoric or, for that matter, the artifices (like metaphor) used by writers of tragedies—remain possible and useful in nonmetaphysical contexts. Indeed, in a sense Aristotle's dialectic comprises various formal "approaches" that may consist in attacking and defending a specific proposition or thesis. Thus, Aristotle's "topics" constitute a formal repertory of probable principles, and elaborate the dialectic of an "applied logic." Disputation replaces dialogue.

Aristotle's justification for the treatise on *Topics* is highly revealing (*Topics,* I, ii). The treatise is useful, he says, for exercise, conversation, and philosophical science: (1) Once we possess method, we can argue more effectively on the subject at hand; (2) If we take stock of the common opinions of others, we can meet fellow men on their own terrain and not have to rely on strange-sounding arguments; (3) As for philosophical science, once we see the two sides of a question, we are better placed to separate the true from the false in each instance. Training in "applied" dialectic makes one think better, renders one more persuasive, and protects one from error. Let me reproduce here the final "advantage" of this kind of dialectic; it concerns us directly: Dialectic is applicable "to the first principles of each science [as indeed Aristotle has shown its applicability in the elaboration of dialectic itself!], since we cannot say any thing about these from the appropriate principles of a proposed science, as they are the first principles of all, but we must necessarily discuss this through probabilities in the singulars. This however is peculiar, or especially appropriate to dialectic, for being investigative, it possesses the way to the principles of all methods" (ibid.).

Whereas for Plato language-in-form—e.g., dialogic discourse—could be *revelatory* of the nature of truth, for Aristotle language is susceptible of modification in ways that make of it an *instrument* of truth. Aristotle is careful to distinguish between dialectic and philosophy in Book Gamma of his *Metaphysics* (ii): the latter leads directly to truth, the former is purely *critical*. Yet one does not become a philosopher without understanding the workings of the syllogism. Aristotle does not entirely reject Plato's ideas, but, in practice, he devotes his attention to the kinds of knowledge the application of syllogistic reasoning engenders, since, by definition, legitimate philosophy remains immune to dialectic criticism. Knowledge so engendered is, in effect, "intelligibility." Intelligibility becomes, in Aristotle, a function of rationality, and rationality in turn operates upon "things" that it must conceive of as whole, not separated into abstract forms ("ideas") and matter.

Underlying Aristotle's rationalism, then, is the principle that, to all intents and purposes, things may be conceived as being endowed with an essentially mechanistic nature. Reason, when properly applied, explains the mechanism of reality, i.e., "principle" and "causes": "there is always a mover of things moved, and the first mover is itself unmoved" (*Metaphysics,* Gamma, viii). That is, what accrues to the investigator is his apprehension of a series of coherent operations. Consequently, just as Plato's dialogue incarnates, so to speak, his philosophical viewpoint, so Aristotle's application of reason *shapes*—makes relevant—the reality upon which it exercises itself. Reason is investigative; what it shapes constitutes effective knowledge. Aristotle describes and gives value to the quality of this shaping in Book Mu of the *Metaphysics* (x), where he refutes those Platonists who negate the "effective reality" of the object of rational thought. He prizes speculative investigation and admits the reality of knowledge, and so claims that the object of this investigation cannot be deprived of "substantially real" status without the investigation itself being rendered useless: "If we do not believe in primary beings as separate and as being in the way in which particular beings are, *we undermine primary being in the way in which we wish to speak of it*" (italics mine). Science requires our seeing things a certain way; we value scientific knowledge; the conclusion is inescapable. Though the power of knowledge is general, *actual* knowing works upon singularized objects— matter; therefore, thanks to intellectual activity, matter is in a sense transformed or made into the universal, that is, "interpreted" in terms of the kinds of mechanical operations or logic reason is capable of describing.

A kind of dovetailing or mutual interdependence between the substantial reality of things and their intelligible properties underlies Aristotle's "scientific" procedure. His *Metaphysics* is designed to permit and to further scientific disciplines based on the exercise of reason. We return then to our point of departure: the importance and the nature of Aristotle's concern with language. I have tried to show Aristotle's preoccupation with syntactic form and the relationship between considerations of syntax and the essential structure of his thought, as this thought engenders meaningful and useful knowledge. With Aristotle one envisages the possibility of a type of knowledge that, while still governed by a metaphysical view, does not necessarily depend formally upon such a view at every stage. In practice, bodies of knowledge may exist

—or at least appear to exist—for their own sake. Such "independent" knowledge is converted into disciplinary "activity," which in turn engenders its own momentum. Thus, knowledge can be seen as cumulative, that is, as something to which more data can be added and into which these data may be processed. One must respect only the invariable principles of true philosophy and the needs of the specific discipline involved.

Yet Aristotle—no more than Plato—did not see fit to study language as an autonomous subject-matter. His treatment of linguistic structure remains emphatically and irreducibly linked to the main philosophical concerns or biases I have summarized. His views on language are in fact most stimulating and original when he describes what, for us, constitute the linguistic justifications that support his understanding of rational process and his appreciation of the metaphysical and social uses of that process. Yet, in a sense, Aristotle prepared the way for the later study of language by giving scientific— or disciplinary—form to a number of activities involving language which, before him, had been mostly ignored or even deprecated by systematic thinkers. Realizing that language expresses opinion ($\delta o \xi a$), Aristotle endowed both rhetoric and poetics with a new disciplinary status within the framework of his philosophically oriented methodology. Thus, whereas for Plato poetics and rhetoric stand for valuable activities only to the degree that their practitioners serve the cause of his monolithically absolutist philosophy (and its moral counterpart),[6]

6. A thorough study of Plato's "literary doctrine" is given in Paul Vicaire, *Platon, critique littéraire* (Paris, 1960); the problematics of ancient dialogue are examined in J. Andrieu, *Le Dialogue antique: structure et présentation* (Paris, 1954).

Aristotle is enabled by his methodological stance to examine and describe poetics and rhetoric as well as to determine their relevance within his equally universalist, though less absolutist, metaphysical scheme.

A word concerning Aristotle's writings on rhetoric and poetics is now pertinent. Though Aristotle's study of these disciplines—like his study of dialectic—involves close scrutiny of linguistic phenomena, he interprets these latter in terms of the needs of the disciplines examined. Thus, as we saw, problems of syntax are resolved into the larger concerns of logic (not related to questions of Greek structure), and so, by extension, technical questions of language—e.g., the operations of the figures—are subsumed into the generic purposes of rhetorical persuasion or poetic form. Aristotle has no philosophical difficulty in asserting the dignity of rhetoric. Truth may be preserved by opinion, hence it must be defended by human activity, so "if judgments are not given as they should be, it must be the speakers themselves who are responsible for the defeat" (*Rhetoric,* I, i). Rhetoric is the art of defending truth competently in discourse, whether in the forum or in the court of law; it consists in making the truth patently relevant to people who, whatever their merits, are more concerned with the business of day-to-day living than with philosophical speculation. With Aristotle, then, one observes the creation of disciplinary specialties which, in turn, are incorporated into the general philosophy that they represent on various planes of human activity. On the surface, Aristotle's view seems more fragmentary than Plato's, but such is not really the case. His teachings, though less uncompromisingly absolutist, remain unified in the metaphysical attitudes referred to above.

Poetry stands in close relation to philosophy too. Philosophy aims to know and possess the truth; the kind of knowledge whose modalities I examined leads to the truth and thereby constitutes its own end. Poetry is an activity that produces a work distinct from its agent, an *opus.* Such works aim to represent universal truth through creative transformation of the particular, that is, in effect, by concretizing the universal within an organic structure whose parts stand in a special, meaningful relationship to one another and to the whole. Works of art appeal to men through the pleasure they afford; this pleasure is of the highest sort since, in fact, it constitutes a source of truth by making men aware of truth. Aristotle, we recall, stresses not the artist but the objective work and the effect this work produces upon the spectator. One is tempted to remark that given the nondialogic structure of Aristotle's discourse, such a theory of poetic activity is necessary, whereas for Plato it would not make sense. Aristotle *observes* what he himself does not *do.* Generic structures in poetry depend on the quality of pleasure sought: comedy and tragedy are thus distinguished (e.g., *catharsis*). Compositional rules may be derived by understanding clearly the implications of the distinctive features that characterize the various genres.

The relationship of rhetoric and poetics to truth and the functions Aristotle attributes to these activities in his studies of their properties underlie and inform all his technical remarks. The metaphor is a case in point. Aristotle describes metaphor in chapters xxi and xxii of the *Poetics;* he does so analytically and functionally, in terms of the attributes of the figure and its generic uses. More important, he states his love of the metaphoric style, which, he says, is the property of a "rich nature," since the discovery of suitable metaphors implies the poet's capacity to "perceive relationships." Formal attributes, then, and function make up the figure called metaphor. Technically, what a metaphor does determines what it is. On a higher level of analysis, however, the workings of metaphor illustrate—indeed exemplify—intellectual process in discourse. Thus, throughout Book III of the *Rhetoric,* Aristotle praises metaphor because, when properly used, it provides for a rapid conceptualization of relationships, a nonlinear demonstration. Through metaphor the dynamic relationships in nature may be conceived and conveyed in discourse with the smallest deformation; the concrete retains its concreteness and yet functions as imitating the universal.

Aristotle's treatment of metaphor is therefore extended in two directions: (1) the description of purely formal attributes that, as practiced by countless compilers of handbooks, will lead to the view of "style" as static ornamentation; and (2) the deeper functional view of metaphor that, in describing how metaphor works in specific cases, shows the true instrumentality of discourse in its mediate role between being and philosophical knowledge in expression. Does not metaphor in fact translate—both actually and symbolically—the way gifted men conceive the "pure act," which for Aristotle meant the identity of thought and matter? In these latter considerations at any rate Aristotle clearly joins his master Plato and the best traditions of Greek thought, since he has chosen to reconcile technical questions with philosophical concern. But modern readers cannot afford to denigrate Aristotle's impressive scientific—or purely descriptive—achievement. By valuing knowledge and by stressing methods suitable to the acquisition of knowledge in the domain of language, Aristotle has set the tone for all subsequent research. Because Aristotle emphasized so overtly the necessary connection between knowledgeable understanding and general philosophic view, later investigators have sometimes proclaimed their anti-Aristotelianism by naïvely holding that such connections might well be spurious. A rereading of Aristotle does much to convince one that a philosophical underpinning governs the work of all linguistic scientists and literary analysts, be they systematic, impressionistic, or pragmatic. It behooves us all to be as fully aware as possible of our viewpoint and its implications.

Grammar and Premodernity. During the two millennia intervening between Plato and Aristotle and the early modernity of late Renaissance and Baroque Europe, men were conscious of an endless dialectic between cultural continuity and historical change. The Platonic and Aristotelian principles discussed above underwent important situational modifications. A literary tradition evolved in which this dialectic of continuity and change itself acquired a fundamental stability which in turn welcomed and incorporated creative innovation by utilizing it to perpetuate its own dynamism. Dante saw himself as Vergil's pupil and colleague, but he also considered himself as having progressed beyond the kind of experience available to Vergil. Similarly, the scholastics' "improvement" upon Priscian's grammar depends on that grammar—and the tradition through which it reached them—and on their own interpretation of Aristotle.

Although the main lines of the Western cultural expansion are familiar, brief recapitulation at this point is pertinent. Greek learning or literary art—however we wish to label it;

Chrétien de Troyes spoke of *chevalerie*—was assimilated and given new focus by Rome, whence it spread, thanks to the Latin language, to North Africa, Iberia, Gaul, Britain, Italy, and the Balkans. The Christianization of the Empire implied, as well, the eventual desecularization of this literary culture and its fusion with Hebraic tradition (from St. Augustine to St. Isidore of Seville and Bede). The political disintegration of Rome and the temporary eclipse of centralized cultural activity in the West permitted the rise of new vernacular languages. These vernaculars were increasingly tied to new European political centers of gravity, though a thoroughly transformed Latin tradition, based on the modes of antiquity, continued to grow in importance, first in marginal lands, then, finally, in new power centers. No single Romance text, no matter how early or how humble, can be said to be free of learned—i.e., Latin—"influence." Yet writing in Latin shrank in generic volume as literary composition in the vernaculars grew in importance. As French, Provençal, Castilian, and Italian expanded, they incorporated more and more of those linguistico-cultural values that, previously, had been the preserve of Latin. The cultural state, which had been bilingual in ancient Rome, where all educated men knew Latin and Greek, became "bilingual" again, with Latin opposed to one or more vernaculars. (Because of Church influence, non-Romance areas, like England and Germany, underwent a parallel experience.) Yet the bilingualism of medieval Europe was fundamentally unlike that of antiquity in that whereas Greek borrowed little from Latin, the Latinization of the European vernaculars led to a total revision of Latin. To be sure Latin continued to be used in chanceries and in the Church; it remained a literary vehicle too. But, as the new national tongues widened their cultural rôle, Latin became increasingly specialized as the ideal vehicle of the new speculative philosophy—as the regimented language of pure thought.

Concomitantly with their expansion as cultural vehicles, the several European vernaculars underwent serious modification. Modern French and Spanish are different in scope from tenth-century *francien* or the eleventh-century folk-speech of northern Castile. Furthermore, each has outdistanced its medieval literary rivals, Provençal and Galician. They acquired new, complex levels of usage and of social acceptance, which, in turn, resemble the broadest Latin usage of the Augustan Age. Given the history of the modern vernaculars, however, their stylistic differentiations could never be maintained for long periods of time with anything like the consistency of the distinctions observed in Latin letters.

A sense of the premodernist cultural context and its relevance to our subject-matter may be grasped by reviewing the traditions of disciplinary activity associated with "grammar" from post-Aristotelian antiquity down to the dawn of modernity. Such a review provides a graphic illustration of the cultural tradition just described and, in conjunction with what was previously said concerning Plato and Aristotle, completes our picture of the historical basis upon which linguistic and literary study rests.

The word *grammar* must be used with great caution. The term has meant many things at different times and places. Modern linguists and grammarians, when writing of the history of their discipline, generally credit Aristotle with distinguishing between noun and verb—though the distinction between ονομα ("name") and ρῆμα ("verb") is present, in germ at least, in Plato—and the stoics with formulating the notions of "rule" and "exception"; that is, they have searched through the writers of antiquity and recorded the various breakthroughs of method and terminology that, in an evolutionary perspective, may be viewed as constituting the patrimony of their disciplines. (Because of his well-known distinction between languages that said *oc, oïl,* and *si,* Dante is often considered to be a forebear of nineteenth-century comparative linguistics.) Yet both Plato and Aristotle subordinated linguistic to other concerns; neither was a grammarian. For that matter the stoics were not "grammarians" either, though their understanding of "analogy" (αναλογία) and "anomaly" (ανομαλία), as well as their distinction between "the signifier" (Το σήμαινον) and "the signified" (Το σημαινό-μενον), certainly helped theorists express the concepts of parts of speech, of gender, of declension and conjugation, and of tense and number. The stoics' active emphasis upon comprehending the workings of language indicates that they were more· grammatically inclined than other thinkers, though their debt to the Platonic ideal of truth and the Aristotelian doctrine of reason is large. The discipline that we, following the ancients, call "grammar" (Γραμματική, *grammatica*) was founded and maintained on the basis of an old cultural value judgment, namely, that brute speech required refinement and perfecting, that without such refinement language was inadequate to cope with the needs or capacities of man: "Grammar is the art of speaking and of writing well."

"Grammar" must first be understood as the hard-core expression—as a continuum of related and flexible doctrines—

of traditional attitudes concerning the purpose of language in human society Among the ancients there were no "pure grammarians"; there were commentators more or less exclusively concerned with language and its technical modalities. Only the didactic aspect of their activity—that is, the actual teaching of their pupils—was specialized. But even then the greatness of a Quintilian lies precisely in the relevance he ascribes to grammatical study when he elaborates his—and Rome's—social ideal, the *peritus dicendi*. Yet, with the passage of time, this traditional grammatical activity did acquire a kind of recognizable shape as a study with roots firmly embedded in the cultural soil. Thus, Dionysius Thrax (first and second century B.C.) dealt with the sounds and grammatical forms of Greek, while Apollonius Dyscolus (second century A.D.) studied syntax. Both grammarians were analytic and descriptive, in the Aristotelian sense, and were widely copied in Rome; their approach was virtually empirical, though underlying their work was the self-imposed task to perfect language (Greek), to make it a more worthy literary instrument. The Roman imitators of the stoic and Alexandrine grammarians used their sources in order to do to Latin what had been achieved with Greek. The anonymous author of *Ad Herennium* is a Roman patriot. For Varro (first century B.C.) the object of grammatical investigation is the defense of *latinitas,* which he defines as "natura, analogia, consuetudo, auctoritas."

Ancient grammar, in practice, is most closely identified with literary composition: belles-lettres or speech-writing. The tradition of grammatical investigation works hand-in-glove with, on the one hand, the established canon of highly regarded literary works and, on the other, the criticism of new works. This literary–grammatical tradition is the cultural counterpart to the absolute identification, in classical Greek thought, of intellectual activity and "philosophy." As an activity, then, grammatical investigation was both stable and essentially normative, though, by definition, it shared in all the vicissitudes of the cultural process. Rather than abstracting the grammatical "precepts" of the art's practitioners and listing their insights alongside their weaknesses, it would be more useful to describe qualitatively the work of a typical grammarian. One such figure was Priscian, the sixth-century author of *Institutiones,* a compendium of ancient grammatical theory and practice that exerted considerable influence in the medieval schools. In addition to the eighteen books of the *Institutiones* (see the edition by Martin Hertz, in Heinrich Keil, *Grammatici latini,* II-III [Leipzig, 1855–1859]), Priscian has been attributed works entitled, symptomatically, *De Figuris numerorum, De metris Terentii,* and *De præexercitamentis rhetoricis,* among others.

In the *Institutiones* Priscian summarized and rephrased the grammatical lore of his predecessors. But—and this is significant—his is no slavish or purely academic recapitulation. His intentions are explicitly to provoke a rebirth of decaying literary studies by translating (*transferre*) into Latin the best Greek works (see his Preface, entitled "Iuliano Consuli ac Patricio"). Furthermore, he adopts a critical view concerning earlier grammatical studies; previous Latin writers, overcome by their love of Greek sources, copied not only the light of their wisdom but also their errors. Priscian proposes to emend Latin grammar by incorporating the corrections of Herodian and Apollonius, and make "emendations according to the

fixed laws of reason" ("certisque rationis legibus emen-
dasse"). The discipline, we read, has known progress over the
years; Priscian praises those more recent authors who have
improved upon the ancients: "auctores, quanto sunt iuniores,
tanto perspicaciores." He thus emphasizes both the stability of
grammar and its cultural purpose and inherent adaptability.

A glance at Priscian's subject-matter will serve to illustrate
our view of the peculiar status of traditional grammar, that is,
its disciplinary rôle and its nature as an activity of the spirit.
If literary studies have decayed, it may be because the study of
grammar has been imperfectly carried on. Thus, his "Latin" is
not the "Latin" of our textbooks, i.e., a historical language,
possessing a grammatical structure, a lexicon, and a phonology; it is "language" (along with Greek), namely, the incar-
nation of definable expressive possibilities, universal in nature,[7] worked out in specific literary compositions and subject
to further improvement. "Language" is at once an ideal and a
continuing *corpus* of achievement; the "history" of Latin can
be no other than the glory of its canon of authors: for Priscian, not surprisingly, Homer and Vergil are equivalent.

The eighteen books treat of "linguistic" subjects according
to the terminology Priscian and earlier grammarians translated from the Greek: the first book deals with sounds ("De
voce") and letters ("De litera")—the two are distinct but inseparable. Following books treat of the syllable, of diction, of

7. The first sentence of Bk. I, i, "De voce," reads: "Philosophi
definiunt, vocem esse ærem tenuissimum ictum vel suum sensibile
aurium, id est quod proprie auribus accidit." This statement is as
universalist as any found in our modern, scientific textbooks of phonetics, and, in essence, as universalist as the most characteristically
Aristotelian medieval thought.

the sentence, of nouns, adjectives, and conjunctions, and finally of the "construction and ordering of the parts of speech" (syntax). His approach is worth a closer look. Thus, characteristically, Priscian speaks in Book V (56–67) of "figures"; the rest of this book is given over to gender (1–45), number (46–55), and case (68–81). By "figures" Priscian understands—rather idiosyncratically—something resembling our "word-formation" or "compounding." *Magnus* is "simple"; *magnanimus* is "composite" or "compound." *Magnanimitas* is not a compound like *magnanimus* because, though one can say *magna,* one cannot say **animitas; magnanimitas* is rather a "derived compound" (*decomposita*), since it is built on *magnus* and *animus* and then patterned on substantival forms in *-itas.* But this section is interesting for its procedure. It contains an exhaustive repertory of forms that fit Priscian's typology, as well as, admittedly, a number of marginal cases; that is, it contains a repertory of good usage. Cicero, Cato, and others are quoted. This usage is further substantiated by direct appeal to mental process. The first paragraph of the second section explains and classifies these "figures" in terms of how we "actualize" them in our understanding. Thus *parricida* is a compound of *parens* and *cædere;* both elements are integral "et intellectum habent plenum." The verbal idea, or semantic component, of each element is formally attributable to the two words in question. The etymology is thus both "right" and "wrong," by today's standards: *parens* has formally nothing to do with *parricida,* though obviously the two terms are genetically and semantically related.

Priscian's manner of presentation involves formal definition, relation to mental process, and appeal to usage; reason, understanding, and tradition, then, combine in his depiction of Latin as "language." His grammar is consequently comprehensive rather than exclusive. Yet, literary tradition, rather than purely linguistic description or even mental process, remains the dominant focus. Thus, Priscian has been criticized by later theorists on the grounds that his descriptive categories are too "loose" and that his "Latin" lacks logical rigor. Priscian is not doctrinally "pure." The Platonic question of things and the words that represent them is resolved, essentially, in a Platonic way: words and what they mean are indissolubly linked, even on the plane of analysis. Value is attributed to the proper kind of convention. But the analysis itself is carried out in terms rational enough to remind one of Aristotle. Priscian's *Institutiones* are a compendium of grammatical lore which, on precisely the practical level of living tradition that antiquity cherished, may be worthily compared with Aristotle's *Organon,* on the level of pure thought.

In his "De pontificibus et sanctis ecclesiæ Eboraćensis" (Migne, *P.L.,* CI, p. 843), the Carolingian poet-scholar Alcuin, the father of the ninth-century Renaissance, declares the following authors—among many others—to be in his library:

> Quod Maro Virgilius, Statius, Lucanus et Auctor:
> Artis grammaticæ vel quid scripsere magistri;
> Quid Probus atque Focas, Donatus, Priscianusve,
> Servius, Euticius, Pompeius, Comminianus.
> Invenies alios perplures, lector, ibidem
> Egregios studiis . . . [ll. 1553–58]

Innumerable analogous references to works of antiquity (as well as, naturally, to the works of the great Church doctors,

Jerome, Ambrose, and Augustine, whose very existence stands
as a testimonial to the reconciliation of Christianity and pagan
letters) may be found in medieval texts. Donatus, in fact, in
Romance garb as "Donat" or "Donet," was a name synony-
mous with "primer." Ancient theories of language and grammatical tradition were made congenial to the European
Middle Ages by intermediaries like these and others, including, with Alcuin, Isidore of Seville and Bede. Chrétien de
Troyes considered his twelfth-century France to be heir to the
humanitas of Rome and Greece: "Par les livres que nos avons
/ Les fez des anciens savons / Et del siegle qui fu jadis."
"Chevalerie" originated in Greece, and thence went to Rome:
"or est en France venue / Dex doint qu'ele i soit maintenue"
(*Cligés*, ll. 25 ff.).

The medieval assimilation of ancient grammatical and literary tradition—especially in the new vernacular tongues—
has been studied variously by a number of scholars, chiefly
Ernst Robert Curtius and Erich Auerbach. Thus, it has been
shown that Bernard of Chartres—as recorded by Abelard's
pupil, John of Salisbury (1110–1180)—taught the old doctrine according to which one ought to imitate the ancients in
order to become a model for posterity.

In his *Les Arts poétiques du XIIe et du XIIIe siècles*
(Paris, 1924) Edmond Faral has written of the transfer into
vernacular poetic usage of specific literary devices. *Annomina-
tio* is a case in point. A Latin construction of the following
type:

Hunc sibi *Roma* vocat; *Romam* subit; omnia *Romæ*

based on an obvious principle of phonetico-syntactic variation,
generates an Old French counterpart:

Qui *amis* a, mout en vaut plus;

Pur *amis* vient om al dessus.

En bon *ami* a bon tresor;

Bons *amis* vaut sen pesant d'or.

—*Éracle,* ll. 4110–13

The famous image of the present as a dwarf perched on the towering shoulders of the ancients is, properly speaking, an invention of the Middle Ages.

The most significant medieval treatise on literature is Dante's *De vulgari eloquentia*.[8] We must now attempt to describe how this work fits into the grammatical tradition inherited from antiquity by the Middle Ages.

As his title indicates, Dante treats "eloquence" in the vernacular, a subject which, he says in his opening sentence, nobody has dealt with before. By "eloquence" he means, with Priscian (Keil, II, p. 194), the *rules* thanks to which eloquence in discourse is achieved. By "vernacular," naturally, he refers to an Italian colloquial: what the child learns in imitating his nurse. He opposes *gramatica*[9] to the vernacular, that is, the language of the élite, as learned after many years of study: the language possessed by the Greeks and by the Romans. In fact, *gramatica,* at its most characteristic, is Latin,

8. In subsequent discussion of *De vulgari eloquentia,* I shall refer to the edition by Aristide Marigo (Florence, 1938). Also, let me here record my debt to Roger Dragonetti's helpful essay "La Conception du langage poétique dans le *De vulgari eloquentia* de Dante," in *Aux Frontières du langage poétique,* Romanica Gandensia, IX (Ghent, 1961); see my review in *Romance Philology,* XVIII, No. 1 (August 1964), 117–24.

9. This is Dante's spelling; the variant *grammatica* is more usual elsewhere.

which by Dante's time had become the learned language of philosophical speculation. Dante does not explicitly state that Italian derived from Latin. He rather conceives of both as having existed always side by side. The "vulgar" or "vernacular" is inherently nobler than Latin. The French scholar André Pézard has explained this nobility by stating that, for Dante, the truly noble vernacular was identical to the linguistic faculty placed in man by God.[10] Yet Dante is fully conscious of the linguistic pluralism of his age (I, vi, passim). After the destruction of Babel the first human speech gave way to others which in turn split into still others: thus the Spanish, the Provençal, the French, and the Italian languages must have derived from a common tongue, since they share so many words (*Deum, celum, amorem,* etc.), but their present use of *si, oc,* and *oïl* illustrates their separation. Our "idiom" has broken down into three kinds of speech, and even these latter may be further divided into multiple dialects, as Dante shows with respect to Italy (I, x). Dante proposes to create an Illustrious Vulgar, that is, to exploit fully the resources of the noble tongue—man's natural faculty of speech, as given by God— in rule and in example. Thus, the use to which he puts the grammatical tradition is, in the highest sense, a creative one; the area in which he operates is that in which literature and speech fuse, and in which this fusion is shown to correspond to the innermost nature of the human spirit. Like Plato's, Dante's view of language reconciles the ideal and the real in

10. See "La Langue italienne dans la pensée de Dante," *Cahiers du Sud,* XXXIV (1951); also Dante, *Œuvres complètes,* ed. by André Pézard, Bibliothèque de la Pléiade (Paris, 1965), p. 553; and, by the same author, the controversial *Dante sous la pluie de feu* (Paris, 1950), especially I, iv–v, and II, i–ii.

terms of specific human possibilities and needs (I, ii-iii). Like Aristotle, he works his doctrine out rationally, with method; though, unlike his scholastic predecessors and contemporaries, he subordinates "reason" to literary ends that are worked out in the same text. But unlike both Plato and Aristotle, Dante recognizes history, in a biblical sense.

Recent works—those of Dragonetti and Pézard in particular—have stressed the poetic character of Dante's linguistic theory. The concept of the Illustrious Vulgar owes much to Dante's meditation upon Genesis. Poetic activity may restore the pristine purity human languages lost after the Fall. Original speech derives from Adam's first response to God; it was endowed with a "certain form" ("dicimus certam formam locutionis a Deo cum anima prima concreatam fuisse" [I, vi, 4]), which pervaded it entirely and which consisted in a "natural and necessary relation between sign and sense" (Dragonetti, p. 19) as well as between speaker and interlocutor. Each utterance—spoken and heard—implies a total dialogic reconciliation, in love. (Dante's Christian doctrine thus permits him to view discourse as exemplary rather than as purely functional; one recognizes the Platonic underpinnings in his attitude.) *Gramatica,* having been formally purified above and beyond what has been accomplished by the vernaculars, remains *essentially* cut off from the authenticity of the Adamic linguistic experience precisely because it is learned; *in posse* the vernacular offers the only chance to recover, through poetic activity, the lost speech of Grace.

Dante's historical view is qualitative rather than chronological. Thus, the vulgar is anterior to, and more universal than, *gramatica,* despite its several-staged corruption over time. One understands that the kind of perfectibility Dante attributes to the vernacular is generically different from that which had been accorded Latin, and, in making the distinction, he not only separates what we today would call "literary" and "philosophic" language, but also is the first to point out, critically, the limitations of the latter. By Dante's time medieval Latin had virtually become identified with scholastic speculation (see below), whereas the vernacular had been used to create many important literary works. The linguistic split, along qualitative lines, had to be made theoretically and systematically in order to justify the practical divorce, as well as to take stock of the real, essential potentialities of the vernacular against the backdrop of the medieval pluralistic linguistic situation. Appearances to the contrary, Dante's preference for the vernacular implies in no way that he was prepared to sacrifice the principle of unity he so jealously guarded in other, nonlinguistic domains. The "unity" preserved by scholastic Latin, he felt, was of another, perhaps spurious, order, whereas true, or essential, unity could be found in the vernacular.

But—to use his own terminology—Dante is obliged to "grammaticalize" the vernacular—for literary purposes, to be sure, and for the reasons just outlined; he does not propose to subject the vernacular to the scholastic speculative grammaticalization. The grammaticalization in which he is engaged is designed to rescue the poetically symbolic potentialities of the vernacular. His efforts are thus dictated by his primordial concern for unity.

It is at this point that one can take stock of Dante's involvement with the grammatical tradition as it was inherited from antiquity and reshaped by earlier medieval thinkers and men of letters to suit their purposes.

Underlying all medieval grammatical theory, both "literary" and "philosophical," is the doctrine present in Priscian that grammatical principle is universal: words, intellectual process, and the authority of (poetic) usage combine to produce correction. What is said, when it is properly said, reflects universal linguistic principle. But Priscian was concerned only with literary Latin (and, by extension, with Greek). He had nothing to do with the linguistic variety—generic or national —facing medieval practitioners. Furthermore, Priscian's grammatical categories are philosophically loose; their coherence is provided by the cultural process that constitutes their context. Nevertheless, the medieval grammarians adopted his premises even though many of the more philosophically inclined criticized Priscian's lack of rigor. Grammar is universal; languages differ from one another only accidentally.[11] Dante explained linguistic differences as due to the corruptions caused by time and distance and by frivolous human will. The vernacular therefore must be made subject to the same intense care as that lavished by grammarians on Latin. Through exercise of an illumined reason, the grammarian may return to the long-forgotten principles of language and then use these principles to undo the damage wrought by corruption. Thus, medieval literary theory adheres to the traditional view that language is *rediscovered,* rather than "cre-

11. "Et sic tota gramatica que est in uno ydiomate similis est illi que est in altero, et una in specie cum illa, diversificata solum secundum diversas figurationes vocum, que sunt accidentales gramatice." (From Charles Thurot, "Histoire des doctrines grammaticales au Moyen Âge," in *Notices et extraits des divers manuscrits latins de la Bibliothèque Impériale et autres bibliothèques,* p. 125; quoted by Dragonetti, p. 41.) Medieval grammarians were fully conscious of the problems attending linguistic pluralism, and faced the question squarely. (Further discussion, below; see fn. 18.)

ated" *ab ovo*. Yet, unlike the scholastic theorists, Dante does not deny tradition as such. For him, grammar preserves the past intact: it is through grammar that culture is maintained and it is through grammar, as literature, that a community of men may be formed. Dante and the schoolmen are very close; but at the point of contact they are, in practice, widely divergent.

One understands, then, that Dante has fully preserved the old unitary notion of language and that he and his contemporaries made generous use of the ancient grammatical tradition in their own teachings. Furthermore, one sees the necessary spiritualization of this lore and its application to the medieval linguistic situation. Dante's Illustrious Vulgar is called upon to fulfill a poetic purpose itself linked to his understanding of a Christian and (supra-)national community; he refuses to base his Illustrious Vulgar on any single Italian dialect, preferring rather to utilize elements from several. (In practice, however, Dante wrote in refined Florentine.) He devotes as much attention to questions of poetic form as to linguistic doctrine. He thus duplicates, in a sense, Priscian's concern for poetic authority, and shows what he believes to be the meaning of tradition. Dante's sense of unitary culture is as fully represented in *De vulgari eloquentia* as his Christian sense of political unity is manifest in *De monarchia:* the Illustrious Vulgar is to common colloquy what the Empire is to Florence. In each case the latter must be subsumed into the former in order that authenticity and justice may prevail.

Let us now examine the theoretical basis of medieval linguistic speculation as it is expressed by some of the scholastic philosophers. These Latin writers, steeped in the grammatical tradition against which many of them react (in highly symptomatic ways), provide a new scientific context for the discussion of the problem of language. Inasmuch as their own expressive vehicle, scholastic Latin, was *grammatica* incarnate, it may be said that their grammatical doctrine at once remained within the tradition I have described and deviated from it. They were forced to cope with that tradition as well as with the new pluralistic linguistic situation predominant in medieval Europe. Consequently, whereas Dante's "Platonic" or "poetic" view reinterpreted the process of grammaticalization in specifically literary terms, the scholastic philosophers adopted a contrary view: their denial of "culture"—whether implicit or explicit—signifies a return to a *purified* Aristotelian, or mechanically *rational,* mode.

The language of scholastic philosophy was of and for specialists. As the refined vehicle of thought, the Latin of scholastic philosophy is called to reflect upon itself, as instrumental *ratio* and, we can see today, as part of a philosophical tradition, a dialogue of philosophies. In recognizing the limits of reason, scholastic philosophy attributed to it well-defined ends. As St. Anselm himself pointed out with great clarity, the Word itself (*Verbum* or *logos*) is the object of eternal thought; that is, it is God conceived by Himself, and the Holy Ghost is the love of God for the Word. The importance of the Word carries over to *words.* However no human word (*locutio*) can convey what God is: theological phrases are figures of speech (see *Monologium*), albeit necessary ones. What Gilson has called a belief in the "universal character of rational truth" justifies the use to which the schoolmen put the Latin language that had been transmitted to them from antiquity. Within, then, the essentialist philosophical framework of medieval theology, *ratio* was assigned the task of engendering —with greater or lesser limitations imposed upon it by the theological context—certain kinds of understanding. The certainties available to discursive reason were, in fact, those actively achieved by the great doctors thanks to—and within— the body of discourse of their *œuvre*.

Medieval scholasticism undertakes a dialogue with the logical tradition begun by Aristotle, but transmitted to it through a variety of agencies (neo-Platonism, Boethius, later on even the Arabic and Hebrew schools) including the grammar-centered curriculum of late antiquity (Priscian, Cassiodorus, Isidore, and Bede). Initially, then, the schoolmen participated fully in the cultural process of premodernity.[12] It is not my intention to trace the history of this participation, rather only to exemplify it. St. Anselm's *De grammatico* (ca. 1070) provides a good *entrée en matière*.[13]

Anselm's dialogue opens with the student's enquiring of his tutor whether *grammaticus*—explained by Priscian as a common noun signifying a substance (Keil, II, ii, 58)—is in fact a substance or, as the logical tradition would have it, a paro-

12. I have quoted the passage from Chrétien de Troyes' *Cligés* concerned with this very involved participation. Étienne Gilson mentions analogous statements in the *Chronicle of Saint Gall,* in the *Speculum* of Vincent of Beauvais, and in the *Grandes Chroniques de France;* see his *Medieval Universalism and its Present Value* (New York and London, 1937), pp. 8 ff.

13. In the following analysis I have relied extensively on the excellent edition and study by D. P. Henry, *The "De Grammatico" of St. Anselm: The Theory of Paronymy* (Notre Dame, 1964). Page references will be made to this work. See also the review by Aldo Scaglione, *Romance Philology,* XIX, No. 3 (February 1963), 483–86.

nym, a word, to be "classed with 'white,' which . . . was said by Aristotle to signify a quality and nothing but a quality" (Henry, p. 89). Anselm rejects the grammarian's view that all names signify substance; but of course what Anselm in fact is doing is establishing a logical basis for discourse (*significatio per se*) "which he opposes to *usus loquendi*," the grammarian's descriptivist ideal (ibid., p. 90). Anselm rejects the loosely ordered poetico-cultural authority stressed by Priscian. As Henry points out, Anselm's dialogue copes with the student's question in such a way as to establish "various meanings of 'meaning' . . . : there is the secondary (*per aliud*) sense of 'meaning' which involves, where this is possible, generalization from concrete utterances, *usus loquendi;* this is contrasted with the primary (*per se*) sense of meaning which embodies the requirements of the word's satisfactory functioning in the [truly logical] language. The latter is the concern of logicians, and he leaves the conclusion to be drawn that the first typifies the activities of grammarians" (p. 94). Anselm follows Boethius and declares that the dialectician is concerned not with *signatum* or *res* but with "meanings" contained in words *per se,* as words, and, in answer to the question: "Quid est grammaticus?" replies: "Vox significans qualitatem." The *quale* or *habens grammaticam* takes precedence over secondary denotation, the *quid.* Syntactic function—i.e., "substantiveness"—is thus separated from purely referential meaning, yet, curiously, syntactic function is itself discussed in purely lexical terms, on the level of the *word.*

The unitary medieval spirit thus provides the context for a generic opposition—which this spirit *contains,* however—that profits, in effect, from the *de facto* linguistic split into

Latin versus the vernacular. It would be easy to document the transformation of medieval Latin effected by the schoolmen who, by and large, believed that, in keeping with their notion of the universality of *ratio,* their Latin language *in posse* did "contain" logic. Henry reminds us that "the Latin of Boethius' time had no corresponding paronym [*to virtus*], since he tells us that a man having *virtus* was called *'sapiens'* (wise) or *'probus'* (honest); *'virtus'* could hence not be considered by him in connection with paronyms. Yet in medieval [scholastic] Latin the corresponding paronym (*'virtuosus'*) exists and is used freely" (pp. 81 f.). The proliferation of such word-derivation—along the lines of Priscian's "figures" in *-itas*—that later was to incur the mockery of Rabelais and Locke, proves that the schoolmen thought one should "make artificial additions to the language in an attempt to ensure that it reflects" logical problems. To an important degree, the drama of scholastic discourse resides precisely in this linguistic coinage, in the effort of these philosophers to actualize, in their usage, the linguistic state they knew, rationally, to be "true."

The great men of the twelfth-century "Renaissance"—one thinks especially of John of Salisbury—succeeded in reconciling their philosophic concerns (and the linguistic implications of these concerns) with their love of the grammatical tradition and its literary character. But already in the twelfth century one can detect, in the flowering of logic, the kind of specialization that eventually would lead to a serious revision of the grammatical tradition. In his *Geschichte der Philosophie* (I, 4th edition [Berlin, 1871]; English trans. by G. S. Morris [New York, 1877]), Friedrich Ueberweg describes the rise of nominalism as a conscious doctrine in opposition to realism; the nominalists attributed to Aristotle the teaching that logic deals with the proper use of words, that genera and species consist in merely subjective collections of the various individuals designated by the same name, and that universals are possessed of no real existence (Ueberweg, tr. Morris, p. 371). As we observed, Anselm's antinominalism led him to deal problematically with dialectic. Abelard's position in the debate is not easily ascertained. According to John of Salisbury, Abelard located the universal, not in words (*voces*) as such, but in words employed in sentences or judgments (*sermones*) (ibid., p. 392). His perhaps was an effort at conciliation. In any case Abelard's dialectic is founded on the proper application of words, first syntactically and then—this is the focus —"semantically," and such an application depends on one's knowing the peculiarities of the objects represented by words. Verbal convention has its roots in the objects it expresses and is controlled by them. *Sermones* constitute a higher level of expression than mere words, despite their being themselves made up of words, because words-in-the-sentence are, in fact, predicable of objects in such a way as to contain universality. What is defined by the word equals "the word explained in respect of its meaning (not in respect of its essence—'nihil est definitum, nisi declaratum secundum significationem vocabulum')" (ibid., p. 393). Logic and a kind of "syntactic activity" or evaluation thus go hand in hand during the first period of scholastic philosophy. Seen from a linguistic standpoint, the insight, though not followed through, is profound. Abelard quite suggestively recognizes the importance and the distinctiveness of the *sermo;* he nevertheless subordinates this syntactic consideration to what, for him, remains fundamental: the word. Thus Abelard's *sermo* constitutes what Rémusat has called the "expression of the word"; this expression is active: it both "reveals" and "affirms" the universal categories. Abelard's thought, however, conceives of universals as "existing," though not independently, as emanations of the divine mind. This somewhat Platonic view does not so much contradict as complement the doctrine we have just reviewed. Theological concerns consistently govern the best scholastic thinking, and should be viewed as the point of departure—as well as of reference—of that thought, at its most complete. Curiously, Abelard quotes Priscian (XVII, 1–4) that general and specific forms are conceived in the divine mind before they assume corporeal shape.[14] Priscian's context is "literary" and "linguistic," Abelard's is primarily philosophical, but, incidentally, "linguistic" too. Both employ a neo-Platonic notion in order to adumbrate a kind of dualist framework that permits each to organize his subject-matter—literature and thought—in a coherent way, and thereby to side-step the crisis affecting their respective disciplines. However, the framework chosen effectively curtails the pure descriptivism of their linguistic analysis. Abelard's views explain why the schoolmen, in subjecting logic to review, were obliged to subject both Latin and, analogously, linguistic theory to revision.

Abelard provides numerous acute examinations of the meaning of words like "some such" (*quidam*), "and" (*et*), "of," "on" (*de*), "all" (*omnis, totum*). He felt that no sure knowledge may be attained without such previous critical dis-

14. Abelard, *Introductio ad theologiam,* in *Opera,* II, ed. Victor Cousin (Paris, 1859), p. 109.

cussion of language. Like Anselm in the *De grammatico,* Abelard thus investigates—at least preliminarily—the meanings of grammatical and syntactic forms *as such,* i.e., their relational and functional nature. In the work, then, of both Anselm and Abelard, one discovers a sense of linguistic structure which, though applied in fact to Latin and rendered subservient to other than purely linguistic purposes, nevertheless is extraordinarily modern in conception. This sense of linguistic structure—of syntactic *relevance*—remains latent in their thought; that is, it does not engender an autonomous linguistic science, but, one realizes, without it scholastic logic would hardly have developed as it did.

As Philotheus Boehner and Walter J. Ong have pointed out,[15] the concern manifested by scholastic thinkers for the properties of terms, or "modes of words," constitutes a very definite addition to Aristotelian logic, despite Kant's—perhaps misquoted—*boutade* that nothing had been added to Aristotle "during the course of centuries." Father Ong considers Petrus Hispanus (ca. 1210–1277) to have been "the most important [and typical] of all scholastics," precisely because he systematized, in logical terms, the kind of grammatical considerations I have alluded to here. Though the systematization achieved by Petrus Hispanus was not grammatical in order, it nevertheless produced a kind of feedback into the more ostensibly "linguistic" grammatical theory and practice called *grammatica speculativa.*

15. Philotheus Boehner, *Medieval Logic* (Manchester and Chicago, 1952) and, especially, Walter J. Ong, S.J., *Ramus: Method, and the Decay of Dialogue—From the Art of Discourse to the Art of Reason* (Cambridge, Mass., 1958).

A brief summary of portions of Petrus Hispanus' *Summulæ logicales*—following Father Ong (pp. 65 ff., especially)—is nevertheless in order. One recognizes traces of arguments present in Abelard. "Whiteness," like Anselm's *grammaticus,* is a quality, since "what the adjective 'white' designates does not exist in a substantive way as white*ness;* only white things exist." But "whiteness" is a formal "reprocessing"; "it is made into a substan*tive* or substance-like term, a noun," hence, "conceptualized as 'being *per se*' [cf. Anselm] . . . [it] can be talked about directly, . . . i.e., made the subject of assertions" (e.g., of sentences). Terms, then, must be treated logically as though they were substances. The linguist speaks today of "grammatical *facts,*" analogously, though these clearly are on a lower level of abstraction. (No linguist can afford to ignore factual reality to the extent that some later Parisian scholastic logicians were prepared to do when, in their syntactic disputes, they declared that *ego amat* was just as "grammatical" as *ego amo* [Ong, p. 75]: the linguist takes account of the redundancy; the logician deplores it. Yet both the linguist and the philosopher require the concept of "grammaticalness.")

The logical distinction between substantival signification ("substantiveness") and substantivity corresponds to the difference between the modes of words and of the things signified. Logical terms in Petrus Hispanus tend to be "made over by analogy with substance, . . . that is, unit beings not inhering in something else" (ibid., p. 68); they are seen, then, either as subjects of sentences or—following Aristotle's emphasis—as predicates. Thus, universalized, terms are "considered . . . as predicates, which, by various linguistic or logi-

cal devices, have a definite relation to the subject or subjects of
which they are predicated" (Boehner, p. 28, quoted by Ong,
p. 67). One begins to understand the scholastics' constant syn-
tactico-grammatical bias. Petrus Hispanus is careful to distinguish signification (the word, or sign, signifies a thing) and
supposition (the substantive term—itself already significant
—is accepted in place of something). "Signification belongs
to the word (*vox*), whereas supposition belongs to the terms
(*termini*)." Signification, then, is essentially a lexical matter
of equivalences ("Plato" equals the "being Plato") whereas
supposition implies a kind of lexical syntax, as it were: "*Man*
runs" is understood as "Socrates, Plato, and the rest of men"
(ibid., p. 66). A sort of economy is at issue here, a terminological economy, or a relational grammar–syntax operating,
however, on the lexical level, that "deals for the most part
with the extension or range of predicates in reference to individuals" (Boehner, quoted by Ong, p. 67). Thus, the difference between substantival signification and substantivity
(and what is implied by each—things, words, and kinds of
words) is established in order to provide for a more searching
investigative instrument—or logical language—which in
turn is to be relied upon to make largely quantitative statements about the realities around us.

Father Ong shows that the "terminist logicians thus tried to
develop a formal, quantified logic which maintains at the
same time an awareness of the elaborate structure in which a
substance is modified by or 'stands under' (*sub-stare*) its acci-
dents or modifications. This way of dealing with wholes,
without, as it were, dismantling them . . . is a part of the
attempt to develop a formal logic relatively close to ordinary

language (that is, without special symbols, but only with specially defined words)" (p. 69). He points out that later adversaries of this kind of logic (e.g., Ramus) were inspired by the objection, precisely, that the kind of discourse actually produced by these logicians was too far removed from ordinary speech to be properly convincing. In the hands of the scholastic logicians, then, Latin became a kind of "seminatural" language—a specialized prolongation, of course, of the traditional cultural language, but also a surprisingly close forerunner of the symbolic language of today's logic. The later humanist tradition would seek to "restore" the literary–rhetorical—or eloquent—quality[16] of the expression of antiquity in its own Latin usage and, in so doing, would render somewhat obscure the paths leading from scholastic to modern thought. But clearly, certain attitudes toward language present in scholastic philosophy, as well as a number of im-

16. A problem I have not dealt with here, but which nonetheless remains very important to an understanding of the genesis of scholastic logic as well as of its originality, concerns the confused interpretation given by the scholastics to Aristotle's carefully delimited concepts of logic and dialectic. The scholastics do not distinguish between the certainties dealt with by logic and the probabilities that are the domain of Aristotelian dialectic. Though rejecting the rhetorical tradition as such, the scholastics actually incorporate its theoretical basis into their logical framework. Father Ong examines the question with considerable thoroughness, pp. 59–65, concluding: "Here in the thirteenth century [Petrus Hispanus], when the goddess of reason makes her most definitive appearance in scholastic philosophy in the most distinctive and influential of all scholastic manuals, she is supported not on the pillars of science, but on the topics or arguments of a merely probable dialectic or rhetoric" (p. 65). The later humanists will, however, attempt to restore rhetoric in its pristine form, though, naturally, their mentality will bear the trait of this scholastic confusion which, by their time, will have become a tradition.

portant implications of these attitudes, would certainly filter through to modernity.

As has been pointed out, the structuralist bent of medieval logic—inherited from Aristotle, but amplified in characteristic ways—caused the practitioners of that logic to stress what I have called syntactic relationships over other features of language (e.g., *Ego amat = Ego amo,* minus undesirable redundancy). When the chips are down, Anselm rejects Priscian's authority; he does so on the same grounds invoked by Priscian himself against certain of his own predecessors. Yet, as I have suggested, scholastic syntax was designed in virtue of its repercussions upon fundamentally lexical values: words, as verbal relationships, but only to the extent that such relationships permitted insights into the material world—the world, precisely, of substantial matter. Father Ong has put the question very eloquently: "any effective logic is . . . desperately engaged in quantity and hence in the material world. Logic is a study of the reflection of this material world . . . in the structures of the mind" (p. 74). Therein lies the *raison d'être* of the anticultural bias so dramatically expressed in thirteenth-century logical philosophy and in the struggle against the literary grammatical tradition. In contrast, the kind of linguistic relationships—at once dialogic, or poetic, and historical —that Dante outlines in *De vulgari eloquentia* are of an entirely different order. The Illustrious Vulgar is justified on purely qualitative grounds.

Logical considerations of the type I have referred to led to the creation of *grammatica speculativa* in thirteenth-century Europe. *Grammatica speculativa* — a body of grammatical doctrine whose creation must be understood in the framework of what Gilson called the "exile of *belles-lettres*" that took place, despite the misgivings of certain great scholastic thinkers like Roger Bacon, after about 1230[17]—constitutes, for the historian of linguistics proper, the most important linguistic repercussion of the new logic. The practitioners of *grammatica speculativa*—sometimes known as the *Modistæ*—criticized Priscian. Though he had, himself, invoked the "laws of reason," Priscian was not rational enough: it was felt that what he taught was deficient because only those who provide the causes for the phenomena they describe may legitimately be called teachers.[18] Though Priscian and Donatus remained as part of the curriculum, they were joined in the fourteenth century by the speculative Latin grammars of Alexander of Villedieu (ca. 1170–1250) and Évrard of Béthune: the verse *Doctrinale* and the *Græcismus*. Siger de Courtrai and Thomas

17. See Étienne Gilson, *La Philosophie au Moyen-Âge,* 3rd ed. (Paris, 1947), p. 401, and the chapter entitled "L'Exil des belles-lettres," pp. 400 ff.

18. Cf. fn. 11. Also: "Unde constructiones multas dicit, quarum tamen causas non assignat." See L. J. Paetow, *The Arts Course at Medieval Universities,* University of Illinois Studies, III, No. 7 (Champaign–Urbana, Ill., 1900), p. 35, a work described by Gilson as "fundamental." The passage is quoted by Gilson, ibid., p. 404. This objection to Priscian reminds one of the criticisms the eighteenth-century philosophical grammarians—e.g., Thomas—leveled at Vaugelas' theory of *bon usage;* see Ferdinand Brunot, *Histoire de la langue française des origines à 1900,* VI, No. 2, by A. François (Paris, 1932), especially the chapter entitled "La Grammaire et les grammairiens." Paetow is quick to point out that the "new grammar" of Alexander of Villedieu, in verse, provides general rules of syntax better adapted "for boys who learned [Latin] as a foreign language" than the works of Donatus and Priscian, which "had been written for students whose native tongue was Latin" (p. 33). Cf. D. Reichling, *Das Doctrinale des Alexander de Villa Dei* (Berlin, 1893), pp. vii–xv.

of Erfurt (whose mid-fourteenth-century *Summa de modis significandi* has often been attributed to Duns Scotus) may be said to represent the high-water mark of this new tradition. The emergence of *grammatica speculativa* took place in an intellectual atmosphere of great tension between the followers of the belletristic grammatical tradition (that had flowered in the twelfth century) and the newer philosophically oriented view of language. The latter held that the attainment of philosophical purposes hinged first of all on a ground-clearing operation that would eliminate "what is not philosophy." Paris "fought" against the more conservative Orléans, "logic" against the "authors," in a battle of the books recounted—most symptomatically—in a mid-thirteenth-century *vernacular* poem by Henri d'Andelys that sympathized with the traditionalists and was entitled *La Bataille des sept arts.* Gilson describes this poem: "On y voit les Classiques en déroute, des étudiants ès arts ... ne s'intéressent plus qu'à la philosophie" (p. 412). The absolutism of both schools testifies eloquently to the latent polarization of literature and pure thought during the Middle Ages, but, even more significantly, this absolutism also bears witness to the complementary nature of the two trends within the medieval unitary spirit. Both "schools" reflect the age's sense of unity, though each illustrates a different emphasis placed upon a factor—or set of factors—in the tradition.

What did *grammatica speculativa* set out to do? In theory at least the poets and the philosophers were not all that far apart. Dante would certainly have subscribed to Roger Bacon's statement that: "Grammatica una et eadem est secundum substantiam in omnibus linguis" (Gilson, p. 405; cf.

Paetow, pp. 26, 41, especially 44 ff.). But although Bacon defended the cultural importance of literary study, as a philosopher and logician, he was obliged, in his grammatical theory, to emphasize precisely what Dante, the equally universalist poet, would not stress. The poet's "discovery" of grammar differs in kind from the philosopher's—despite the latter's claim: "Non ergo grammaticus sed philosophus . . . grammaticam invenit." By applying to their very specialized Latin their revised Aristotelian method, the speculative grammarians attempted to utilize the idea expressed by Bacon in order to found a science of grammar—a coherent set of rules—according to which pure thought could be channeled most effectively into highly formalized expression. They meant to teach young students the "Latin" they needed to know in order to perform adequately as pupils in the arts course. They made short shrift of linguistic diversity (the *fact* of Bacon's *omnibus linguis*), and they explained variations by "accident" ("licet accidentaliter varietur"). Speculative grammar turns out to be the pedagogic arm of a logical philosophy which felt impelled to consummate its victory over the literary tradition by redefining the *usage* of learned speech (*usus loquendi*) in terms of its own specialized technical preoccupations.

The universalism underlying *grammatica speculativa,* unlike Dante's, is purely intellectual, never poetic in the sense described above. We are a far cry from Plato who, of course, recognized that poetry could at times be philosophy—or be made to serve philosophic ends. Speculative grammar considers the syntactically conceived parts of speech as pure modes of signification, i.e., as they express the several aspects of being and thought, analytically. As Gilson has shown, grammar is the study of *modi significandi* and, as such, it fits into a program leading to—and including—logic (*modi intelligendi*) and even metaphysics (*modi essendi*). Scholastic grammar thus adumbrates a coherent, though limited, theory of language, a *Sprachphilosophie,* the like of which had not been seen before, not even in Aristotle. Scholastic grammar has a concrete *disciplinary* quality about it; it is based on the principle of universal categories *and* on the expressive possibilities open to the "seminatural," re-worked language that medieval Latin, to a considerable extent, had become. Scholastic "language"—its *langage,* in the Saussurean sense—constitutes an attempt to minimize the "inconsistencies" of the language-in-history of the looser grammatical tradition. Thus, the *modista* Siger de Courtrai (ca. 1300) distinguishes between *modi significandi,* thanks to which words (*voces*) have function as parts of speech, and *modi signandi,* the level of word as designator of things (lexical value); both "modes" are related to modes of understanding, i.e., to structures of the mind.[19] Like Saussure, Siger de Courtrai appeals to a structural formulation in order to impart coherence to statements concerning language: logic—or instrumentality—is the keystone for the scholastic, psychology for the German linguist.

As a discipline, *grammatica speculativa* is characterized by definite methodological and pedagogical principles, within an intellectual scope that includes metaphysics and logic but that, by the same token, feels it necessary to eliminate poetry and even eloquence. The establishment of the highly structured

19. Cf. G. Wallerand, *Les Œuvres de Siger de Courtrai* (Louvain, 1913), pp. 34 ff., and the text of *Summa modorum significandi,* pp. 93 ff.

discipline known as speculative grammar consequently results in both an increased level of disciplinary independence for "pure" grammatical study and a more intense degree of integration of that discipline into the philosophical concerns of scholastic thought. Many substantial and qualitative differences between, "grammar," "metaphysics," and "logic" are—at least provisionally—resolved in practice by disciplinary reference to the various planes of activity which, taken as a whole, are felt to constitute a cohesive, well-organized, and properly directed intellectual enterprise. The "violence" done to Latin by the speculative grammarians was understood to be entirely justified in terms of their wider philosophic (and pedagogic) goals; they were able and willing to sacrifice *usus loquendi* (e.g., "Ego amat") when, as they understood it, the "correctness" of usage conflicted with what, for them, was superior correctness. Speculative grammar thus purchases a higher degree of stringent coherence at the cost of appearing —when compared, say, with Aristotle or even Priscian—psychologically naïve.

Implications. Justified theoretically by the contrasting doctrines of Plato and Aristotle, as these were adapted into the vital cultural process, the new medieval play of diversity-in-unity at once represented and utilized the linguistic situation to which it was subjected. It would be quite inaccurate to claim, however, that the Platonic absolutist mode "became," in written discourse, the poetry of Dante, nor, *a fortiori,* may one identify the mechanist mode of Aristotle purely and simply with the analytic philosophy of the schoolmen. Such a statement would hardly do justice to the complexities involved. Yet the concatenation of circumstances embodied in the medieval understanding of the cultural tradition to which it belonged and which it reinterpreted in the light of its needs rendered possible a split between poetic and philosophic discourse. By positing the existential "truth" of maternal speech, the poet emphasized what may be called the synthetic or symbolic view of language one finds expounded and illustrated in Plato's *Cratylus,* whereas the philosopher–logician stressed the Aristotelian analytic, or disciplinary, view. The one opposes the other far more pertinently than, say, in the *Institutiones* of Priscian, where literary culture itself remained primary. But any depiction of this historical "split" would have to take into account its structural corollary, namely, that the theoretical implementation of the poetic, symbolic view is expressed in highly analytic terms. Dante's *De vulgari eloquentia* would be inconceivable without Aristotle and even without scholastic *grammatica speculativa.* It is no accident that Dante wrote the work in Latin. Meanwhile, as we observed, the transcendent goals of understanding that inform scholastic philosophy are conceived, if not expressed, in terms that ultimately go back to Plato. "Reason," as defined by Aquinas, is very limited indeed: it is destroyed in understanding. (Likewise, Vergil may not accompany the poet in Heaven.) One thinks of the inevitable silence of mystical contemplation, of St. Anselm's remark concerning the "figurative" or symbolic nature of human language when faced with the struggle to convey the meaning of the Word through mere discourse (*Monologium,* pp. x, xxix ff.).[20] One recalls his statement

20. St. Anselm's *Monologium* is available, in English, tr. by S. N. Deane, in *Proslogium; Monologium; An Appendix, In Behalf of the Fool, by Gaunilon; and Cur Deus Homo,* 2nd ed. (Chicago, 1910).

about the unity of God's essence: "Unum est quidquid essen-
tialiter de summa substantia dicitur."

The Platonic and Aristotelian strands thus fuse in medieval
thought and expression, but as vital traditions, they each are
identified with specific generic traditions within that thought
and expression. As we have observed in connection with
Dante and the scholastics, the notion of grammar maintains
its basic cultural sense throughout the Middle Ages—Priscian
is not so much abandoned as superseded by the great vernacular poet and his logician predecessors and contemporaries.
The principle of "grammatical universalism" is never attacked; what is meant by such unity is made more explicit.

Dante's intuitive understanding of the potential truth of
the vernacular leads him to "grammaticalize" it, that is, to "restore" the purity of speech through an act—*the* act—of poetic
creation. (See, in this connection, Dante's letter to Can
Grande.) The idea of (dialogic) communication in Dante is
incredibly rich in implications of all kinds; these range from
the total understanding such poetic communication is designed to *achieve* and *represent* to the smallest details of
poetic devices borrowed by the poet from the learned literary
tradition of antiquity and from his Provençal and *dolce stil
nuovo* forebears. Epistemological concern and technical art
are, so to speak, actualized and given transcendental relevance
in the poetic text of the *Commedia.* Exemplification of the
highest sort takes precedence over analytic dissociation.
"Grammar" stands for the active forging of poetic discourse,
and poetic discourse is that which synthesizes our understanding of the human drama: truth. Dante's "poetry" has much in
common with Plato's "philosophy."

59

Grammar as viewed by scholastic logic—in the fullest sense, not the narrower, though related, sense of practical *grammatica speculativa*—corresponds to a much more segmented concept of cognition. In the context of logical investigation the notion of grammatical universalism provided theoretical justification for a kind of linguistic experimentation which demanded, in effect, a reshaping of Latin to fit definite disciplinary and pedagogic needs. When received grammatical tradition stood in the way of the progress of the new logic, it was cast aside. What was said had to be made consistent with what should and could be said, in logical terms. An already somewhat specialized learned language was made even more specialized, in the name of universal—i.e., logical—principles. The mechanistic and quantitative side to Aristotle's "method"—the instrumental character he attributed to discourse—was thus stressed by medieval logicians who saw, in language, a means of combating falsehood and championing truth systematically with such quantitative means.

Given the nature of the medieval arts course—theology was in fact isolated in its own faculty (see Paetow and Ong) —the discipline we have called logic took on an increasingly independent character. *Grammatica speculativa* thus could become a preparatory discipline with respect to the logic on which it was based, an "antigrammatical" grammar whose coherence depended less and less on the cultural tradition than on the philosophical curriculum of which it was a part. The segmented nature of the curriculum thus contributed to the creation of equally segmented intellectual activities. The *idea* of such activities or "disciplines" is very much a medieval invention.

It does not require too great a projection of a modernist point of view to find, in the medieval intellectual and linguistic ferment, a series of links between antiquity and our own age. The similarities between Plato's view of language and philosophy and Dante's notion of the Illustrious Vulgar, with its poetic implications, reveal the presence of a continuity that will constantly affect the very nature of literary creation—both in contrast and in conjunction with philosophy—in the West. By the same token, the successful adaptation of the ancient cultural tradition into the medieval context will contribute to the equally constant play between innovation and tradition that characterizes modern intellectual activity as much as it did the medieval, though, of course, in radically new ways. However, the medieval linguistic split—Latin versus vernacular—though by no means complete, constitutes a real factor which, along with the ancient-versus-modern dichotomy also felt by writers of the Middle Ages, helped polarize and give new relevance to the linguistic doctrines of Plato and Aristotle. When dealing with language, Platonic thought concentrated on the linguistic act—dialogue—and the exemplary relationship between that act and truth as symbolized in the essential nature of words. But, during the Middle Ages, the Aristotelian notion of language as instrument, in conjunction with the old grammatical tradition, led to disciplinary segmentation which, in turn, provided for a fledgling "science" of grammar at least potentially more independent than any previous grammar had been. Already in Priscian, but especially after Anselm, grammatical commentary takes on a disciplinary character—it makes statements—reminiscent, above all in the scholastics, of the economical, structuralist type one associates with modern linguistics (e.g., the concept of meaning per se). Finally, the medieval disciplinary viewpoint, already firmly entrenched in Dante's time, is precisely that which governs, formally, Dante's *De vulgari eloquentia*. The ideas explained and defended in that work are organized, so to speak, in an analytic framework fully consistent with the usual medieval *tractatus*. What Dante says and how he says it, then, together provide the first great and coherent example of what we now call "literary theory" or "criticism." Thus, to a very considerable degree, the Middle Ages helped formulate the topic with which the present study is concerned. As it is applied in the medieval period, the old tradition of grammar at once "incorporates" and tends to "become" two qualitatively distinct disciplines. Or, seen in yet another perspective, the "activities" we call poetry and logical speculation—both intimately concerned with language—engender two disciplinary approaches to the problem of language that, critically and theoretically, are to be distinguished: poetics, or literary theory, and linguistic philosophy.

Modernity

The Renaissance saw itself as "restoring" letters. From the point of view of the present study, it is more profitable to view the fifteenth and sixteenth centuries as the period in which the stability of the Western cultural process, as described previously, broke down, and new unifying principles were sought, with varying degrees of success. Renaissance critical philology certainly helped "restore" the letters of antiquity, but, at the same time, this critical spirit interrupted the kind of historical continuity obtaining between pagan and Christian antiquity and the European Middle Ages. Also, the Renaissance saw the definitive victory of the various vernaculars and, consequently, the development of new kinds of linguistic study as well as their rapid extension. Nebrixa's Castilian grammar was presented to Queen Isabella in 1492; Juan de Valdés' *Diálogo de la lengua* (ca. 1535) praises the idiosyncracies of Spanish. In Italy Pietro Bembo's *Prose della volgar lingua* (1525) shows that the *questione della lingua* interested all educated men. Grammars of French proliferated,[21] as, for that matter, did those of other languages—some even exotic. The substance contained in the premodern unitary attitude toward language was progressively sapped.

The genuine cultural expansion characteristic of Renaissance Europe entailed important qualitative revisions of what, in fact, was to be construed as culture. A work like Joachim DuBellay's *Deffence et illustration de la langue françoyse* (1549) illustrates such revision. Medieval *"episseries"* are rejected; classical and Italian models are praised, new forms and new values are specifically programmed, and, to a

21. Both Nebrixa and Juan de Valdés offer an antischolastic viewpoint in their respective treatments of Castilian. However, within the literary or cultural framework in which they operate, each adopts a characteristic attitude. Nebrixa is analytic, as Priscian was. Valdés is decidedly more Platonic; he discovers the essence of Castilian—its "usage"—in the language of Spanish proverbs. A close comparison of the two men provides an important insight into the modes of grammar during the early Renaissance. As for French grammatical activity—much, one should add, accomplished by Englishmen—one may refer to the list drawn up by Mildred K. Pope, in her *From Latin to Modern French* (Manchester, 1934), pp. xxv ff. Miss Pope gives four titles antedating 1500, and some eighteen dating from the sixteenth century; all these deal specifically with French.

considerable degree, justified on the grounds of their newness. Cultural nationalism tends to replace the rather spontaneous cosmopolitanism predominant in medieval Europe. The literatures of Italy, Spain, England, and France share only a common sense of their own relationship to the literature of antiquity and to the other European literatures. The ways these relationships were implemented in practice are highly idiosyncratic and must be interpreted in terms of each specific national "tradition." Calderón (1600–1681), Corneille (1606–1684), and Milton (1608–1674) are contemporaries. Their differences are at least as important as their similarities, though each was thoroughly familiar, in his own way, with the common cultural heritage.

The question of linguistic use is important, since, during the Renaissance, patterns of thought appear to be more ostensibly related to given ends than ever before. What *is* is rather more a function of what one wishes to do than previously. Though the Renaissance shows great interest in the qualities of things—their qualitative properties or thingness—the period cultivated an increasingly quantitative manner of dealing with things, conceptually or analytically. Renaissance literary discourse and analysis reflect what Father W. J. Ong has called this "quantification of thought." [22] Purely quantitative attempts at imitation of the ancients give us—especially in France and Italy—innumerable neoclassic tragedies and epics, and schematic, or "methodical," and quantitative literary theory comes into its own (e.g., the "three unities"). Ambigu-

22. See his previously quoted *Ramus: Method, and the Decay of Dialogue* . . . (Cambridge, Mass., 1958), especially Book II, and Book III, chap. xi.

ous reconciliation of quantity and quality also characterizes the linguistic analysis of the period. The Latin grammatical model was used, so to speak, "symbolically" as the analytic base for the description of a wide variety of tongues, both European and exotic. Or, as this model proved impractical, other biases prevailed: (1) the "traditional" approach, involving complex genetic relationships between languages that were shown to derive, say, from Hebrew, or (2) a more philosophical view dependent upon rather more logically construed "general grammatical principles," usually calqued, however, upon Latin usage. In each case quantity enters into the problematics to be dealt with and some attempt is made to resolve the questions it raises by appeal to an a priori qualitative affirmation. One is struck by the systematic nature of these efforts—in this sense they are modern—but also by their almost gratuitous arbitrariness. We too tend to conceive of linguistic realities in ways we find useful, but by definition our techniques are meant to conform more closely to whatever the implications of our conception might be.

Seventeenth- and eighteenth-century thought concerning language may be interpreted, in general, as an attempt—or series of attempts—to deal cogently with ambiguities of the type just referred to. Or, in other words, it may be seen as an effort to overcome the fragmentation that followed upon the disruption of the medieval cultural unity described above. The modern view of language rests on a kind of dynamics which contains, or utilizes, the crisis that characterizes the modern understanding of reality. The medieval resolution into tradition of cultural continuity and historical transformation, which allowed for the diversity-in-unity reflected in the grammatical theories of Dante and those of the schoolmen, thus gives way to a number of possible, almost ad hoc, resolutions that depict, in one way or another, a permanent dialectic between conceptual order and the complex multiplicity of reality.

The Rationalist Mode: Thought, Grammar, Expression. The tradition that extends from René Descartes (1596–1650) to Jean-Jacques Rousseau (1712–1778) offers, within the framework of a single country, an insight into the formulation of the modernist approach to language, and, moreover, it illustrates the effect such a formulation had upon later developments in both linguistics and literature.[23]

Space does not permit a detailed analysis of this period here. Subsequent discussions of Condillac and Coleridge will offer a fuller account of the problems raised. However, the basic issues should first be defined in a general way.

In a brief letter to Father Mersenne, dated 20 November 1629, Descartes counters a proposal that had been made to him concerning the possibility of creating a new, universal language.[24] Though he rejects the proposal, he claims that a truly universal language is possible, provided one finds "la Science de qui elle dépend." This "science of language" would be entrusted with the task of making men aware of the "universal language" they all speak. Its function lies in pointing

23. The recently published, and very interesting, study by Noam Chomsky, *Cartesian Linguistics: A Chapter in the History of Rationalist Thought* (New York, 1966), endeavors to show the relevance to contemporary linguistic theory of rationalist and Enlightenment thought concerning language. See also Roland Donzé, *La Grammaire générale et raisonnée de Port-Royal* (Berne, 1967).

24. *Correspondance,* ed. Charles Adam and Gérard Milhaud, I (Paris, 1936), pp. 89–93.

out the correlation between thought process—the bedrock of Descartes' doctrine—and the linguistic forms men use. It is necessary that the thought process be exactly symbolized in words and grammar in order that language might become truly instrumental, and peasants better equipped to "juger de la vérité des choses, que ne font maintenant les philosophes" (p. 93).

The allusion to peasants suggests that Descartes is referring here to a natural language. Linguistic "symbolism" and "instrumentality" are reconciled in Descartes' belief that a language that would properly represent the generating of authentic thought would, by definition, serve to judge the truth of things. Put another way, such a language would produce discourse consciously and necessarily emblematic of mental process and so would constitute the tool of that process. Finally, though philosophy provides the criterion for the "langue universelle," a special science is required to implement the idea.

These notions are fraught with important implications. First, language is viewed as operating on two levels: that of absolute form—i.e., the linguistic categories identified with the production of thought—and that of ordinary usage, the contingent or "imperfect" forms preserved by tradition which, when systematized, we call, respectively, English, French, or Latin. The latter level, subject though it is to "significations confuses," is not to be denied outright, since historical languages constitute the repository of civilization. As Descartes ruefully admits, his linguistic idealism is fit for a "pays des romans." Second, though Descartes' dualist focus enables him to preserve a universalist view of language as well as to recognize obvious linguistic pluralism, he is thereby forced to elaborate a method by which, in fact, his dualist interpretation may be shown to be effective; a linguistic science is thus called upon to mediate directly between man and language. This science regulates, as it were, the dynamics of man and expression. The universalization of language—the linguistic order —is accomplished by revealing the "ordre entre toutes les pensées qui peuvent entrer dans l'esprit humain." In short, what may be implicit in the scholastic analysis of *usus loquendi* and *modi significandi* becomes explicit in Descartes' view. By extension, the semidisciplinary status accorded *grammatica speculativa* within the old arts curriculum acquires here a far greater methodological autonomy.

The *Grammaire générale et raisonnée,* by Lancelot and Arnauld (1660), of Port-Royal, takes up Descartes' challenge.[25] These writers envisaged their task as relating reason and *bon usage,* that is, the "proper" or refined speech of the royal court. They attempted to "universalize" French discourse by systematizing loose usage according to rational principle. The Port-Royal grammar categorizes its subject-matter as Descartes had suggested: universal rational process, essentially creative in nature, is worked out in terms of idiosyncratic French linguistic procedure, and our understanding of the latter is, concomitantly, to be shaped by rational process, thanks to logical formulations. An illustration is in order. Defending Vaugelas' celebrated rule that a relative clause may not follow a noun that is not modified by an article, the Port-Royal authors examine nine so-called "exceptions" to the rule

25. Edition used: Antoine Arnauld, *Œuvres,* XLI (Paris, 1780), pp. 1–84.

(pp. 42 ff.). They declare, e.g., that the French phrase *Je suis homme qui parle franchement* is perfectly correct, since, logically, *homme* is an attribute determined by *je* (cf. *Je suis homme qui AI vu bien des choses*). The "exception" is not genuine. Other so-called exceptions are merely "left-overs of the old style, in which articles were almost always omitted." Such "bizarreries de l'usage" are condoned but must not be permitted to interfere with one's appreciation of the deeper system of rules.

If the Port-Royal grammarians found their philosophical justification in the Cartesian system—and, as we saw, Descartes does provide such justification for a mediating grammatical science possessing great disciplinary autonomy—their techniques of analysis and their understanding of linguistic tradition owe much to formulations like those of the Spanish disciple of Ramus, Francisco Sánchez de las Brozas (Sanctius). Sánchez' *Minerva: seu de causis linguæ latinæ,* first published in Salamanca in 1587, was frequently reprinted in France, Holland, and Germany throughout the seventeenth and eighteenth centuries.[26] This work deals with Latin. Sánchez defines grammar, quite traditionally, as "ars recte loquendi" (I, ii), but immediately sets a new tone, by adding: "Cum artem dico, disciplinam intelligo; est enim disciplina scientia acquisita in discente." Sánchez' "discipline" corresponds to Descartes' "science." The study of Latin grammar is "methodical," i.e., based on principles of general linguistic analysis. Earlier in the same chapter Sánchez had said:

26. Edition used: Franc. Sanctii (Brocensis), *Minerva seu de causis linguæ latinæ commentarius,* add. by Gaspar Scioppius and Jacobus Perizonius, ed. by C. L. Bauerus (Leipzig, 1793).

"Grammatici enim . . . sermonis Latini custodes sunt, non auctores." This opposition reminds one of earlier scholastic statements to the effect that "grammarians" (i.e., the literary grammatical traditions) are not the custodians of language, that the true custodians must be "philosophers." Sánchez' "grammarians" are opposed to "authors" (the literary tradition) in a similar way—"method" is thus contrasted with and preferred to the looseness of cultural traditon. His "grammarians" are in fact philosophers-concerned-with-language, autonomous "specialists," in the modern sense of the term. Nowhere is the mediating quality of "universal" grammatical study more clearly delineated. Furthermore, just as Sánchez worked with "language" through, and in, Latin, so the Port-Royal grammarians worked through, and in, French. Both Sánchez and his Port-Royal disciples achieve a kind of mutual contamination between their universalist principles and the historical language they study. The former focused on an abstractly viewed "Latin," the latter considered the virtually "perfect," or essentially stable, French *bon usage* of the classical moment. Latin or French, so understood, both lend themselves to such universal, methodical analysis, and this analysis itself helps characterize what Latin, or French, really "is."

"General grammar" thus constitutes a temporarily successful attempt to parry the dangers of fragmentation that inhere in the modern experience of language. The analytic techniques used as well as their wider philosophical contexts are clear. Yet certain ambiguities persist. The Port-Royal grammar manages to reconcile Cartesian thought, the new universalist grammatical science, and the *fact* of French usage within a framework that itself tends to regard cultural process—or history—as fundamentally stable. This reconciliation will not last, since, during the eighteenth century, the modernist crisis proved to be stronger than the bonds designed to restrain it.

Eighteenth-century "philosophical grammar" continues the Port-Royal tradition. The "sublime genius" of the *Grammaire générale et raisonnée* was admired because, as the grammarian Thomas put it, "les écrivains de Port-Royal ... eurent toute la logique que pouvaient avoir les bons esprits de ce temps-là." [27] This statement, however, hardly attributes to Lancelot and Arnauld the last word; progress has been achieved since their work. The successors of Port-Royal attempt to deal even more systematically with the relationship between the nature of language and French usage than their predecessors had done; they sharpen their analytic tools.

The most celebrated philosophical grammarian of the Enlightenment was César Chesneau DuMarsais (1676–1756), contributor to the *Encyclopédie* and author of the very influential *Traité des tropes* (1730).[28] According to DuMarsais, grammar examines the relation "que l'esprit conçoit entre les mots, selon le sens particulier qu'on veut exprimer." It accomplishes this task by analyzing the form of linguistic conventions in given languages so as to understand how man produces discourse. In his *Encyclopédie* article entitled "Construction," DuMarsais isolates "natural constructions"—those that correspond to the "état des choses"—and "figurative constructions." The former are "uniformes dans toutes les langues," while the latter abound in specific discourses. Tropes

27. Brunot, *Histoire de la langue française,* VI, No. 2, p. 900.
28. Edition used: C. C. DuMarsais, *Œuvres,* III (Paris, 1797), pp. iii–xii, 13–262. See also Gunvor Sahlin's exhaustive study, *César Chesneau du Marsais et son rôle dans l'évolution de la grammaire générale* (Paris, 1928).

—the figures—are thus worked into his general linguistic theory: they derive from the mental activity underlying the linguistic activity of individuals. "Natural constructions" do not exist in reality: they constitute a formal coefficient to basic linguistic principle—they are what is universal in language, what French, Spanish, and Latin share. "Figurative constructions" are existentially more genuine; they comprise what is particular to real discourse. Both "constructions" are thus, in fact, categories of grammatical analysis.

DuMarsais approaches these two categories by contrasting them with one another and by appealing to a third, which he calls "usual constructions." (One is again reminded of Saussure's *langage, parole,* and *langue.*) The "usual construction" equals the "manière ordinaire de parler des honnêtes gens de la nation dont on parle la langue," that is, the speech, or *langue,* of our "average native speaker." "Usual constructions" —i.e., common French usage—are composed in part of underlying "natural constructions" and, in part, of "figurative constructions."

DuMarsais also provides a fairly sophisticated account of the speech act. Speech takes place thanks to certain mechanisms which require the speaker to "analyze" his thought— i.e., undergo a formal process of enunciation—and the interlocutor to do likewise: mental process governs such "analysis." Encoding and decoding of messages reflect mental process, approached formally and analytically.

Yet, like most philosophical grammarians, DuMarsais pays heed to usage mainly in order to direct it. His predilection for "natural constructions"—logic—is evident. Thus the grammarian's analytic basis constitutes a normative ideal, and grammatical mediation becomes truly effective. One is free to readjust one's "speech" in conformity with the "natural" ideal.

Unfortunately, the linguistic situation in eighteenth-century France was far less monolithic than in 1660. Though the personal taste of DuMarsais caused him to associate proper French usage with the language of belles-lettres and of the *philosophie* of his day, one detects in his grammatical viewpoint a view of language that stresses instrumentality. DuMarsais offers support to the neologists of the time who wished to reform French usage in order to make of the language a more adequate instrument of scientific and philosophical investigation. The neologist position was violently attacked by those who, like Voltaire, sacrificed "reason" to their wish to preserve French usage exactly as it was in Racine's day. In the article "Langues" of the *Dictionnaire philosophique* (1769), Voltaire expressed his fear that, should changes be introduced, nobody would understand "les bons écrivains du grand siècle." This "traditionalist" attitude rejects effective grammatical mediation. Thus, Voltaire, who had praised Abbé Girard's *Synonymes français* (1718), on the grounds that it helped to "faire subsister la langue française," abandons the same author when he published his typologically oriented *Vrais Principes de la langue française* (1747).

But the modernist crisis comes fully out in the open when, as the century progressed, the mediation of philosophical grammar is denied on other, more serious, grounds.[29] Des-

29. Another, also significant, factor in the eighteenth-century "crisis" was perhaps DuMarsais' inability to write a "complete"

cartes, we recall, had "utilized," or resolved, the crisis by identifying mental process *in the individual* with universal principle, and his grammarian successors had worked into this identification their understanding of general linguistic, as well as of French, procedure and usage. Thus, in the Cartesian analysis, linguistic activity could be seen as symbolizing mental process as well as being instrumental to it.

The crisis is hinted at in Diderot's *Lettre sur les sourds et muets* (1751). Diderot declares that French syntax is best suited to philosophy, whereas English, Greek, and Latin are "les langues de la fable et du mensonge." Consequently, innovation in French may be permitted provided one's innovations are "harmonious" and "analogous" to the "nature" of French. But, in fact, Diderot is merely giving free rein to his own creative verve. Whether it is he who adjusts his style to the genius of French or whether it is French that he molds to his own use is a very moot point. In any case, an aesthetic factor seems to determine the relationship between what he writes and the language he uses—or "serves." The matter turns on Diderot himself. The authenticity of what he writes depends on his fidelity to himself, and when—as is at times the case—such fidelity comes into conflict with received rationalist tradition, then the latter is to be sacrificed. For Diderot, as for Descartes, discourse translates the writer's *act* of understanding, and so it is at once instrumental and symbolic. However, in Diderot, its symbolic authenticity must be above reproach or its instru-

---

French grammar. His remarks, interesting though they are, are scattered in numerous articles and publications. Given the orientation of his thought, could he, in fact, have composed a general grammatical treatise?

mentality will suffer. Consequently, Diderot stresses a kind of rhetoric that guarantees such authenticity. The *necessary* link between universal "reason" and an individual's mental process is broken. The "philosophy" that so perfectly suits French thus is transposed into an essentially literary key.

As one would expect, Rousseau is even more radical. The aestheticization is complete. All pretense that truth possesses some objective status apart from the individual's convictions is dropped.[30] Rousseau thus carries the Cartesian linguistic— minus its mediating nature which, of course, he summarily rejects—to its logical expressionist conclusions. Language is so entirely a matter of personal identity that he disavows tradition and, in fact, regards it as pernicious. By the same token, he forbids that Émile be taught foreign languages. Thus, in defense of the *Discours à l'Académie de Dijon* (1750), Rousseau declares: "J'ai surtout voulu rendre exactement mon idée; je sais, il est vrai, que la première règle de tous nos écrivains est d'écrire correctement, et, comme ils disent, de parler français: c'est qu'ils ont des prétentions, et qu'ils veulent passer pour avoir de la correction et de l'élégance. Ma première règle à moi, qui ne me soucie nullement de ce qu'on pensera de mon style, est de me faire entendre: toutes les fois qu'à l'aide de dix solécismes, je pourrais m'exprimer plus fortement ou plus clairement, je ne balancerai jamais; pourvu que

---

30. The final sentences of Rousseau's *Confessions* (1788) illustrate his systematic rejection of the "objective" or "factual" truth: "J'ai dit la vérité. Si quelqu'un sait des choses contraires à ce que je viens d'exposer, fussent-elles mille fois prouvées, il sait des mensonges et des impostures, et s'il refuse de les approfondir, et de les éclaircir avec moi, tandis que je suis en vie, il n'aime ni la justice ni la vérité."

je sois bien compris des Philosophes, je laisse volontiers les Puristes courir après les mots." [31]

Rousseau mythologizes language. He uses the philosophical jargon of his day—superficially, he "innovates" very little, neither lexically nor syntactically—but he resets this vocabulary in a completely symbolic framework. He replaces Descartes' rational process with something one might call the structure of his sensibility, and he builds, on this very personal basis, his "general" attitudes. Language is thus meant to be *expressive* of the truth of *his* understanding. By stressing the writer's need to struggle and to forge his own rhetoric, Rousseau carries the Cartesian notion of linguistic creativity to an extreme point, and, of course, announces the kind of expressionism that dominates much modern literary creation. In subverting analysis to his transcendental and synthetic purpose, Rousseau eliminates a number of contradictions that had plagued the Enlightenment, but he also annihilates much of what the Enlightenment stood for. From Rousseau onward, it makes sense to speak of writers in terms of highly personal "languages" coequal to the sum of their writings. Such languages have usually been considered as material for literary critics, not as the stuff of "true" linguistic study.

In the remainder of this section I shall discuss two modern attempts—one philosophical, the other literary—to provide a coherent view of linguistic phenomena. Both these attempts cope, in characteristic ways, with the crisis I have described.

31. The text is quoted by Ferdinand Gohin, *Les Transformations de la langue française pendant la deuxième moitié du XVIIIe siècle* (Paris, 1902), p. 44. According to Gohin it is to be found in vol. VII of the Geneva edition of Rousseau, p. 158 n.

Both accept, and utilize, the fundamental modernist postulates. The results are very different, but not, it would seem, irreconcilable.

The Analytic Mode of Condillac. A lucid and prolific writer, a great pedagogue, and an original thinker, Condillac (1715–1780) more or less successfully grafted important principles borrowed from the British empirical tradition upon the rationalist framework of the French Enlightenment. His *Traité des sensations* (1754) is fairly well known, but his linguistic theories and their implications have been less thoroughly studied. Several of his most important treatises deal explicitly with language in an epistemological and psychological context that summarizes the best the period had to offer. His *De la Grammaire* and *Traité de l'art d'écrire* (both eventually published in 1775) as well as his *Logique* (1780) and *La Langue des calculs* (1798) develop philosophical grammar to logical conclusions as well as Condillac's own fundamental maxim: "Toute langue est une méthode analytique, et toute méthode analytique est une langue ... l'art de parler et ... l'art de raisonner ... [sont] un seul et même art." [32]

Following Locke's *Essay Concerning Human Understanding* (1689), which he read in Pierre Coste's translation (1700), Condillac's *Essai sur l'origine des connoissances humaines* (1746) relates the "history of understanding." He re-

32. *La Langue des calculs* (posthumously printed in 1798), I, i. (Quotations from Condillac are taken from the edition of his works in three volumes, by Georges LeRoy [Paris, 1947–51].) Condillac's notion of language as "method" stems from his rejection of the Cartesian doctrine of innate ideas. If the structure of thought cannot depend upon mental structures—i.e., in the mind—then it makes sense to correlate the structures of thought with those of language, which, of course, lend themselves to observation.

jects Descartes' innate ideas, preferring to operate solely with what can be observed. "Understanding" exists in the functions attributed to it: judgment, affirmation, reason, analysis. But how does man pass from the simple exercise of his elementary faculties to true reflection, i.e., endow his mental activity with objective coherence? Or rather how may this step be made without appealing to some overriding metaphysical principle? In answer, Condillac declares outright that man—humanity and the individual—succeeds in dominating the reality surrounding him by linguistic means. "Lier nos idées," e.g., our transformed sensations, is the job of reason, and reasoning is to utilize signs. The semiotic facility functions with three kinds of sign: (1) accidental signs—those in which certain objects are associated with particular circumstances; (2) natural signs, or the cries that nature has established for the feelings of joy, fear, pain, etc.; and (3) institutional signs (*signes d'institution*) which we ourselves have chosen and which exist arbitrarily in relation to our ideas (*Essai,* I, II, iv). Reflection, which takes place thanks to the third type of sign, is our freedom, our way of *"composer* et *décomposer"* our ideas in order to compare them "sous toutes sortes de rapports, et en faire tous les jours de nouvelles combinaisons" (I, II, vii). Analysis and the construction of "general ideas" serve to put "de l'ordre dans notre esprit."

Locke's *Essay* (III, ii) suggests that language offers men a means to dominate their ideas, but Condillac develops this notion radically. The quality of one's reflection is closely related to the quality of the signs one uses. Thus, in his *Traité des systèmes* (1749, 1771), Condillac mocks the word-games that characterize so much metaphysical speculation: "Voulez-vous apprendre les sciences avec facilité? Commencez par apprendre votre langue" (xviii*a*). Condillac's antimetaphysical position is the reverse of the Port-Royal doctrine which, we saw, defined "thought" in a more a priori fashion. "Reason" in the Cartesian tradition is more absolute than in Condillac, for whom it becomes mainly a procedure or a process. According to Port-Royal teachings as well as those of DuMarsais, thought and language are identified with one another, but the latter is produced in conformity with the possibilities open to the former. (Hence the underlying ambiguity of DuMarsais' linguistic "freedom.") Condillac believes in truth; he is no relativist. However, his "truth" is first of all that which is not false, and then knowledge whose justifying value resides above all in utility. Utility is a principle which he identifies with active and deeper understanding. In this sense, Newton's physics is "true." Consequently, DuMarsais and Condillac agree that languages are systems of thought, but their theories of linguistics differ radically. DuMarsais' grammar examines languages in order to establish how the mind "conçoit entre les mots." Condillac eliminates this kind of dualism entirely in order to focus upon the rational process itself. Condillac's linguistic theory is central to a broad system of thought; it is also far more ostensibly historical than that of DuMarsais.

Descartes studied his own "history," of course, so as to detect in the mass of phenomena around him what was "true." There is something tragic about the Cartesian concept of self, since, for Descartes, the self exists authentically only to the degree the individual succeeds in understanding himself as the representative of certain universal qualities which, in a sense, supersede him. Descartes tells his "story," but in telling it, he relates the drama of his own consciousness confronting something superior to himself which, ultimately, he has to identify with himself. His history ignores chronology. Similarly, DuMarsais can see in linguistic convention—usage—only the superior rules of language which govern such convention. Whenever convention is deficient, the grammarian must come to the rescue—hence his efforts to conjoin usage—what is said—with the "construction naturelle."

Condillac attributes a very different function to history. In writing the history of understanding, Condillac must demonstrate how, over all time, man learned to do what he knows how to do. His vision is cumulative. Condillac's temporality is double: one *is* what one *was*. Each man is the history of his species. Therefore, Condillac devotes the second part of his *Essai* to summarizing the history of what he calls "le langage et la méthode." This second section of his work incorporates the multiplicity of the modern linguistic situation—the fact of many languages—into a panoramic vision that eliminates the drawbacks of such multiplicity by according each isolated factor a goal and a precise value. The historian does not distinguish between ideas and words; he describes how, thanks to words, men have in fact produced ideas and how they continue to do so.

According to the Cartesian grammatical tradition, to "better" one's language means to "purify" it, to adapt it to a preconceived ideal. This doctrine allowed Diderot—and especially Rivarol—to proclaim that French was the most philosophical language, since its syntax most closely resembles "natural syntax." Condillac sees the danger of such claims; he mocks them: "Nous nous flattons que le Français a, sur les

langues anciennes, l'avantage d'arranger les mots dans le discours, comme les idées s'arrangent d'elles-mêmes dans
l'esprit .... Cependant nous avons vu que, dans l'origine des
langues, la construction la plus naturelle exigeoit un ordre
tout différent" (*Essai,* II, I, xii). Condillac does not deny the
possibility of bettering one's language, but such improvement
must be accomplished in terms of precise goals. One cannot
compare two languages like French and Latin, he avers, because the advantages of each are so different; every language
has its own genius which derives, precisely, from its history
(loc. cit.). Condillac thereby parries Diderot's nascent aestheticism and channels into instrumentalist modes the individualism that Rousseau would invoke in defense of his aesthetic
reëvaluation of the Cartesian linguistic position. Condillac,
like Rousseau, agrees that each man has his own language,
that this language constitutes his identity, and that one's language is determined by the passions of the speaker (II, I, xv).
However, the nature of linguistic signs is such that they are
arbitrary the first time they are used, but the combinations
finally "autorisées par un long usage" determine the genius of
a language—its tradition—whether the language is that of
the individual or of an entire people. Condillac's historicism
thus prevents him from following Rousseau in his personalized symbolic usage. Learning to speak is an essentially creative activity. Traditional usage may consequently be discarded,
but not merely in order to "se faire une loi d'attacher toujours
aux termes des idées toutes différentes de celles qu'ils sig-
nifient normalement." That would be "une affectation puérile
et ridicule." To improve one's language involves giving it
"clarté" and precision; it is necessary to "reprendre les ma-

tériaux [de nos connoissances], et d'en faire de nouvelles combinaisons, sans égard pour celles qui ont été faites" (II, II, xxvi). Creation or production for their own sake are meaningless; one creates *for* something. The first rule, once again, involves ridding oneself of useless prejudice: "Les philosophes, honteux d'avoir médité inutilement, sont toujours partisans entêtés des prétendus fruits de leurs veilles." The task is not always easy.

Condillac is the most Aristotelian of Enlightenment figures. For him language is best envisaged as instrumentality, that is, as the only sure instrument we have to reach truth. Language is also expression, but Condillac, allowing for this doctrine, downplays it. He is not primarily concerned with the expression of conviction in which Rousseau indulges, though, on other levels, he cannot but admit the literary legitimacy of such expression.

To exercise oneself in the proper use of signs develops one's intellectual capacity, and, concomitantly, such exercise provides good models for the use of others. This ancient and medieval idea is fully reworked by Condillac. Since the art of reason is identified, in history, with a well-fashioned language, the first steps in the establishment of a given science consist in constructing a language capable of fomenting its development. This thesis of Condillac was borrowed by Lavoisier and Guyton de Morveau when they set out, systematically, to provide a specialized nomenclature in order to advance the science of chemistry (*Méthode de nomenclature chimique* [1787]). Condillac himself composed his treatise on political economy, *Le Commerce et le gouvernement* (1776), because the language of economics "remained to be set down" (see his preface). Condillac's modernity is self-evident. Unlike medieval theorists who saw to it that their students imitated the ancients in order to become themselves models for posterity, Condillac speaks of "sciences," i.e., of coherent systems of discourse that actively mediate between man and reality, "objectively." For Condillac, such sciences must be "invented" in the modern sense—"created," not "restored" or "found." The kind of discourse each represents must be amenable to—in fact must engender—additions, subtractions, and other modifications.

Condillac is certainly the most authentic "linguist" among Enlightenment thinkers. The influence of philosophical grammar is undeniable.[33] The well-made language is approached through its formal characteristics, which Condillac analyzes. After studying primitive man's passing from the "language of action"—the language of symbolic gesture—to the "language of articulated sounds" by *describing* the formal features that characterize it, he stresses syntax, because, e.g., word-order provides evidence for the slow transformation of the human spirit in its use of signs. He explains usage and its linguistic rôle. The language of action expresses the simulta-

33. In the opening paragraphs of his *De la Grammaire* Condillac praises the Port-Royal grammarians for having "les premiers porté la lumière" to elementary grammatical study; DuMarsais is seen as having "recherché en philosophe les principes du langage" and lauded for exposing "ses vues avec autant de simplicité que de clarté." Condillac regrets DuMarsais' not having written a "grammar." He adds: "D'autres ont travaillé en ce genre avec succès ... Cependant j'avoue que je trouve point, dans leurs ouvrages, cette simplicité qui fait le principal mérite des livres élémentaires." One imagines that Condillac's predilection for DuMarsais reflects the latter's willingness to equate expression with human sensibility (see *Traité des tropes,* I, iv, v, vii).

neity of thought: complex thoughts are translated into a single cry or gesture. During the period of transition between the language of action and that of articulated sound, a kind of bilingualism occurred that resulted in a preservation of usages more proper to gesture even when articulated sound had, to all intents and purposes, won out. Hence, truly adequate speech—the speech of philosophy—must be made to depend on suitable analytic procedures sufficiently powerful to replace the simultaneity of the language of action by the genuinely linear, or consecutive, quality of the language of articulated sound. Adequate discourse thus consists in an adequate inter-penetration of "conventional" or "historical" linguistic form and thought process. The organization (*liaison*) of ideas in sentences constitutes "reason" transformed into "efficient form." Consequently, for Condillac, the form of language ex-ists on two distinct, though interrelated, levels: (1) that of the formal system that evolves in time and that may be identi-fied with the various tongues (Latin, French, English, etc.); and (2) that of inner form, or the form of the discourse which itself is elaborated in the process of its production.

Condillac's bias remains philosophical, though, as we have seen, he stresses the dual dimension of history and psychology. He is consistently antimetaphysical. In his *Traité des systêmes* he quotes the metaphysicians only in order to refute them. Thus, very curiously, Condillac's "philosophy" leads him to speak highly of men of letters. He respects poets and orators for having discovered, long before the philosophers, the proper method in composing their works: "Ils ont eu l'avan-tage d'essayer leurs productions sur tout un peuple." Condillac recognizes the existence of different genres; he isolates three

84

types: the didactic, the narrative, and the descriptive. But nothing prevents a didactic text from being "poetic," nor a description from being "scientific." Condillac distinguished between "poetry" and "science" only in terms of the goals they are assigned. He recognizes the fundamental rôle of culture because culture best symbolizes the complexity of man, Condillac's irreducible point of departure. The last few sentences of his *Essai sur l'origine des connoissances humaines* show his very modern appreciation of the problem of culture and his analytic approach to this problem:

> Je finis par proposer ce problême au lecteur. *L'ouvrage d'un homme étant donné, déterminer le caractère et l'étendue de son esprit, et dire en conséquence non seulement quels sont les talens dont il donne des preuves, mais encore quels sont ceux qu'il peut acquérir: prendre par exemple, la première pièce de Corneille, et démontrer que, quand ce poëte la composoit, il avoit déjà, ou du moins auroit bientôt tout le génie qui lui a mérité de si grands succès.* Il n'y a que l'analyse de l'ouvrage qui puisse faire connoître quelles opérations y ont contribué, et jusqu'à quel degré elles ont eu de l'exercice: et il n'y a que l'analyse de ces opérations qui puisse faire distinguer les qualités qui sont compatibles dans le même homme, de celles qui ne le sont pas, et par-là donner la solution du problême. Je doute qu'il y ait beaucoup de problêmes plus difficiles que celui-là.

How close this sounds to Rousseau's personalism, yet how different it really is!

In his *De la Grammaire* Condillac gives the standard rationalist definition of grammar; it is "un système de mots qui représente le systême des idées dans l'esprit," and the art of writing "n'est que ce même systême, porté au point de perfection dont il est susceptible." The "system of ideas" is the same for all men everywhere—"chez les peuples sauvages et chez les peuples civilisés"—but the linguistic extension of this system differs. Thus, as has been indicated, Condillac is obliged to devote more attention than his predecessors to the nature of the "extension." The study of grammar becomes, then, the study of the methods men have followed in the analysis of thought. The first part of *De la Grammaire* deals with the "analysis of discourse" (I, pp. 428–460), i.e., the signs furnished by languages enabling us to analyze thought; and the second, lengthier, part (pp. 461–513) is given over to the "elements of discourse," namely, the "rules our language prescribes in order to endow the analysis of our thoughts with the greatest clarity and precision." Condillac's "French" is a far more tangible category than the very sketchy "French" one finds in the Port-Royal *Grammaire;* the subject is examined in greater detail because it has become a more completely defined "subject-matter." [34]

Much depends, of course, on Condillac's doctrine of history, which itself amplifies considerably upon Descartes' identification of the mental process of one man with that of humanity in general. With Condillac, "individualism" and "interpersonalism" are subsumed into the categories—system of ideas and historical language—discussed above, but they nevertheless retain a sort of conceptual independence. The individual is recognized as such. However, in proper modern fashion, the individual is the key to the universal. The following passage

34. The matter may be put this way. The Port-Royal grammar establishes grammar as a *discipline;* Condillac's grammatical discipline, however, is shown by him to create its subject-matter, *as such.*

in *De l'Art d'écrire* (I, i) illustrates the point; note Condillac's use of "nous":

> Si nous réfléchissons sur nous-mêmes, nous remarquerons que nos idées se présentent dans un ordre qui change suivant les sentimens dont nous sommes affectés. Telle dans une occasion nous frappe vivement, qui se fait à peine apercevoir dans une autre. De-là naissent autant de manières de concevoir une même chose, que nous éprouvons successivement d'espèces de passions. Vous comprenez donc que, si nous conservons cet ordre dans le discours, nous communiquerons nos sentimens en communiquant nos idées.

But if philosophy is to make any sense at all, the "truth" of the individual must be apprehended in "interpersonal" terms. Rousseau, we saw, handled the same problem in his rhetoric by aestheticizing his subject-matter. Condillac remains faithful to analysis; he objectivizes *his* subject-matter by interpreting it analytically, in historical terms.

Condillac thus preserves the Cartesian notion according to which science—in this case grammar—mediates between man and reality. However, in Condillac we note a reversal of emphasis. His science of grammar posits a "realistic" view of language. Language itself is objectified; it exists. The factual, historical quality of language is what allows Condillac to speak generally, in interpersonal terms, of the "rules" our language—French—prescribes for us. Condillac's antimetaphysical stance causes him to stress functions over a priori abstract categories. Words and objects are essentially what men, individually or collectively, make of them, in time and space. They cannot be defined or hierarchized in perpetuity, though austere study may reveal the sense of their operations. What remains constant in all this flux is the speech act, i.e., the generation of thought in discourse and its communication. In short, then, Condillac justifies the founding of modern linguistic science, as a branch of philosophy. It is in this context that his above-quoted statement makes clearest sense: "Voulez-vous apprendre les sciences avec facilité? Commencez par apprendre votre langue." Unless the operations undertaken—or represented—by the individual can be explained—i.e., analyzed—in interpersonal terms, philosophy will remain helpless, even obscurantist. Condillac's grammar insists, then, upon that which is systematic and consequently amenable to description and evaluation.

De l'Art d'écrire extends to literature the doctrines discussed above. Writing, of course, implies for Condillac the qualitative perfection of linguistic possibilities. He is concerned, once again, with *expression,* in analytic terms. The art of writing is thus made to serve what he calls *la plus grande liaison des idées,* a universal formal principle. Condillac casts aside much deadwood inherited from the older poetic and rhetorical tradition. His "art of writing" expresses a normative intent, to be sure, but this intent is implemented by analytic and historical techniques. It is virtually a "science of literature." The volume analyzes many textual specimens, for example; each illustrates a point to be explained and is judged to be successful or to have failed with respect to the adequacy of its linkage of ideas.

Condillac insists that the poet study his language, not ancient models. His bias becomes clear in his final defense of the *loi de la liaison des idées.* This law, he writes, "should constitute no obstacle to genius; this vice can be attributed only to the rules which rhetoricians and grammarians have proliferated to such a degree only because they sought them out in places other than the human spirit." To respect this law means, in effect, to perfect one's creative powers—the same as are put to use in the generating of discourse. The neoclassic doctrine of imitation disappears, then, as a creative principle, along with the stable universe for which it was designed. Condillac proposes that the dynamics of language take the place of the old doctrine of imitation. The idea is very modern. The step from Condillac's "Study your language" to the modernist "Create your language," especially when these phrases are inserted into the context of his analysis, is a very short one indeed.

Condillac's *liaison des idées* is closely related to the romantic transcendental organicism one finds expressed, for example, in Coleridge. However, his emphasis remains analytic and thereby differs qualitatively from the romantic stress of synthesis. Whereas *De l'Art d'écrire* deals explicitly with what individual writers ought to do, its doctrines are elaborated in historical, interpersonal terms. Condillac's historical structures are fascinating. His almost nineteenth-century theory of the "three ages"—infancy, healthy maturity, and decline (cf. Auguste Comte)—governs literary judgment, and explains the eighteenth-century's relationship to the admired masterworks of the seventeenth. The latter constitutes the "second age" whose productions incarnate a harmony of subject, purpose, and means; this harmony determines "le naturel propre à chaque style." Furthermore, the structural order of literary works depends on patterns of "associations of ideas" that themselves vary, over time, like the "spirits of great

poets." Poetry is a constant; nonetheless, "different circumstances have given our poetry a character distinct from that of
ancient poetry." Condillac points out that our poets have lost
the resources of mythology, so they must now seek others in
philosophy; Italian poetry differs from French poetry "because it began in different circumstances."

Remarks of this kind abound in *De l'Art d'écrire*. Eighteenth-century cultural relativism thus blends with that century's very modernist optimism concerning the universality of
man. (See, in particular, the brilliant last chapter of *De l'Art
d'écrire*, appended at a later date and entitled "Observations
sur le style poétique, et par occasion, sur ce qui détermine le
caractère propre à chaque genre de style.") Poets must discover for themselves "le naturel propre à chaque genre," and
they do so by observing the "circonstances qui ont concouru à
former le style poétique" ("Table").

The "art of writing," as Condillac conceives it, offers a kind
of objective correlative to literary creation, which is itself
viewed essentially as an activity summarizing what one's culture on the whole has produced. And, when interpreted in
reference to the objective "art of writing," the possibilities exploited by the past may provide an understanding of the possibilities open to the present and the future. The art of writing
thus becomes an instrument too. The analysis of possibilities,
it is assumed, leads to an unprejudiced—hence *truer*—understanding of genuine realities.

To summarize Condillac's contribution, let us repeat his insistence that all thought, expressed in language, is necessarily
linear, or consecutive, in character. This idea dominates his
Essai sur l'origine des connoissances humaines and is analyti-

cally, or scientifically, implemented in the pedagogical works on grammar, the art of writing, logic, and "la langue des calculs." These works—and *L'Art de penser* as well—are specialized; each offers a disciplinary analysis of one aspect of the total intuition. On one level, then, Condillac distinguishes between the specialized "science" and his global view of knowledge, i.e., the means of expression open to his "philosophy." On another level, however, these works point to a different distinction: discourse is typified as "literary" or "mathematical." Condillac's "arts" recall the old medieval *trivium* and *quadrivium*. The *study* of discourse, in practical terms, is subdivided into two general approaches, each concentrating on isolable formal aspects of discourse which, in turn, must be related to qualitatively determined mental categories. The *Traité des systêmes* describes these categories (xvii, in the 1771 version):

> Dès que nous connoissons l'art de donner à chaque pensée son caractère, nous avons un système qui embrasse tous les genres de style ... Dès que nous savons donner au discours la plus grande clarté et la plus grande précision, nous savons l'art de raisonner ...

Each discipline thus comports two principle points of focus: discourse is analyzable in terms either of (1) its style and character or of (2) its clarity and precision. The distinction suggests a superior generic opposition between works that call the reader's attention primarily to themselves as works and works that direct his attention to the material they treat. Whether predominantly "literary" or "mathematical," all discourse lends itself to such dual analysis. Newton's physics posesses "style" too, though it functions referentially. Corneille's plays are notable for their "style," but are also approachable in terms of the "reason" they utilize or, so to speak, contain.

The essential modernity of Condillac's techniques of analysis, *as such,* resides, therefore, in their dualist structure. Organized in this way, these techniques, when applied to language itself, provide classificatory frameworks as well as sophisticated disciplinary justification for a cumulative, historically oriented, formal science of language and of literature. Each technical perspective is related to a broad, total view; every formal characteristic possesses, as it were, an analytic counterpart. From Condillac onward it is possible to affirm that the more rigorously organized a discipline—i.e., the more perfect its "language"—the less likely it is to fall prey to the dangers of aestheticism and fragmentation. It is also true, however, that, like Condillac, each subsequent modern approach to the problems of language and literature will have to cope in some relevant way with the equally grave dangers of stressing either the interpersonal or the individual to the exclusion of the other. The latter provides a necessary existential authenticity, whereas the former, by definition, contains a broader, more amenable or verifiable objectivity.

Synthesis and Symbolism in Coleridge. Romantic theorists of language operate with categories and principles closely related to those discussed in previous sections of the present chapter. However, the Aristotelian emphasis upon instrumentality one finds developed by Condillac is replaced, to a large extent, by a more Platonically conceived symbolism. Descartes' linguistic doctrine, we recall, tended to balance—if not really reconcile—both these biases, but, as we observed, the equilibrium was disturbed by developments in Enlightenment thought. Thus, the German theorists of language, in the late eighteenth and early nineteenth centuries, share Condillac's historicism. However, unlike Condillac, the historicism of a Herder, an A. W. von Schlegel, or a Humboldt depends on a transcendentally conceived geneticism: "spirit" (*Geist*), interpreted in a national, social, or even broadly human context, unfolds itself over time and in culture to inform, with varying modalities, languages viewed, increasingly, as historical organisms. Romantic "philology"—historical linguistics and literary history—is usually considered as the starting point of modern linguistic and literary research. But later, positivist scholars, blinded by their scientific claims, have usually praised the romantics for their disciplinary discoveries and orientations. Every linguist is aware of Grimm's "law" and of the early, halcyon days of comparative Indo-European grammar, just as students of literature regard highly the romantic "discoveries" of medieval literature and poetic theory. All too often the theoretical underpinnings of romantic philology have been either minimized or, worse, entirely forgotten by subsequent generations for whom the technically oriented notion of "discipline" or "science," inherited from the Enlightenment, has once again taken precedence over general philosophical attitude.

Romantic linguistic theory is clearest and most cogently expressed in Wilhelm von Humboldt's (1767–1835) influential *Ueber die Verschiedenheit des menschlichen Sprachbaues und ihren Einfluss auf die geistige Entwicklung des Menschengeschlechts* (1836).[35] The title of this work be-

35. The attraction exercised by this work upon subsequent thinkers may be imagined when one cites the names of just a few of those

trays its modernity. "Verschiedenheit" indicates the work's concern with linguistic variety, or pluralism, as well as with a unitary view of this diversity. The essay is historically oriented: the "development, or evolution, of humanity." And the history is "spiritual." Condillac's analysis is set into a transcendental organicist context. Thus, in Section I, Humboldt declares: "Language is the organ of the inner being; this very being, to the extent that he succeeds little by little in recognizing his inner self and in exteriorizing himself." The individual provides the point of departure for approaching the universal, as in Descartes and, for that matter, in Rousseau. But instead of relating the individual to universal rational process or to a given structure of sensibility, Humboldt relates him to an essentially transcendental "creativity principle" which, itself, is the animating force in history. Condillac's "analytic," or disciplinary, mediation is downplayed by Humboldt. In Section III of *Ueber die Verschiedenheit,* he adds: "The production of language is an intimate necessity of human nature, not only a social commerce for communication, but rather an entity based in its very essence, required for the working-out of man's spiritual potentialities." Most interesting is Humboldt's well-known distinction between *ergon* and *energeia.* Thus *ergon* corresponds to language seen as the passive instrument of collective man—interpersonality—whereas *energeia* defines language in its function

---

who declare their debt to Humboldt: Hugo Schuchardt, the great Romance linguist; Benedetto Croce; and now, recently, Professor Chomsky (op. cit.). We may also mention here the earlier *Ueber das Entstehen der grammatischen Formen und ihren Einfluss auf die Ideenentwicklung* (1822).

as the creative act of the individual (Section VIII). Humboldt declares that in essence language is not an action or product (*Werk*), but a "creative potentiality," an activity (*Tätigkeit*), a fertile and organized—or "regulated"—"productive capacity." Consequently, as one might imagine, the study of language—e.g., comparative linguistics—is no longer, in this view, a mediating *discipline* between "man" and "language," as philosophical grammar was; it becomes rather a source of information, or knowledge, and, as well, an essentially symbolic *illustration* of the philosophical intuitions just stated. Within the romantic framework, disciplinary mediation is transferred to domains other than grammar or "general linguistics." In literature, for example, the notion of "creativity" was identified with firmly grounded aesthetic principles.

Space does not permit a detailed analysis of this very important problem. For reasons appropriate to the present study, I propose to summarize very briefly the literary theories of Samuel T. Coleridge (1772–1834), without question the romantic critic who most influenced modern Anglo-American literary theory.

Coleridge's debt to German romantic thought is very great. It is now widely conceded that many of the "new ideas" presented in the *Biographia Literaria* (1817) and other critical works were borrowed, often with little or no acknowledgement, from the Schlegels and Schelling, especially.[36] However, his real originality consists in his synthesizing, within a relatively coherent bloc of doctrine, currents of idealist theory

36. See René Wellek, *A History of Modern Criticism:* 1750–1950, II, *The Romantic Age* (New Haven, 1955), pp. 151–87.

with the kind of modernism represented by the Franco-British empirical philosophers of the late Enlightenment.

One recognizes the fine hand of post-Kantian philosophy in Coleridge's distinction between "imagination" and "fancy." Imagination is the faculty of genius; fancy, the faculty of talent. Imagination is the power of unity—a monolithic, creative, monistic drive imparting life and higher order into an otherwise confused and incomplete reality. Thanks to imagination, works of genius actively attain the realm of the transcendental Idea and necessarily embody an essential organic unity. Through imagination—i.e., symbolizing capacity—the individual is generalized on the highest level, remaining, through a dialectic process, both intensely personal and completely universal. "Fancy" in some ways is more difficult to define. Briefly, it involves the intellectual ordering, or combining, within specific works, of psychological associations (cf. Condillac's "logic of the passions"). "Fancy" is, *mutatis mutandis,* the "imagination" of eighteenth-century empirical psychology, that is, an "imagination" whose symbolizing power remains finally contingent upon its ultimate instrumentality as determined by analysis. But the romantic Coleridge goes beyond analysis. Within his coupling of imagination and fancy, imagination is seen as active, truly creative, whereas fancy is passive and arbitrary. Genius, then, forges new realities, transcending space and time, while talent merely "juxtaposes"—sometimes in novel and witty ways—elements of memory.

"Fancy" is the category that Coleridge uses to emprison Condillac's "analysis." What, in literature, is subject to analysis is the product of fancy, hence to be subordinated to imagination. German literary theorists of the time distinguished between outer structure in art and "inner form"; the structure may be analyzed in terms of its elemental parts, but imaginative genius has infused into these parts a whole greater than their sum.

Literature or "poetry" is seen as the realm, par excellence, of creative imagination, i.e., as the domain in which human creativity at its highest and most noble exercises itself. The notion is Platonic, but given Coleridge's modernist expressionism—cf. Rousseau—poetry takes the place of Plato's "philosophy." The authenticity and value of poetic expressivity are taken, so to speak, for granted. Thus, Coleridge's example and much romantic practice have tied Anglo-American literary theory to a conception of the poet as a "creative metaphysician," his works as embodiments of truth and beauty. In Coleridge there is little to distinguish "between psychic processes and capacities and the finished product, the work of art, which, in literature, is a structure of linguistic signs" (Wellek, p. 165). Nor does Coleridge's aesthetic outlook permit him to see the relationship between poetry as language and other types of discourse. On the contrary, he is led to widen as much as possible the gap between the "articulate language" of poetry and ordinary language. Whereas Condillac had held that poetry, *in given circumstances,* differs from prose in "style" and "end" (*fin*), but principally in "degree of art," Coleridge bases his distinctions upon a theory of "end," or "object," and "function" [37] in which ethicophilosophical considerations are blended into psychoaesthetic ones (beauty–good–truth–

37. Edition used: *Biographia literaria,* chap. xiv (London, 1876), pp. 147 ff.

pleasure). Condillac had endeavored to establish analytic bases of distinction between poetic language and the language of other genres, but the upshot of his argument remains that poetry as such is less distinctive, after all, than habit might suggest; poetic dignity suffers, but poetry does remain an integral part of general language. Coleridge, however, stressing the dignity of poetry, isolates it within the categories of discourse and endows it with proportions approached best from other than linguistic angles. In Coleridge's view poetry acquires a series of qualities and comes to embody certain values that have little or nothing to do with linguistically formal properties as such.[38] Thus "language" is an ingredient of poetry to the same extent that "passion" is, or, for that matter, "personality" and "character"; "language" is one of the non-metaphysical components that Coleridge, in his system, places at the service of the ideal.[39] In a sense Coleridge justifies those

38. In "On the Principles of Sound Criticism," Preliminary Essay, Coleridge writes: "All the fine arts [music, painting, etc.] are different species of poetry."

39. Hegel, representing the *ne plus ultra* of the German romantic position, carries this viewpoint to its extreme conclusions, "freeing" poetry from dependence on language altogether; the latter, as sound, is mere *accidentellere Aeusserlichkeit* to the "inner representation" which is the soul and essence of poetry. See Hegel, *Vorlesung über die Æsthetik*, 3, in *Sämtliche Werke*, XIV (Stuttgart, 1926), p. 226; cf. Wellek's treatment, op. cit., pp. 322 ff. On the secondary, or analytical, level Coleridge speaks of language in terms reminiscent of Condillac, but only very briefly, and he quickly returns to familiar, nonlinguistic principles: "The definition of good prose is—proper words in their proper places;—of good verse—the most proper in their proper places; . . . The words in prose ought to express the intended meaning, and no more. . . . But the great thing in poetry is, *quocunque modo,* to effect a unity of impression upon the whole. . . ." *Table Talk,* "July 3, 1833" (London, 1923), p. 238.

modern linguists who distinguish between "linguistic" and "extralinguistic" elements in verbal works of art.

To switch now to the higher level of the Idea, we note that in Coleridge's system the groundwork is laid for the future prominence of one feature or *implication* of language that, by and large, tends to receive less than proper attention from the new scientific linguist–grammarians of the nineteenth century: I refer obviously to "meaning." The history of this word is by no means clear, but one can easily assume that, for Condillac and the Enlightenment, meaning as such presented few great theoretical problems. If anything, it had to do with such pragmatic qualities as clarity, precision, and exactness, although, to be fair, we must not forget that Condillac, like his age, was preoccupied by the conventionalized *flatus voci* of traditional metaphysics, as well as by the relativity of values. But "meaning," as we have come to understand it, is simply not one of Condillac's concerns. Nor, to the superficial reader, does it seem to affect Coleridge. Nevertheless, when Coleridge writes, in *Biographia Literaria* (chap. xiv), that "GOOD SENSE is the BODY of poetic genius, FANCY its DRAPERY, MOTION its LIFE, and IMAGINATION the SOUL that is everywhere, and in each; and forms all into one graceful and intelligent whole," the important adjective *intelligent* stands out. Intelligent of what? Signifying what? The problem of meaning arises. Coleridge's "esemplastic" imagination (in *Biographia Literaria,* chap. xiii) is what it is and does what it does in order to furnish intelligence of beauty and truth——of a truth

---

And, in "Allsop's Recollections," we find Coleridge believing "that processes of thought might be carried on independently and apart from spoken or written language" (London, 1917), p. 420.

belonging to an order different from, and superior to, the order from which derives the absolute, demonstrable truth of science. The celebrated essay "On Poesy or Art" (Lecture XIII of the 1818 Course) sums up Coleridge's position.

This incomplete and somewhat disorganized essay begins, curiously enough, with a brief description of human communication: "Man communicates by articulation of sounds, and paramountly by the memory in the ear; nature by the impression of bounds and surfaces on the eye, and through the eye it gives significance and appropriation, and thus the conditions of memory, or the capability of being remembered, to sound, smells, etc." The following sentence goes on to describe art as "the mediatress between, and reconciler of, nature and man." Art is no more and no less than "the power of humanizing nature, of infusing the thoughts and passions of man into every thing which is the object of his contemplation . . . it stamps [the elements that it combines] into unity in the mould of a moral idea." Communication, man, nature—the three terms of the modernist position—are thus welded by art into the transcendental form of a "moral idea." It is in this welding that—as we understand the term—meaning lies. Art is the "middle quality between thought and a thing . . . the reconciliation of that which is nature with that which is exclusively human" (i.e., understanding through language). In art it is not the thing represented but the "re-presentation" of the thing that interests us. Only the beautiful in nature deserves to be imitated; beauty is, "in the abstract, the unity of the manifold, the coalescence of the diverse; in the concrete, it is the union of the shapely (*formosum*) with the vital." Mere nature, *"natura naturata,"* is of no value; the artist "must master the essence, the *natura naturans"*; his work reconciles "the external [with the] internal," and, to a considerable extent, it does so unconsciously. And, in the following passage, Coleridge reaches the heart of "meaning":

> The artist must imitate that which is within the thing, that which is active through form and figure, and discourses to us by symbols—the *Natur-geist,* or spirit of nature, as we unconsciously imitate those whom we love; for so only can he hope to produce any work truly natural in the object and truly human in the effect. The idea which puts the form together cannot itself be the form. It is above form [i.e., structure], and is its essence, the universal in the individual, or the individuality itself,—the glance and the exponent of the indwelling power.

These Germanic phrases underscore the dynamically symbolic —or essentialist—nature of works of art. Dynamic because essences are conceived in terms of relations (things–man), essential because the symbols operative in the work point to or incarnate the one, whole *Naturgeist* or idea. Criticism in the service of the idea and, by implication, of art, proclaims the effectiveness or ineffectiveness of the symbolic organization of the work, that is, whether it succeeds or fails (synonyms, for Coleridge, of good or bad) in its task of creating beauty, in "reducing many to one." To return to the rather mysterious first sentence of "On Poesy or Art," we must conclude, then, that symbols constitute the effective fusion of human and natural communication. Poetry is the highest form of cognition. "Meaning," however—the term we use nowadays to designate this effective fusion—is, in Coleridge's view, essentially extralinguistic. Not extralinguistic in Condillac's pragmatic sense, though, because, for Coleridge, symbols seem to derive in large part from the nature of human communication, which, as he himself has written, resides at its most basic in the "articulation of sounds." The process of meaning seems here to be partially drawn from, and parallel to, linguistic operation (seen as "communication"), but, as we have seen, it serves different ends. Coleridge has not resolved the problem of poetic meaning; indeed, he merely raises the question, and, at that, only implicitly. But he has done much to present Anglo-American criticism with the dilemma it still faces, namely, the relationship between language and poetic meaning and value. In fact, by grappling with this problem, twentieth-century critics have learned to manifest deeper interest in the workings of signs—linguistic and other—even though their taste for transcendental philosophy has, in recent years, considerably declined. The linguistic bias of modern criticism in both the United States and Great Britain is distinctly semantic. Meanwhile many modern critics, as distinct from professional linguists and certain academic investigators of literature, seem to have inherited from Coleridge a certain distrust of analytic techniques that focus on purely linguistic or grammatical relationships in literary works; these critics transplant to their criticism Coleridge's specifically "poetic" distrust of demonstrable knowledge, the very kind of knowledge professional linguists tend to aim for. This too has contributed to the separation of the fairly well-defined linguistic disciplines and the highly idiosyncratic brands of literary analysis.

When applied, by Coleridge, to literature, romantic geneticism leads to a kind of aesthetic monumentalism. This is the result of that thought's fundamental transcendentalism. The literary critic, qua critic, becomes concerned with isolating the formal coefficients, in the literary work, of the creative genius that has produced it. Despite Wellek's previously quoted claim to the contrary, the modern American critic's concern with the literary work as a "structure of linguistic signs" derives directly and logically from Coleridge's identification of "psychic processes and capacities and the finished product." *ergon* is thus itself seen as a symbol for *energeia:* "creativity" and "genius" are manifest in the poem.

Coleridge's aesthetic is not a genuine "discipline" as is Condillac's "grammar" or "art of writing." Yet, in the transcendentalist framework, it plays a rôle analogous to that played by these disciplines in Condillac's philosophy. It provides for coherence in an otherwise fragmented reality. Underlying Coleridge's aesthetic is a conceptual cogency that posits a dynamic permanence governing human linguistic activity in all its variety; the individual is given relevance in terms of a universal principle that works itself out in history by and through individuals. Every "poem" is at once a personalized "history" and a manifestation of the Ideal. This doctrine incorporates the modernist crisis into a kind of historical dialectic, a dynamics that exalts the "truth" of the individual at the same time that it subsumes that truth into a higher order. Coleridge's thought is rooted in romantic linguistic theory and its philosophical counterpart, but, just as in Plato, language is seen by Coleridge as functioning in ways that culminate in non-language: pure contemplation.

In conclusion it must be said that the modernist destruction of the former cultural continuity and its subsequent rephrasing of the old tension between unity and fragmentation lead to a differentiation of "philosophy" and "poetry" very reminiscent of that obtaining in the late Middle Ages between the scholastics' instrumentalist view of language and Dante's poetic view. Platonic "symbolism" and Aristotelian "instrumentality'" seem indeed to be isolable constants in the Western understanding of language; possibilities tend to cluster about these two poles. However, now that certain basic modernist attempts at formulating new, coherent views of language have been described, it is clear that the very real relationships between these two poles are at least as important as what differentiates between them. What I have somewhat loosely called "history" has replaced the premodern "cultural continuity." The "individual versus interpersonal" dichotomy is a historical phenomenon, and, according to one's perspective, it is resolved in historical terms. Similarly, whether metaphysical— i.e., literarily aesthetic—or antimetaphysical and "disciplinary," the modern attitude toward language always implements a historical viewpoint that, in fact, automatically conjoins all possibilities, even when these are otherwise opposed. Consequently, the various activities known as literary theory and criticism or "linguistics," as developed over the past century and a half, are by definition complex. Even so highly specialized an activity as "historical grammar" depends at least as much on Humboldtian constructs as on Enlightenment empirical science. Although, for a number of reasons to be analyzed in due course, practitioners of these activities have usually preferred to adopt an exclusivist stance with respect to colleagues in other—even "related"—fields, such an exclusivism is untenable. As we have seen, the needs of specialization cannot legitimately be confused with the supposed nature of modern intellectual activity, especially when the exercise directly concerns language, since what counts, after all, is the very *fact* of such activity, not, ultimately, its "products."

THE STUDY OF LANGUAGE AND LITERATURE

In Chapter One of this study we reviewed, all too briefly, the history of the idea of language in the Western tradition, as well as the early attempts to define, and study, literary and philosophical expression. The unitary force represented by the notion of "culture" in medieval Europe and the more modern concept of "history"—in several ramifications—have been explained in the context of the broad problem of language. We have observed the vitality of what I have called the Platonic and Aristotelian modes. Certain constants of thought seem, as it were, to straddle the boundaries of "premodernity" and "modernity." Finally, the idea of "discipline," that is, of a coherent *mediating* science in the domain of language, takes hold during the seventeenth and eighteenth centuries. The various linguistic disciplines assume different forms. The form depends entirely on the practitioner's view of history and cultural process, and on his attributing certain values—goals, purposes, tastes—to "language" and "expression." Rousseau's "language" is quite different from Condillac's; the former is consequently concerned with questions of rhetoric, the latter with a kind of grammar.

During the eighteenth and early nineteenth centuries, however, "literature"—or "literary criticism"—and "linguistics," as we now understand these terms generally, became, in principle, fairly well-defined, independent activities. Despite obvious dissimilarities in mental outlook a mid-twentieth-century Prague school structuralist considers Grimm and even Jones as a "predecessor," as one concerned with problems basically the same as those with which he is concerned. The modern literary critic feels analogous kinship with Lessing, Diderot, and Coleridge. The fact that such specialization has occurred is a consequence of the kinds of world-view we have alluded to in our depiction of the modernist attitude toward language. Both activities are products of the Enlightenment and romanticism.

By definition specialization tends to be exclusivist. The historian of language describes himself as something differing in kind from the historian of literature, unless, as was sometimes the case in nineteenth-century Europe, the historian of language—e.g., Friedrich Diez (1794–1876)—considered himself as principally a historian of culture, and thus implemented his historical investigations by technical studies of linguistic *and* literary problems. Generally speaking, though, it is quite accurate to say that over the past two centuries hard-core activity centering on something called "language" came to differ considerably from the activity centering on "literature." Such, we observed, was not the case with Condillac, who attempted to provide a systematic view of literature and language in conjunction with one another and with the history of thought.

Exclusivism, in linguistic study, has been a matter of general assumption as well as of technique. The linguistic disciplines generated a momentum of their own which, over time, contributed much to characterize the "language" they studied. I do not intend here to summarize the history of modern linguistics,[1] but rather to indicate the general direction of the disciplines we call linguistics—their momentum—and, within this momentum, the considerable variety of approaches thanks to which a number of literary problems were, in fact, looked into by linguistic scholars. (The question of literary criticism itself will be examined in later sections of this review.)

The Assumptions and Techniques of Linguistics and Some Literary Ramifications

Most early linguists reconcile, with greater or lesser rigor, the rationalist–empirical analysis of Condillac with the wide historical framework of Wilhelm von Humboldt. That is, they combine the ideals of descriptive analysis one associates with Enlightenment science with a genetically oriented appreciation of historical dynamism. The early successes in comparative and historical phonetics and grammar endowed "philology" and linguistics with an autonomous personality that rendered these "methodological" sciences quite respectable. It would be impossible to overestimate the importance of formulations like Rask's (1787–1832) and Jakob Grimm's (1785–1863) sound-shift (*Lautverschieberung*) "laws," which,

1. For a general review of the history of modern linguistics, consult Carlo Tagliavini, *Panorama di storia della linguistica* (Bologna, 1963); Holgar Pedersen, *Linguistic Science in the Nineteenth Century,* tr. by J. W. Spargo (Cambridge, Mass., 1931); also Thomas A. Sebeok, ed., *Portraits of Linguists: A Biographical Source Book for the History of Western Linguistics, 1746–1963,* 2 vols. (Bloomington, 1966), as well as the multivolume *Current Trends in Linguistics* (The Hague, 1963—) now appearing under T. A. Sebeok's general editorship.

when published in Grimm's *Deutsche Grammatik* (1819, *1822*, 1840), depicted (1) the phonetic relationship—differences and correspondences—between Germanic, Latin, Greek, and Sanskrit in terms of a cyclic progression of unvoiced to aspirate to voiced and back to unvoiced consonants; and (2) the shift, within given Germanic dialects, of certain consonants, resulting in the differentiation of German from English and other Germanic dialects. Formulations of this type gave credence to the doctrines that: (1) languages may be profitably approached as systematic organisms, especially on the level of sound; (2) phonetic evidence offers the surest insight into language mechanisms; and (3) the interpretation of such evidence, when carefully implemented, is relevant to the solution of other historical problems, say, in ethnology, literary history, comparative religion, etc. The Enlightenment and romantic notions of a general linguistics—a "science of speech" or "philosophy of language"—did not disappear. But under the sway of comparative linguistics and its success, so to speak, in the field, *Sprachphilosophie* declined considerably in importance. Scholars held increasingly that the empirical study of languages must precede general statements concerning language. Nevertheless—and this seems to be a condition even of the most empirically inclined linguistics—general assumptions were still made. These assumptions were more and more tailored to fit the practicing linguists' understanding of linguistic operations and their methodological requirements.

The doctrine of language as system—a system at once self-sufficient and linked to other forces—has in one form or another dominated linguistics during the past century and a half. The romantic *Volksgeist,* the midcentury Darwinian "biological code" (laws), and twentieth-century "structure" have ruled entire epochs of linguistic study. Each relates the possibility of linguistic system to an imaginative concept that, in turn, tends to predominate in research for a generation or two. Certain realities of language are sacrificed in order to make the system as visualized function smoothly: e.g., the starred forms so prevalent in neogrammatical writings resulted directly from the mechanical diachronic phonetic laws constituting the core of the neogrammarian outlook. Furthermore, the very idea of language as system, as a bloc of reality possessing inherent order and to be analyzed totally and methodically, whatever the fad of the moment and its modalities of application, has entailed the companion notion of interpersonality. In short, language qua object of linguistics has become a kind of entity in itself, related to, yet in a sense distinct from, the larger, more fluid concept of total language.[2] In other words, linguistics in general has shaped the raw material it has set out to study, and it has done so with remarkable consistency throughout the past hundred and fifty years.[3]

2. Studies like Willard Quine's *Word and Object* (New York and Cambridge, Mass., 1960), the speculative essays of Ernst Cassirer and Susanne Langer, or the works of critics like R. P. Blackmur and I. A. Richards, all dealing with language, show that each approach tends to be monolithic in effect, yet highly particular in scope. The idea of language—as interpreted by linguists and nonlinguists alike —has become in our day an extremely fragmented concept.

3. Amado Alonso, for one, noted this tendency in Saussure: "Una de las características de la mentalidad de Saussure es que cada distinción y cada delimitación de hechos está ya como encarnada en sus exigencias metodológicas, de modo que sus doctrinas han nacido más de las necesidades técnicas de la investigación que de la contemplación filosófica del objeto." "Prólogo a la edición española" of Saussure's *Cours de linguistique générale/ Curso de lingüística gen-*

"Interpersonality," as I shall use the term here, remains a key criterion of the general "linguistic" view of language.

In the broadest sense "interpersonality" involves first of all language abstracted out of the context of individual speakers or "creators"; these latter, in whom of course the concrete phenomena of language reside, may be taken into consideration only to the extent that the raw phenomena they present can be classified in terms of given common elements or denominators. In Ferdinand de Saussure's (1857–1913) celebrated classification, the concept of *langue,* set, it is true, in relief against both *langage* (language as faculty, the gift and generalization of speech) and *parole* (i.e., individual, concrete manifestations), sums up "interpersonality" and, to boot, claims the major share of Saussure's attention as a practicing linguist. *Langue,* Saussure repeats, may be classified positivistically within the scheme of human activities, but *langage* is *unclassifiable,* and, as Amado Alonso has shown, *parole* "is in itself heterogeneous" (p. 21). Although a linguistics of *parole* is feasible, true—orthodox—structural linguistics is concerned with *langue* (see *Cours de linguistique générale,* "Introduction," chap. iv). Saussure stresses the interpersonality of *langue:* "The study of speech *{langage}* comprises two parts: the first, and most important, deals with *langue,* which, in essence, is social and independent of the individual. . . . *Langue* is therefore something which . . . is common to all individuals [although] located outside the will of the individuals in whom it is deposited."

---

eral (Buenos Aires, 1945) p. 10. (The original French version of Saussure's magnum opus, compiled by Charles Bally and Albert Sechehaye, was published in Paris, in 1916.)

The twentieth-century American school, as represented especially by the tone-setting Leonard Bloomfield (1887–1949), his followers, and successors—the prophets of taxonomic structuralism in the United States—has tended to avoid the associationist–spiritualist debate stirred up in Europe by the neogrammarians, the Saussureans, and the "idealists" (Vossler, Spitzer, Amado Alonso), by deliberately ignoring and by agnostically refusing to recognize the legitimacy of the quarrel. Yet, partly by default, partly by local tradition,[4] and mostly by preference, American linguistics has overwhelmingly dealt with interpersonal linguistic structures. Bloomfield's *Language* (1933) constituted the Magna Charta of American linguistic research for an entire generation. Bloomfield's even earlier rejection of "Wundtian mentalism," indeed his refusal to consider any kind of spiritualist speculation on the grounds that there are "too many mentalisms," relieved a subsequent generation of scholars of the burden of dealing with the nonmechanical, rather more transcendental considerations of language that, in post-Enlightenment and romantic Europe had stimulated so much "wasteful" discussion. Bloomfield's "mechanism" is far less justifiable on purely speculative grounds than on strictly pragmatic ones. When faced with certain questions, Bloomfield, even more decisively than the Saussureans, would reply that they were simply not his concern.[5] Psychological considerations, with the possible excep-

4. E.g., the immediate necessity in America to do much fieldwork with rapidly disappearing indigenous languages.

5. See the following articles published in the journal *Language:* "Why a Linguistic Society?" I, No. 1 (1925); "Twenty-one Years of the Linguistic Society," XXII, No. 1 (January–March 1946) ("Linguistics has come more and more to resemble, in its social complex-

tion of various brands of behaviorist experimentation, virtually disappeared from linguistics as practiced in the United States during the period 1930–1955. Indeed, apart from anthropology, among the humane disciplines only philosophy—mainly as represented by certain positivist logicians—has, until very recently, succeeded in interesting a number of American linguists.[6]

Bloomfield's *Language* and various theoretical articles, whatever their methodological importance in America, are hardly revolutionary documents. *Language* is rather a synthesis and a program, a concise formulation of trends, aspirations, and tastes prevalent in American linguistics for a number of years. William D. Whitney (1827–1894), a nineteenth-century Yale Indo-Europeanist admired by Saussure, had stated already in the 1860's that "comparative philology [was] the forerunner and founder of the science of human speech" ("the linguistic science").[7] Whitney insists repeatedly on the scientific nature of his discipline, although, praising Humboldt, he declares, in fine nineteenth-century periods, that the scholar must aim "to trace out the inner life of lan-

---

ion, the type of the better established branches of science—say physics, chemistry, and biology."); "Secondary and Tertiary Responses to Language," XX, No. 2 (April–June 1944), and Leo Spitzer's rejoinder: "Answer to Mr. Bloomfield," XX, No. 4 (October–December 1944), a polemic concerning "mechanism" versus "mentalism," typical of the time.

6. One thinks, for example, of the late Uriel Weinreich; see "On the Semantic Structure of Language," in *Universals of Language,* ed. J. H. Greenberg (Cambridge, Mass., 1963), pp. 114–71.

7. W. D. Whitney, *Language and the Study of Language* (New York, 1867), p. 3. This work was originally presented as a series of twelve lectures in Washington, D.C., and Boston, in 1864 and 1865.

guage, to discover its origin, to follow its successive steps of growth, and to deduce the laws that govern its mutations, the recognition of which shall account to him for both the unity and the variety of its present manifested phases; and, along with this, to apprehend the nature of language as a human endowment, its relation to thought, . . . and the history of mind and of knowledge as reflected in it" (pp. 6 f.). In short, Whitney's outlook, like Bloomfield's, is "scientific," but unlike Bloomfield's position, which supports no philosophical stand, Whitney's position is "mentalist." Let us not forget, though, that Whitney's lectures and book make up, in large part, an apology for his own work and a plea for the status of his discipline. He is trying to convince a midcentury American audience of the legitimacy and utility of linguistics with respect to other accepted sciences like ethnology, psychology, and history. This explains his effort to incorporate "linguistic science" into the general intellectual and spiritual concerns of his time. Whitney's considerable originality as a linguist lies, as even Saussure has pointed out, in (1) his recognition of the arbitrary nature of linguistic signs and structure, and (2) his appreciation of language as a conventionalized institution possessing features analogous to other human institutions. Like Humboldt before and Saussure after him, Whitney willingly concedes, on the theoretical plane, "that everything in human speech is a product of the conscious action of human beings" (p. 50), but, faced with the exigencies of the discipline, he immediately adds: "we should be leaving out of sight a matter of essential consequence *in linguistic investigation* [italics mine] if we failed to notice that what the linguistic student seeks in language is not what men have voluntarily or intentionally placed there. . . . A language is, in very truth, a grand system, of a highly complicated and symmetrical structure; it is fitly comparable with an organized body" (p. 50). And furthermore: "Now it is this absence of reflection and conscious intent which takes away from the facts of language the subjective character that would otherwise belong to them as products of voluntary action. The linguistic student feels that he is not dealing with the artful creations of individuals. So far as concerns the purposes for which he examines them, and the results he would derive from them, they are almost as little the work of man as is the form of his skull. . . . Hence the close analogies which may be drawn between the study of language and some of the physical sciences. Hence, above all, the fundamental and pervading correspondence between its whole method and theirs" (pp. 51 f.). Whitney is admirably clear, though somewhat hesitant. In the final analysis, the study of language differs from other sciences by the nature of the raw material examined: linguistics need copy no other science. Linguistic science remains *sui generis,* as respectable a branch of human learning as any other, since its aim—"the increase of knowledge, and the advancement of man in comprehension of himself and of the universe"—is precisely the aim of all true sciences. He sets the problem up in perfect focus: "Beyond all question, it is this coincidence of method which has confused some of the votaries of linguistic science, . . . leading them to deny the agency of man in the production and change of language, and to pronounce it an organic growth, governed by organic forces" (p. 52). This viewpoint, which Whitney condemns on the basis of "the ultimate facts" of linguistic reality, he accepts and commends with respect to the method linguists must follow in their actual practice. The distinction is both necessary and possible for Whitney, because, writing in the earliest days of American linguistics, he must take stock of the dialogue I have been discussing in these last few pages.

In Bloomfield, however, the primacy of what Whitney might have called "method" is taken so completely for granted that it dislodges the philosophical concern whose legitimacy Whitney still must recognize. Bloomfield merely subscribes wholeheartedly—almost as though to a dogma—to the methodological trend previously expounded with great clarity and to a large extent condoned by Whitney.[8] The tradition, especially in America, is an old one, as time is measured in the history of modern linguistics. The question of interpersonality remains, then, one of goals and methods, and, naturally, is intimately linked to the ways linguists understand their discipline. We must recall Saussure's memorable and generous dictum to the effect that, unlike other sciences whose approach is necessarily controlled by the material studied (chemistry, anatomy), linguistics is the science in which the point(s) of view will always shape or define the material to

8. Speaking of the "school of modern philosophers who are trying to materialize all science," who deal exclusively with "purely material effects" and "physical causes," Whitney declares: "With such, language will naturally pass . . . for a physical product, and its study for a physical science; *and, however we may dissent from their general classification, we cannot quarrel with its application in this particular instance*" (ibid., p. 49; italics mine). Bloomfield's echoing of this doctrine is well known. Typical of his outlook is his 1927 remark, "A grammatical or lexical statement is at bottom an abstraction" (*Journal of English and Germanic Philology*, XXVI, No. 3, p. 445), a statement that, among others, shows very well Bloomfield's "metalinguistic" and operational solution.

be studied, such is its very nature (*Cours,* "Introduction," chap. iii, p. 22): the "normal" procedure is reversed.

The several pages Whitney gives over to writing and to literature are more interesting for their highly symptomatic omissions than for their inclusions (see pp. 447 ff.). "Language" and "literature" (speech and writing) are two separate entities. Writing involves "intentions" different from those predominant in speech, namely, "the desire to communicate to a distance" in time and space. Both writing and speaking, however, serve the purposes of "communication"; that is, Whitney stresses once again the interpersonal over the individual and the creative. He has little to say about literature as such, and what he does say is hardly original, especially when one recalls his fondness for Humboldt. Language *"is* just what the people to whom it belongs have made it by their use. . . . A literature, then, is one grand test of the worth of a language" (pp. 470 f.). This worth is summarized in impressionistic terms: *depth, nobility, subtilty* (sic), and *beauty*—terms, incidentally, that remind one of the *clichés* of much Victorian literary moralism. Whitney comes closer to the spirit of his time in seeing the double-pronged unity-in-duality of speech and writing within the scope of the history of culture. He repeats, in essence, Condillac's judgment on this matter, but his formulation, because of its exclusivism, empties Condillac's judgment—as well as Humboldt's romantic corollary—of real pertinence. In short, the relationship between speech—qua object of linguistic analysis—and literature is conceived, not *linguistically* (except when, in passing, Whitney opines that writing takes "the great step towards its perfection . . . when it accepts a subordinate part, as consort and helpmate of speech" [p. 449]), but *historically*. Interpersonality and its disciplinary concomitant, empirical generalization, win out by default in that, having been transferred to an independently conceived plane of cultural history, literature is rendered linguistically inoperative.[9]

Even during the nineteenth century, however, all was not smooth sailing for the disciples of the great comparatists. As the neogrammarians attempted to rephrase with even greater scientific rigor the discoveries of Rask, Grimm, Bopp, and others, stressing the exceptionless character of "sound laws" and the perfectly systematic nature of "languages," critics proposed counter assumptions. Students of dialects—e.g., Jules Gilliéron (1854–1926)—undermined the very notion of "language" as an organic monolith, progressing implacably over time and space. Pointing out the importance of dialect borrowings, regressions, readjustments in the system, and illustrating such phenomena by precise cartographic references, the geographers showed the concept of language itself to be most problematic indeed or, at best, arbitrary. In fact, it is quite legitimate to speak of a profound *crise de conscience* among linguists during the first decade or so of the present century. Confidence was shaken, and Saussure's teaching certainly was designed to restore a semblance of disciplinary relevance to the many procedures then in use.

Other critics operated on the basis of different assumptions. The great Romance linguist Hugo Schuchardt (1842–1927) rejected the "dogma" of "sound law." With withering wit he

9. This same anthropological–cultural tendency is vastly developed in the linguistico-literary studies of Franz Boas and his school; see also the works of Edward Sapir.

demonstrated that this theory has neither deductive nor inductive justification, that, in fact, it is far more profitable to view language as a social product in continuous, dynamic flux than as a "natural organism." Schuchardt goes back to Humboldt; he strips linguistic research of its Darwinist trappings. Etymological study reaches a high-water mark in Schuchardt, who based his study of words in great part on their associations with the objects and practices of culture (*Wörter und Sachen*).

Yet neither Gilliéron nor Schuchardt was prepared to reject the interpersonalism of scientific linguistic study. On the contrary, both argued in favor of their own techniques by indicating the scientific inadequacy of the assumptions made by the neogrammarians. If, as Gilliéron put it, each word in fact has its own history, then an etymological investigation of that word—bringing to bear upon the analysis every possible bit of relevant information—will reveal the truest kind of *general* linguistic operation. Or, put another way, the history of a single word—especially an opaque word like [Fr.] *trouver*—stands a better chance of depicting linguistic history more genuinely than equations of the type [Lat.] $-\acute{A}-$ > [Fr.] $-e-$ (*MATRE{M}, PRATU{M}* > *mère, pré*).

By the end of the nineteenth century, then, something we may call linguistic science is firmly established, that is, a discipline, or a variety of related disciplines that share the basic assumption that an empirical understanding of linguistic operations precedes the making of general statements concerning these operations. In practice, research varies from the broad-gauged attempts of the "systematizers" to a kind of *pointillisme* characteristic of the etymologists. In the context of this research the concept of language itself undergoes considerable fragmentation, since what constitutes "a language" for, say, the neogrammarian Meyer-Lübke differs substantially from what is meant by the term in Schuchardt. The *fact* that linguistic science shapes, or *determines,* the material it studies becomes obvious and, as we noted, this fact is incorporated by Saussure into his all-encompassing structuralist formulations. Similarly, Bloomfield's mechanism, arbitrary though it may seem to us now, responds to the freewheeling state linguistic research found itself in around 1910. By proposing what was thought to be coherent purely methodological limitations, Bloomfield hoped to eliminate the undesirable anarchy. However, these methodological limitations—far more severe even than those one finds in Saussure—were, in the judgment of many, gratuitously confused with "science"; Bloomfield's rejection of "mentalism" merely substitutes behaviorist psychology for the despised Wundtian brand.

Before examining in greater detail the work of more recent twentieth-century American linguists in connection with literary matters, it would be well to summarize briefly the earlier contributions of certain (mainly European) scholars and schools of thought.[10] I shall limit the discussion to investigators who share the basic assumptions of linguistic research as these have just been reviewed but who, for various reasons,

10. A number of these European scholars—or their disciples—immigrated to the United States in the 1930's. Note should be taken of the enormous debt the American university owes these many men and women who, in most cases, not only became worthy American scholars, but brought with them the varied and precious heritage of their countries of origin, blending the best of their past with the realities and possibilities of their American present. Their contributions to intellectual life in the United States have been incalculable.

either find the "affective" or "creative" functions of speech and literature more to their taste than their somewhat mathematically inclined colleagues do, or attempt to deal with such functions in a less circumscribed methodological framework than one usually associates with hardcore linguistic research. I shall focus on the "stylistics" of Charles Bally (1865–1947) —Saussure's disciple—and on German "idealist" *Stilforschung;* the remainder of this section will be given over to Prague school theory and to the work of one of America's greatest linguists, Edward Sapir.

Symptomatic of the directions taken by the Bloomfield group—indeed of its virtual isolation—is the fact that, to all intents and purposes, Bally's work has been ignored in the United States. Even now its meager *direct* influence is confined largely to a few Romance scholars here. His viewpoint is, of course, Saussurean, but it contains a number of interesting modifications that, at first glance, may seem paradoxical. Like his master, Bally, also a Swiss, chose to work within the limits of *langue,* and his traditional orientation always remained totally psychological (a French trait already clearly present in Condillac). As stated in *Le Langage et la vie* (1913, 1926, 1935), Bally proposes to study "language as the expression of feelings and as the instrument of action," that is, the preponderance, over intelligence, of "affective" and "volitional" elements in the construction and workings of natural language. His mentalist bias is at once antilogical and antiliterary. He rejects "style study," i.e., the study of literary style in its aesthetic context, in favor of "stylistics," which, as he puts it, deals principally with the spoken tongue or with texts only to the degree that they offer examples of the spoken language. His aim is "to draw conclusions from the investigation of current emotive words or expressions which manifest the spiritual and mental attitudes common to, or present within, a linguistic group." From the standpoint of principle, this doctrine seems to resemble the intuitionist theories of the idealists, but in reality, methodologically, it does not. Bally operates within carefully delimited sectors of given linguistic systems and the "spiritual" factors implied, and he is content to describe them as they function. Moreover, unlike Vossler or Spitzer, Bally is resolutely antihistorical: "Stylistics is purely descriptive. What is of the past does not affect it, if this past has not left some [describable] trace in the present." Having chosen *langue* over *parole,* Bally prefers to deal with synchrony and not diachrony. Moreover, his method is typically linguistic, since it is based on effective contrast (oppositions); he uses the term *comparison:* "Un principe important de notre méthode, c'est l'établissement, par abstraction, de certains modes d'expression idéaux et normaux; ils n'existent nulle part à l'état pur dans le langage, mais ils n'en deviennent pas moins des réalités tangibles, dès qu'on observe 1. les tendances constantes de l'esprit humain et 2. les conditions générales de la communication de la pensée." [11] These characteristic "modes of expression" are grouped around two poles: (1) the "intellectual" or "logical" mode, to be employed by the linguist as a norm, permitting first the comparison and then the detection of semantic and affective variants, and (2) "common language," the norm allowing for the description of the "social peculiarities" of linguistic usage. Both

11. *Traité de stylistique française* (Heidelberg and Paris, 1909), I, pp. 28 f.

these poles are evidently "interpersonal"; in effect, they are linguistic measuring rods engendering precise descriptions of aberrant *realia*. Bally's criterion is usage, never grammatical "rule" as such. He also warns against the confusion, when observing literary texts (seen here as sources), between stylistic observation (true stylistics) and the observation of the means of style (literary analysis), since this confusion may cause us to believe erroneously that we are studying the nature of means of expression when, in reality, we are merely studying the use an author makes of these means. "When we examine," says Bally, "whether [a given] expression conforms to the general tone of the work, . . . we practice literary aesthetics, criticism, but not stylistics." Each element studied, then, must be "compared" in terms of strictly categorized oppositions— e.g., synonymy versus antinomy. These comparisons can lead up to cross-language comparisons involving nongenetic relationships between two different linguistic systems. Bally frequently makes use of German to point out the stylistic resources of French.

Bally's curious distinction between spoken and written language is important and well worth extensive paraphrase. Written language is always the manifestation of states of mind, of forms of thought that normally do not find their expression in ordinary language. The context of written language differs from the spoken situation; written discourse is deprived of expressive intonation and mimicry. Moreover, in conversation the situation is almost always given, whereas the writer must create the situation. He may take his time, he may even ask the reader to reread. Thus, for Bally, the true norm of authentic stylistic investigation is contained in the liveliness, the source-ness of speech. By implication the literary analyst must do precisely the opposite.

Against the backdrop of general spoken language Bally places his concept of "ordinary language," a type deprived of all affective value, a kind of linguistic zero degree useful as a tool in comparisons. For example, the syntax of "John loves Mary" is a function of "ordinary language," since in theory, it allows no choice; it is also a frequent construction and can be usefully referred to as a "norm." Yet Bally intelligently denies the existence of *real* grounds for comparison, in a structural sense, between logical syntax and affective stylistics since they constitute two quite different systems of expression. However it remains to be seen to what extent they are really two separate expressive systems and not simply two categories embracing the same raw material.

These working principles lay the groundwork for a science parallel to, but different from, the structural linguistics to which we have become accustomed. Paradoxically, it is Bally's intellectualism that stimulates his concentration upon the affective. His point of departure, the dynamics of Saussure's speech act (*circuit de la parole*), implies that language is the vehicle for the expression of concepts and that these concepts are embedded, as it were, in an all-pervasive affective climate. Bally does not, however, fall into the (linguistic) error of studying as a psychologist the affective states accompanying expression; he rigorously orients his analysis toward the investigation of linguistic structures in themselves and of their general expressive values: "The task of stylistics is to extract what is general in the caprices of personal expression and to state common tendencies; one can say that stylistics investigates in speech and in written works precisely that which least interests a critic or historian of literature." In a sense, Bally deals with the structures of certain linguistic modalities. Thus, for example—space not permitting a detailed summing up of his various results—his table of "evocative effects" includes classification according to tone, temporal strata, region, age group, social classes, social groups, etc. The emphasis is decidedly lexicological, although syntax (e.g., ellipsis, *procédés indirects*) is not entirely neglected.

Bally's work concentrates far more on the expressive resources of French than, as he put it, on the "sublime deformations" of French practiced by Racine, Molière, and Hugo; that is how he intended it and that is how it should be. Nevertheless, students of literary language, particularly in France, have directly or indirectly applied Bally's techniques to the study of literature; the precision of his formulations has appealed to a number of literary scholars. (See the well-known works of Jacques Marouzeau and Marcel Cressot and B. Dupriez' more recent "Jalons pour une stylistique littéraire," *Le Français moderne,* XXXII, No. 1 [January 1964].) In the main they have retained the ancient norm–deviation dichotomy inherited from classical rhetoric, and have considered, say, the language of a given writer as deviant from "standard" French or English. This kind of treatment has indubitably increased our information concerning the various authors studied, but has advanced not one whit our understanding of the linguistic and aesthetic processes involved in literary composition. Nor have these stylisticians of literature been faithful to their master's real originality. Bally consistently focused his attention upon processes (the "etymological instinct," "synonymy," "figures," etc.). Bally's "norms"—his "logical" and "common language"—are not absolutes in any sense of the term. The "logical mode" and "common language" may be avatars of what I have called interpersonality, but in Bally's system interpersonality is essentially part of a dialectic process, a movement (functioning on two levels) through which the "comparative" linguist–stylistician seizes and records the patterns governing the means of expression proper to a given linguistic system and, hopefully, sheds light on the behavior of language in general. In a sense this movement or process is circular (or spiral): Bally begins with a tangible fact of expression, situates it with respect to the two normal "characteristic modes" that, we must remember, "exist nowhere in a pure state" (the first level of interpersonality), and this comparison enables him to sketch out a preliminary qualitative description, which in turn leads to the formulation of the processes involved (the second level of interpersonality). Bally not only respects the concreteness of the phenomena observed, his very abstractions are infused with a sense of the real. In short, he has devised a method that reconciles, *within a closed system,* the individual–interpersonal polarity, but that nonetheless remains faithful, on the plane of method, to the interpersonal character of the structuralist viewpoint as systematized by Saussure.

Critics like Amado Alonso have frequently stressed the similarities and differences between Bally and his contemporaries, the German linguistic "idealists." By and large these similarities and differences boil down to the following: like Bally, Karl Vossler, Leo Spitzer, Ulrich Leo, and Helmut Hatzfeld are "mentalists"; they too stress the affective elements in expression, they too speak of "language" and "life" in somewhat metaphysical terms. Unlike Bally, however, the idealist school rejects positivism as a method and the kind of scientific, or measurable, truth it purports to teach. Moreover, denying—as Croce has done—any essential difference between ordinary speech and literary usage, they deal preferably with the complex language of poets. Much of their work, incidentally, has been done in the Romance field. Thus, they constitute a bridge between the larger body of linguists and certain—mainly academic—schools of modernist literary criticism. Although considering themselves linguists, the idealists have had greater success among the literary critics and historians.

First of all, it must be said that the idealists are a much less tightly knit group than, say, the Geneva school, the Prague Circle, or the Bloomfieldian team represented in *Language*. Affinities among the idealists are quite strong—they share a number of basic attitudes—but their methods specify a high degree of individuality in each member. These methods go back to the theories of Humboldt (see above) and to certain avowed disciples of that master. One remembers, for example, Heymann Steinthal (1823–1899), author of the ethnopsychological *Ursprung der Sprache* (3rd rev. ed., 1877), who "freed" language from dependence on a priori logical categories to an extent previously unknown: "In the matter of language," wrote Steinthal, "there is no difference between its *original* creation [*Urschöpfung*] and the creative act which is repeated daily." This idea was taken up by Benedetto Croce (1866–1952) in his *Estetica come scienza dell'espressione e linguistica generale* (1900–1902) and given new philosophical coherence. For Croce all *use* of language remains essentially expressive, and is therefore governed by an aesthetic system; the reality of language, of course, resides in its use. As a category, language constitutes, therefore, an order of personal creation (i.e., *energeia*). It is not an arsenal of prefabricated weapons, nor is it a mere dictionary, a "cemetery of more or less well-embalmed corpses." Linguistic unity resides in the "inner form" of given pieces of discourse (Humboldt's *innere Sprachform*). It is this inner form that the linguist—aesthetician, or critic, must endeavor, in his investigations, to point out in terms of both structure and meaning.

This all too brief summary hardly does justice to Humboldt, Steinthal, and Croce. I wish nonetheless to stress one essential point, namely, the effort made by these forefathers of the idealist tradition to set up analytic categories, permitting the study of the individual and his dynamic linguistic rôle by establishing an alternative to positivism as a method. It is highly significant that, during the heyday of the neogrammarians (the first decade of our century), the first important theoretical works of Karl Vossler (1872–1949) should deal precisely with "positivism" and "idealism" in the "science of language" (*Positivismus und Idealismus in der Sprachwissenschaft,* 1904, a work dedicated to Croce), and with "speech as creation and evolution" (*Sprache als Schöpfung und Entwicklung,* 1905). In the first of these works Vossler is careful to define positivism and idealism as methods, not as two distinct philosophical systems (though he does distinguish "metaphysical" and "nonmetaphysical"—or "methodological"—positivism). The idealist viewpoint purports to apply correctly "our intuitive powers in the field of objective historical research"; linguistics is one of the historical disciplines—here Vossler does not quarrel with the neogrammarian view—based, however, on the "intuitive faculty." It places the "principle of human causality" in the domain of human reason, i.e., the spirit (*Geist*). On the other hand, positivism is content to describe minutely the facts of given circumscribed problems. It deals exclusively with "knowledge of the material," seen as a value in itself, and ascribes causes to the phenomenological operations themselves or simply refuses to deal with them. Adoption of the "idealist" point of view entails, in linguistics, a complete reversal of procedures. According to Vossler, the positivists (e.g., Meyer-Lübke and his cohorts) have classified linguistic material both anatomically and hierarchically in terms of phonetics/phonology, morphology, syntax, and semantics (the latter virtually neglected), and have claimed that stylistics, which deals with choices determined by aesthetic motivation, should properly fall within the purview of the literary critic and historian and not within the linguist's concern. Vossler, the idealist, takes an opposite tack. He confers pre-eminence upon stylistics, the only discipline capable of providing true explanations of the phenomena described by phonology and morphology (defined as "the lower disciplines," chap. ii). The idealist accepts the general aesthetic classification, since he equates language and "spiritual expression": "The history of linguistic development and change can only be the history of the spiritual forms of expression, that is, the history of art in the widest sense of the word."

For Vossler this view is a prioristic, but perhaps less so than the pseudo-objectivity of empirical positivism. The linguist must depend upon his institutional flair, his grasp of patterns in any given mass of facts, but the results of his analysis, if properly handled, are just as "scientific"—indeed, more so—than the schemes and patterns displayed in conventional descriptive or historical grammars. His method consists in "consciously reproducing the inner process which has led to the 'work of art' " (chap. iii, part 2), that is, which gives coherence to the chaotic facts assembled. This "conscious reproduction" takes stock of the "two distinct moments" or stages through which all linguistic phenomena—whether phonetic, grammatical, or, for that matter, metrical—must pass: "(1) the moment of absolute progress, i.e., the stage of free individual creation, [and] (2) the moment of relative progress, i.e., the stage of so-called regular development, of collective creation, as it were, undergoing a process of life-conditioning" (chap. vii). The bias is unquestionably diachronic; German idealist *Stilforschung,* unlike Bally's *stylistique,* is almost invariably genetic. However, this temporal limitation is compensated for by the wide scope left to Vosslerian analysis. Individual linguistic devices, single poems or novels, and whole language systems are all relevant and treated on much the same level. In practice, though, Vossler's method has a dual, hierarchical focus: the individual work of art and, on a yet higher plan, language as *cultural process.*

Vossler's "method" goes far toward defining the material upon which it is designed to operate. The theory of "two moments" or stages referred to in *Positivismus und Idealismus in der Sprachwissenschaft* effectively sums up his attitude toward the interpersonal versus individual polarity. This attitude is surely even more paradoxical than Bally's. It implies that:

(1) Both factors are cooperative in linguistic history, but remain, so to speak, temporally distinct; the individual would seemingly correspond to the first step, whereas the interpersonal would involve the second step—yet each step constantly involves the other; and (2) Only close attention to the individual as part of the general creative process is capable of shedding light on the interpersonal. The former engenders the latter, and it is precisely the pattern of genesis that lays prior claim on the linguist's attention. Indeed, in later years Vossler greatly amplified his theories concerning levels of genetic patterns; he became almost obsessed with the implications of an internal process governing expression on all strata, particularly the national—hence his doctrine that the expressive potentialities of any tongue are ruled by the "spirit" of the speakers (see the revised *Frankreichs Kultur und Sprache,* 1929). Study of these potentialities with regard to their use— not abstractly—is the study of "national style." In a sense, then, Vossler resolved the paradox by rising above it in his own practice; he came to deal more and more with the interpersonal, but, in so doing, he relied on techniques normally associated with studies of the individual in language. And it goes without saying that none of his experiments or conclusions can be verified mathematically; his later works are not free of mysticism.[12] Thus, each language possesses "a force, a talent, a temperament," in sum, a creative will of its own, analogous to the creative will of the poet; it remains, by definition, interpersonal, but it behaves individually. Without at-

12. Even Spitzer qualified Vossler's extended analyses of national style as "premature": *Linguistics and Literary History* (Princeton, 1948), p. 11.

tempting to resolve, defend, or attack these interesting paradoxes, we may stress, once again, Vossler's constant insistence upon the expressive, that is, the noncommunicative feature of language. Do the reader's difficulties stem from Vossler's desire to study various languages as expressive systems, rather than, primarily, as vehicles of communication? Very possibly. Bally, we saw, relies very heavily upon Saussure's *circuit de la parole* (with speaker and interlocutor), whereas Vossler seldom takes this relationship into account. Indeed, he is most interested by the types of language least contaminated by interpersonal considerations; witness his remark concerning sound and poetry: "In the language of everyday speech the natural forms of expression—sounds, voice, rhythm—are ruled by usage, and constitute the outer forms which have to obey our intentions and needs. In poetry they become the inner and dominant part, to which the rules of syntax and word usage have to adapt themselves" (*Geist und Kultur in der Sprache*). It is this "inner and dominant" rôle of sound in poetry that clearly claims Vossler's main attention. Indeed, it is the very complexity of literary language that draws him to study, in preference to "ordinary speech," the work of major writers (Dante, Lope de Vega, Racine). Curiously enough, it is the generalization of the individual speech-creation that, in large measure, consecrates it and makes of it a subject worthy of Vossler's interest. How many deviant creations have fallen by the wayside![13]

13. A sample of Vossler's approach to straight linguistic problems can be found in his "Neue Denkformen im Vulgarlatein," published as a chapter in *Geist und Kultur in der Sprache* (Heidelberg, 1925). The general thesis of this somewhat Dilthey-inspired article is that Folk Latin—the "language" from which Romance derives—is no

Because of his migration to the United States shortly before World War II, his forceful personality, the large number of his writings appearing in American journals, and his tenure of an influential chair at The Johns Hopkins University, Leo Spitzer's (1887–1960) work is much better known in Amer-

---

simple "corruption" of classical Latin, but instead of a linguistic mode present in earliest Latinity—a mode very different from the Hellenizing classical literary mode that was never really spoken to any significant extent. Vossler explains phonetic, morphological, and syntactic traits in terms of the Folk Latin stylistic mode (norm), showing that the specific linguistic traits of Folk Latin, *as style*, became generalized in new paradigms that would eventually become Romance when the *Weltanschauung* of the speakers of Folk Latin finally came to predominate over the modes formerly dominant in classical style. In short, we have the typical Vosslerian idea that stylistics—the science studying the free choice of real linguistic phenomena—has precedence over syntax, which in turn is merely the science of generalized stylistic choice. Let us paraphrase a few lines from the passages dealing with the Romance future (pp. 67 f.): In the first place we note that the Latin future did not possess a precisely determined structure of flexional patterns. Because of the historical linguistic coupling of the future and the present subjunctive, the future oscillated between a modal and a temporal orientation: on the one hand, *amabo* and *delebo,* on the other hand, *legam* and *audiam.* The endings *-bo* and *-am* counterweigh each other and they tend to mix. In late Latinity all kinds of confusions are noted: *floriet* for *florebit, respondeam* for *respondebo.* . . . Furthermore, the phonetic similarity of *amabit* and *amavit,* of *amabunt* and *amabant* confuses matters, as does that of *leges–leget* and the first conjugation subjunctive: *am–es, am–et,* etc. Nevertheless, the formal tendency of the language could have provided a solution via analogical change, creating a fixed and homogeneous future pattern; for such a solution to have been possible, it would have been necessary for the cognitive tendency of the language to desire it. However, the temporal concept of the future presented signs of weakness and finally succumbed. Just like the prophet in his own country, the concept of future time does not normally enjoy great consideration in the speech of the masses. . . . The lowbrow adopts with respect to future things a volitional, desiring, hopeful, and fearful attitude, ica than Vossler's. It is difficult to evaluate Spitzer's debt to Vossler; their evolutions seem to be more parallel than derivative, and Spitzer has constantly stressed his own originality. Suffice it to say that both were Romance scholars belonging to the same *Stilforschung* trend and that, within this tradition, Vossler dealt with vaster, more general questions, whereas Spitzer, the etymologist and style analyst, preferred specific problems: typically, the study of given semantic clusters, of word histories, and individual stylistic investigations. Of the two Vossler had perhaps the deeper mind, but Spitzer possessed the more brilliant wit, the more clever intelligence.

For convenience sake I shall not deal with Spitzer's earlier

---

not a purely contemplative attitude. . . . To prevent the futurist temporal outlook from being sidetracked along the modal sector of fear and hope, of desire and insecurity, one must dispose of a high level of self-consciousness and discipline; in short, one must possess a philosophical mentality and inner attitude. If we could embrace in a single glance the total use of temporal expressions at the end of antiquity, and if we could compare, with respect to usage, the familiar speech of the masses with the style of prominent and literarily cultivated people, we should, in my opinion, possess, reflected in historical—linguistic nuances and general effects, the deep abyss separating the stoic calm of the great from the feverish and passionate religious superstition of the masses. Phonetic confusion, then, and especially the fact that the futuristic meaning had, in Folk Latin, become so markedly involved with the sentimental facets of duty, affection, desire, anxiety, fear, etc., caused the inflected forms to become superfluous. Indeed, in order to express the newly formed mentality, language disposed of many other means, more original, stronger and more intense: the subjunctive, the imperative, the indicative, the pure infinitive, circumlocution involving *velle* (cf. Rumanian), *posse, debere,* and the like, and finally with *habere.* The infinitive-plus-*habere* construction became the basis for the Romance future in most cases (except for Rumanian). (CANTABO > CANTARE HABEO > [Fr.] *chanterai,* [Sp.] *cantaré,* [It.] *canterò.*)

work; his ideas remained remarkably constant over the years. Furthermore, it was the studies published in English and collectively titled *Linguistics and Literary History* (Princeton, 1948) that had the widest repercussions in the United States.[14] A glance at this volume shows Spitzer's adherence to the basic principles discussed above in my treatment of Vossler. Spitzer also rejects "positivism," especially the brand practiced by Meyer-Lübke and Becker, his professors, respectively, of Romance linguistics and French literature at Vienna. This antipositivist crusade accounts in part for a number of highly acrimonious reviews that did not enhance Spitzer's reputation among his American colleagues (see his review of Hayward Keniston's *The Syntax of Castilian Prose* [Chicago, 1937] in *Language,* XIV [July-September 1938], 218–30). Like Vossler, he refuses to admit any fundamental distinction, save, apparently, one of emphasis, between the study of literature and the study of language per se. But, whereas for Vossler the analysis of literary texts was normally, as such, subordinate to general linguistic speculation, Spitzer, especially in his later years, came to deal more and more with purely literary works in terms of structures and meanings. His influence as a straight linguist—at least in America—has been at best minimal and, in some rare cases, perhaps, damaging (especially to the cause of Romance linguistics), but his importance as a special kind of literary critic has been considerable. Not only

14. References to this volume by other American and foreign scholars have been legion; two reactions deserve special mention however: Jean Hytier, "La Méthode de M. Leo Spitzer," *Romanic Review,* XLI, No. 1 (February 1950), a well-phrased critique of Spitzer's method, questioning its general validity, and, more recently, René Wellek's lengthy and moving necrological statements in *Comparative Literature,* XII (Fall 1960).

does Spitzer combine linguistic study and literary investigation, he actually "crosses the line" separating the two disciplines. Nevertheless, for many nonlinguists in American literary scholarship, Spitzer incarnates "the application of linguistics" to the study of literature. Thus, in the title essay of *Linguistics and Literary History,* Spitzer confesses that the methods and degrees of certainty in both literary and linguistic investigation are fundamentally the same, that the conclusions he has reached concerning Diderot's *Neveu de Rameau* and Racine's *Phèdre* might have been arrived at just as surely by a different approach, but that, having been trained by Meyer-Lübke in Romance linguistics, he prefers a technique he has found useful in etymological research. Criticism, he adds, should deal with the work as such (just as etymology should study the word), not with any a priori judgment or appreciation of the work. Each work is a complete and indivisible whole; its unity is a function of the mind of the creator (Vossler's "creative will"). Everything depends on the coherent spirit of the writer: the plot structure, the imagery, the language—the meaning, in short. Borrowing a notion from etymology, Spitzer calls this inner coherent spirit the "spiritual etymon" of the work, the source of everything else. After many rereadings, the critic–analyst grasps the spiritual etymon, or is led to it, by an intuitive "click," i.e., an instantaneous comprehension of the work's inner principle of order. Without such a "click" no understanding occurs.

Once the work is restored by the critic to its whole meaning (principle of organization), it can and should be integrated into a wider domain: e.g., the entire collected works of the author or the aesthetic spirit of the age and/or nation.

Spitzer's "click" is frequently provoked by a linguistic or

stylistic feature of the work, a trait that, being distinctive, can qualify as a "stylistic deviation," revealing in turn a quirk typical of the writer's mentality. (It is, unfortunately, not made clear from what norm or presumed norm this trait is supposed to "deviate.") Thus he observes in the novel *Bubu de Montparnasse* (1905) of the early twentieth-century French writer Charles-Louis Philippe an "aberrant usage" of *à cause de* ("because of") reflecting the spoken, nonliterary language. He notices that, furthermore, in several instances, the causal relationship is stressed "where the average person would see only coincidence," as in the sentence: "Awakenings at noon are heavy and grimy. . . . One has a feeling of decay *because of* previous awakenings"—*because of* instead of something like *as compared with*. Spitzer goes on to discover a whole pattern of causal relationships set up in Philippe's novels; this pattern points to what "is the matter" with his conception of causality. He then passes "from Philippe's style to the psychological etymon, to the radix in his soul." He calls "the phenomenon in question 'pseudo-objective motivation': Philippe, when presenting causality as binding for his characters, seems to recognize a rather objective cogency in their sometimes awkward, sometimes platitudinous, sometimes semipoetic reasonings; his attitude shows a fatalistic, half-critical, half-understanding, humorous sympathy with the necessary errors and thwarted strivings of these underworld beings dwarfed by inexorable social forces." Another example: "[He loved Bertha's] private voluptuousness when she flattened her body tight against his. . . . He liked that quality which distinguished her from all the women he had known *because* it was softer, *because* it was more delicate, and *because* she was his own woman, and he had taken her virginity." Spitzer completes his explanation: "The pseudo-objective motivation, manifest in his style, is the clue to Philippe's *Weltanschauung;* he sees, as has also been observed by literary critics, without revolt but with deep grief and a Christian spirit of contemplativity, the world functioning wrongly with an appearance of rightness, of objective logic. The different word-usages, grouped together . . . lead toward a psychological etymon, which is at the bottom of the linguistic as well as of the literary inspiration of Philippe." [15]

This typical sampling suffices, I think, to show the kind of study Spitzer has attempted. One sees to what extent he has departed from the usual linguistic concerns, how complete his conversion to literary analysis and commentary eventually become. Applying to Spitzer our interpersonal–individual yardstick, we may safely conclude that (1) his attention was occupied exclusively by the *individuality* of the linguistic or literary phenomena he investigated (in other words, that only specifically individual phenomena really interested him), and (2) interpersonality, which, for him, eventually meant little more than general validity of method, resided entirely in the assent his conclusions could inspire in fellow scholars and readers. Put in another way, Spitzer's concern with the state of his discipline—and with the humanities in general—constituted his principal scientific excuse: for many years the humanities have blindly imitated the positivistic natural sciences; humanistic scholarship has reached a dead end; let us

15. Spitzer develops these conclusions even further in an effort to show how the *"mens Philippina* is a reflection of the *mens Francogallica* of the twentieth century" (p. 14).

therefore try something else. This is a constant theme in Spitzer's writings, at least in America. Meanwhile, his personal taste, his almost mystical reliance on intuition—the most personal form of cognition—his passionate faith in man as creator, led him to probe, in a highly idiosyncratic way, precisely those aspects of human creation embodied in *Wortkunst* that reaffirm the independence of *homo faber,* his freedom from whatever is binding or logical—preimposed—in language. In a sense, Spitzer was the self-styled nongrammarian of the "ungrammatical" principle of linguistic order; he always tried to point out the hidden meanings, as he saw them, of these important, freedom-loving, central, and very lively "deviations."

Spitzer's work has been much praised and much criticized. On the negative side, it has been remarked that his method is really a nonmethod; when imitated by lesser minds it has led to complacency and even to downright incompetence. There is surely something capricious, even anarchical, about the "philological circle" with its "clicks," self-sufficient intuitions, and psychological stresses. Unfortunately, Spitzer—a scholar, we observe, who always freely expressed his concern over the state of his discipline—has left no solid foundation on which to build; he has bequeathed to his successors the disturbing example of his own dazzling brilliance and, less happily, his frequent wrongheadedness. His conclusions are at times puzzlingly contradictory. It seems odd, to return to our previous example, that such a lover of liberty as Spitzer assuredly was should see in the *mens Philippina* a kind of precooked "reflection of the twentieth-century *mens Franco-gallica,*" that this should be Spitzer's last word on the matter, his culminating statement.

Interpersonality never played an indispensable rôle in any Spitzerian linguistic analysis; at most, summed up in a theory of "dry positivism," it acts as a kind of technical bogey in the framework of his "method." Nor did Spitzer rise above the tension as, to a considerable extent, Vossler succeeded in doing; Spitzer is at his best when interpreting specific data. It seems then that the methodological value of his resolutely individualist approach is mainly exemplary. Consequently, we must ask what the positive effects of Spitzer's "example" have been.

On the most general level Spitzer simply carries the antipositivist ball. He has contributed significantly to the maintenance of the individualist alternative within an academic structure largely given over to positivist research. But, more specifically, we must speak of his presence in the United States, a country, let us not forget, where by 1940 the new linguistics and structural descriptivism had entirely merged and literature had been banished from sophisticated linguistic attention, where textual criticism (witness the important Armstrong team at Princeton) dominated medieval studies, at least in Romance, and where, finally, graduate studies of literature were almost entirely given over to intellectual history and to source-investigation. The application of any form of linguistic approach to literature (except, of course, in the establishment of texts) was unheard of. True, the New Criticism had begun to exert some influence in a few American universities, but its efforts and techniques, although waxing stronger, had yet to be universally diffused. Romance linguistics—in many ways perhaps the most literate of the great linguistic subdivisions—was suffering a general eclipse. It was in this atmosphere that Spitzer's originality stood out. Indeed, in his 1947 Princeton lecture ("Linguistics and Literary History"), he justifies a number of autobiographical remarks, claiming, somewhat maliciously but not without a certain truth, that the situation of the then present-day American student was not unlike his own predicament in pre–World War I Vienna. Most important, then, was Spitzer's well-documented claim that minute analysis of given linguistic features present in literary works could lead to deeper, and entirely legitimate, understandings of these works. The interpretations would be acceptable to the more advanced representatives of traditional scholarship *as well as* to the young votaries of the New Criticism. As it turned out, this affirmation offered an exit from what an increasing number of American scholars, critics, and students had come to view as a methodological dead end. Moreover, it jibed perfectly with the concern over "meaning" so typical—even then—of modern Anglo-American literary criticism. Spitzer's shortcomings were overlooked, and, by and large, rightly so, in view of the exciting new possibilities his critical acumen, his great learning, his linguistic flair seemed to open. His conclusions might at times be debated, or even rejected outright, but his essays were never dull; they seemed to call for emulation. Certainly as much as any other scholarly writer, Spitzer contributed to the breakthrough we are experiencing at present, the partial reconciliation of linguistics and literary study. The fact that he did little to promote or encourage lines of research that began to emerge during his lifetime —indeed, there is reason to suppose he did not understand them—remains another matter. Not the least of his many paradoxes is the tragic fact that Spitzer, who had in effect done so much to awaken so many vocations and who possessed such a fine sense of realities, was ultimately unable to do more than disparage the efforts of his most talented younger colleagues. Spitzer was no innovator: he belongs at the end of an often splendid tradition. Nowhere is this truth more evident than in his inability to grasp the new trends of his discipline.

Over the past two decades or so, American linguists have come to know, and to appreciate highly, the work of a number of fellow scholars usually grouped together under the label Prague Linguistic Circle (or, Cercle linguistique de Prague). The Prague Circle derives ultimately from—and reacts against—Saussurean structuralism and certain East European traditions going back to the Russian schools of Jan Baudouin de Courtenay (1845–1929) and Serge Karčevski (1884–1955). Less known in America than, say, Trubetzkoy's "phonology" have been the important literary studies produced under the aegis of Prague school members. Many of these latter—e.g., Roman Jakobson—had previously been in close contact with the Russian formalist group; others, like René Wellek and Jan Mukařovský, were native Czechs strongly interested in literary matters. The presence of Jakobson and Wellek in America, and the extent of their influence here, justifies our reviewing, at this point, the literary activity related to Prague Circle linguistic theory.

The first volume of the *Travaux du Cercle linguistique de Prague* (1929) contains the group's manifesto, its *Thèses* (pp. 7–29). These "theses" attempt to reconcile the synchronic and diachronic study of linguistic structures, as well as comparative and evolutionary linguistics and dialect study. The approach is formally systematic and functional: "La langue est un système de moyens d'expression appropriés à un but" (p. 7). Put another way, the methodology of linguistic analysis is redesigned so as to provide for a globally adequate classificatory system capable of coping coherently with the immense variety of linguistic phenomena empirically and objectively. When handled by the classificatory system, linguistic "facts" are endowed with scientific relevance. Thus, Prague school theory responds in its own way to the disciplinary needs of "linguistics" as well as to the fragmented character of language itself. By classifying and showing the interrelationships that obtain in linguistic phenomena, this theory and practice *systematize* language; language *becomes* "un système de moyens d'expression." One recognizes the heritage of Condillac.

The theses proceed by opposition. After describing the various functions of language (*langue*) in terms of "internal" versus "manifest," "intellectuality" versus "affectivity," "communication" (referential) versus "poetic" (self-directed), the authors go on to show the "system of conventions" attached to each "langage fonctionnel": "oral" versus "writing," "langage alternatif" versus "continuous monologue," "degree of social cohesion existing among the speakers," "interdialect relations," etc. The remarks on "literary language" are very instructive. Exterior—i.e., political, social, etc.—factors do not explain *how* the literary language differs from popular speech. The linguist must recognize that *"la distinction de la langue littéraire* se fait *grâce au rôle qu'elle joue,"* and that this *cultural* rôle possesses formal coefficients: (1) intellectualization, (2) control, (3) norm-creating. Literary language is characterized "par une utilisation *fonctionnelle plus considé-*

rable des éléments grammaticaux et lexicaux" (cf. Vossler) and, on the one hand, tends to expand while, on the other, it tends to be monopolized by the dominant social class.

The history of the literary language is consequently the description of these tendencies *in their operations* over time. This history is legitimate, in fact necessary, if adequate attention is to be paid to what makes English, French, or German what they are—important cultural vehicles. Thus, in the same volume of *Travaux,* one finds Bohuslav Havránek's study, "Influence de la fonction de la langue littéraire sur la structure phonologique et grammaticale du tchèque littéraire" (pp. 106–20). Havránek points out that the grammatical structure of a language is also affected by literary function, not only the lexicon.

The category of literary language—or cultural tradition—is contrasted with "poetic language." These pages (17–21) are among the most valuable in the Prague school repertory. If interpersonality is stressed in the *kind* of function ascribed to literary language, the concept of poetic language effectively incorporates the individualist pole into a broad-gauged disciplinary construct. Poetic language is opposed to the "language of communication": "Le langage poétique a, du point de vue synchronique, la forme de la parole, c'est-à-dire d'un acte créateur individuel, qui prend sa valeur d'une part sur le fond de la tradition poétique actuelle (langue poétique) et d'autre part sur le fond de la langue communicative contemporaine." The relationships are very complex. Our authors hit upon the *symbolic* nature of poetic language when they state: "le langage poétique tend à mettre en relief la valeur autonome du signe, [and] tous les plans d'un système linguistique, qui n'ont dans le langage de communication qu'un rôle de service, prennent, dans le langage poétique, des valeurs autonomes plus ou moins considérables." In other words, the linguistic operations effective in a poetic text are interesting for their own sake and may, in fact, be equated, at least formally, with what poetry is. Meanwhile, the complexities of these operations, when properly understood, provide a precious insight into the workings of language itself. The reality of poetically effective discourse obliges the analyst to relate its different elements to the whole "functional structure" of the work: "Des éléments objectivement [i.e., isolatedly] identiques peuvent revêtir, dans des structures diverses, des fonctions absolument différentes."

One recognizes the modernist organicism built into these doctrines. But critical aestheticism, as such, is minimized in favor of scientific, i.e., "linguistic," observation and classification. The researcher is specifically warned against following the penchants of his own taste (p. 20). Here are a few specific recommendations: (1) Rhythm, meter, and rhyme must be studied in relation to the language's phonological structure, to be sure, but these poetic traits usually involve the grammatical, lexical, and syntactic levels (*plans*) too—thus, (a) if word-order is grammatically irrelevant, chances are it is practically very pertinent, and (b) rhyme reveals a morphological structure both when similar morphemes are aligned (grammatical rhyme) and when such juxtaposition is rejected; (2) poetic semantics has yet to be elaborated—thus, *"Le sujet lui-même est une composition sémantique et les problèmes de la structure du sujet ne sauraient être exclus de l'étude de la langue poétique"*; (3) literary history—and one recalls Coleridge's antilinguistic bias—has traditionally dealt with what literary works have referred to (*signifiés*) rather than that which, in fact, *constitutes* literary discourse, namely, its stress of the sign itself; this is a pity, since *"il faut étudier la langue poétique en elle-même."*

Members of the Prague Circle—especially Mukařovský—concerned themselves with poetics in a considerable number of articles and monographs. The lasting influence of these doctrines may be measured by such recent publications as the volume *Poetics/Poetyka* (Warsaw and The Hague, 1961), the collected papers of the First International Conference of Work-in-Progress Devoted to Problems of Poetics (Warsaw, August 18–27, 1960). However, for our purposes, it is enough to remember that Prague school linguistic theory does in fact remain faithful to the assumptions of scientific linguistic research by positing investigative techniques that shape coherently the discipline's subject-matter, but that include, as well, both perspectives and phenomena of concern to literary critics and historians. Prague school theory is consequently exclusivist in a very creative sense. While defining the linguist's task with commendable rigor, this theory actually opens windows onto other disciplines and matters of general intellectual concern. Furthermore, the kind of analysis adumbrated—the procedure of analytic oppositions or antinomies—is offered as a model for fields other than linguistics.[16] The "structuralism"

16. Thus, Prague school theory succeeds in *integrating* what I have called the interpersonal-individual polarity into its methodology, far more than Saussure had done, when he distinguished between *langue* and *parole*. For Saussure the distinction was tantamount to giving free rein to those who wished to deal exclusively with *langue;* the Prague Circle utilized both poles *in their relation.*

so in favor nowadays, especially in Europe, among anthropologists (Claude Lévi-Strauss), literary critics (Roland Barthes), and even certain philosophers—one thinks of Jacques Lacan and Michel Foucault—may be traced back to the disciplinary paradigm of the Prague Circle.

One is struck, even today, by the notion that literary language must be viewed above all in cultural terms, that is, as a formal function of historical traditions in their expressive relationships. The abstraction is a most useful one and deserves fuller implementation among literary and linguistic scholars in this country, especially since American scholarship can benefit directly from the far from moribund relationship it enjoys with the cultural anthropology of Boas, Sapir, and Conklin. Techniques of analysis expanding somewhat on the purely relational configurations dear to the Prague school theorists must be elaborated. Genetic problems should be worked into the description in pertinent ways, in order to respect the true dynamics of literary and cultural workings. As for "poetic language," the Prague school emphasis upon "creativity" is certainly accurate. The longer view might prefer to consider such "creativity" as specialized, and creativity in general as a necessary factor in *all* linguistic production. However, by dealing with the formal—i.e., patterned—coefficients of poetic language, Prague school theory not only avoids "egocentric aestheticism," but, at least tentatively, reconciles the literary critic's legitimate concern with organically conceived, "monumental" literary works and the linguist's need to understand, in some general way, the operations of language as such works display and utilize them.

The present discussion of the assumptions and techniques of linguistics, and their literary ramifications, should at least mention the very complex figure of Edward Sapir (1884–1939), the scholar who, during his short life, embodied all the potentialities and contradictions of linguistic research in twentieth-century America. First trained in Germanics and Indo-European at Columbia University, Sapir studied American Indian languages under Franz Boas (1858–1942). After spending the years 1910 to 1925 at the Division of Anthropology in the Canadian National Museum (Ottawa), he went, in 1925, to the University of Chicago, then, in 1931, to Yale. Thus by profession Sapir was an anthropologist and a linguist. In addition to numerous articles and monographs, he wrote one book, entitled *Language* (New York, 1921). During his Canadian sojourn Sapir demonstrated his deep interest in poetry and music. A very cultivated person, he wrote poems and composed several analytic studies, including "The Heuristic Value of Rhyme" (*Queen's Quarterly,* XXVII [1920], 309–12; reprinted in *Selected Writings of Edward Sapir,* ed. D. G. Mandelbaum [Berkeley, 1958]) and "The Musical Foundations of Verse" (*Journal of English and Germanic Philology,* XX [1921], 213–28). The final chapter of *Language* is entitled "Language and Literature."

Sapir's *Language* is open-ended. Though he was as aware as anyone of the disciplinary needs of linguistic science, Sapir recognized that no science could possibly embrace, in structural formulations, the dazzling variety of linguistic phenomena. This linguistic work is consequently systematic but in itself not all-encompassing—or exclusivist—as was that of his great contemporary, Bloomfield. Sapir's *Language* virtually bristles with suggestive ideas; there is food for thought sufficient to keep many investigators occupied. With Sapir, one suspects, the principal question concerns the quality of the mental activity he associates with linguistics—the ability to face and utilize complexities, to follow up approaches, that is, to experiment, to think, and to relate. No wonder, then, that one finds in *Language* fresh restatements of the basic issues present in the modern problematics of language: language and thought, culture and linguistic form, the nature of grammatical structure, creativity and expression, unity and diversity in linguistic form—Sapir speaks of all these. He displays the clearest consciousness of linguistic dynamics, whether he writes of historical change ("drift") or of the relationship of grammatical processes and "concepts."

In "Language and Literature" Sapir dwells on what the Prague Circle called "literary language" and "poetic language." He then goes on to relate these to the cultural collectivity and the individual's place within it. His presentation has a dialectic flavor: "Language is itself the collective art of expression, a summary of thousands upon thousands of individual intuitions. The individual goes lost in the collective creation, but his personal expression has left some trace in a certain give and flexibility that are inherent in all collective works of the human spirit. The language is ready, or can be quickly made ready, to define the artist's individuality. If no literary artist appears, it is not essentially because the language is too weak an instrument, it is because the culture of the people is not favorable to the growth of such personality as seeks a truly individual verbal expression" (pp. 246 f.).

Underlying Sapir's doctrine is the very modernist belief that "languages are more to us than systems of thought-transference" (p. 236). Literature, as he puts it, "moves in language as a medium, but that medium comprises two layers, the latent content of language—our intuitive record of experience—and the particular conformation of a given language —the specific how of our record of experience." Dominant in Sapir's thought is the notion that the symbolic function of language is more fundamental than its instrumentality, or rather that the latter is subsumed into the former. Thus, the "truly deep symbolism" of the greatest literary works, though "linguistic," does "not depend on the verbal associations of a particular language but rests securely on an intuitive basis that underlies all linguistic expression." This "intuitive basis" is identified by Sapir—who follows Croce here—with a "generalized linguistic . . . [or] art language" (p. 239). Some artists manage to reconcile the two "layers"—"their personal 'intuition' appears as a completed synthesis of the absolute art of intuition and the innate, specialized art of the linguistic medium"—while others do not. The strain is evident in Whitman; with Heine "one is under the illusion that the universe speaks German."

Many of Sapir's remarks coincide with Prague school theses. Thus, Sapir voices doubts regarding whether "the innate sonority of a phonetic [phonemic] system counts for as much . . . as the relations between the sounds, the total gamut of their similarities and contrasts" (p. 241). Literary styles depend on the language's syntactic structure, but Sapir stresses the play open to the poet who utilizes precisely the constrictions of the language. As for verse, Sapir recommends careful study of the "phonetic system, . . . above all its dynamic features, and you can tell what kind of a verse it has developed—or, if history has played pranks with its psychology, what kind of verse it should have developed and some day will" (p. 246). This is precisely what Roman Jakobson did with respect to Czech verse, and thereby revolutionized

Czech metrical theory. However, unlike the Prague theses, Sapir's remarks on literature are not programmatic. He devoted more attention to the analysis of broadly viewed "cultural constructs," that is, to the ways *"what* a society does and thinks" intersect with the linguistic or semiotic forms—the *hows*—of thought (p. 233). He was preoccupied by the problematics of history—what he calls "the drift of culture" —and, in particular, with the possibility of demonstrating the "series of contours," or "innate form," of culture. If such a demonstration is possible, then, he avers, means could be found to relate these "contours" to linguistic form.

Yet Sapir's sense of culture universalizes language, as did the "history" of Condillac and Humboldt. His accurate identification of linguistic operations with the widest kind of semiotic—or generalized sign—functions does provide a methodological basis for the "linguistic" study of verbal art. His analysis of poetic creation as the creative deployment of resources involving the two "layers" of an inner form versus the outer restrictions of the specific linguistic system (i.e., English, German) remains faithful to the most profitable dualisms modern thought has produced. More than any other American scholar of this century, Sapir showed the way to the genuine issues of linguistic and literary study. His "linguistics" points toward an all-encompassing *philosophy* of language.

Literary Criticism and the Science of Literature in America

With the appearance of tone-setting early critical and imaginative works of T. E. Hulme, T. S. Eliot (the poet's job is to "dislocate language into meaning"), and Ezra Pound, and of reviews like *Poetry* and *The Dial* in the second and third decades of this century, a new literary atmosphere—one of conscious modernism—came to permeate Anglo-American writing and critical thinking. But, whereas the reform of linguistics took place necessarily in the university, the initiative for this transformation of the American literary spirit came from other than academic circles, although, like the linguists, the new men of letters attempted to go beyond nineteenth-century philological historicism. There were few contacts between the literary and linguistic reformers, a situation quite unlike that prevailing in the contemporary Russian formalist group and, later, in the Cercle linguistique de Prague. Pound and Eliot had received a sound, though unspecialized, grounding in Romance—mainly French—literature. Pound concentrated at the University of Pennsylvania in early Romance poetry; Eliot studied under Irving Babbitt at Harvard. French modernism, i.e., art-for-art's-sake, symbolism, and subsequent "schools," became the point of departure in their search for a new poetics and literary order. From 1910 to about 1925, however, these poets and critics were less concerned with establishing a precise critical code than with setting up very general canons of theory and, especially, of practice. Thus, I. A. Richards' *Principles of Literary Criticism* (London, 1924) is among the first landmarks in the trend toward limited systematization characteristic of the New Criticism[17] of the

17. "New Criticism" is a misnomer in the sense that the term, generalized by John Crowe Ransom in his *The New Criticism* (Norfolk, Conn., 1941), says too much and too little: too many individual points of view are summed up by it, and its very "newness" is open to question. The advantage of the term is its obvious cohesiveness and great diffusion.

1930's and 1940's. Significantly, on the purely theoretical level, these works deal more precisely with the two problems most frequently alluded to by Hulme, Pound, and Eliot. Debates focused on the status and value of literature (its inherent independence, as well as its definite relationship to philosophy —mainly aesthetic—and the other arts; its "meaning") and the question of literary language and structure (with the ancillary problems of rhythm, image, and style).

One basic affirmation is shared by New Critics and poets alike. Namely, that literature—i.e., the literary work or, as I shall frequently refer to it, the poem or poetry—possesses some kind of definite identity. It is not to be confused with "history," as Vossler, with typical "idealist" abandon, tended to do. Nor, worse, should it be confused with science. Poetic creation should not be "scientific" either. From these assumptions it follows that the relationship of poetry to language (the latter being, naturally, what differentiates poetry from the other arts) can be approached in two fundamental, though not necessarily unrelated, ways: (1) from the standpoint of poetic language, that is, as language obeying the general and specific conditions of poetic expression (the focus being poetry as such and the purpose illustro-explicative), and (2) from the standpoint of language "behaving poetically," i.e., language, that "abstract" entity, being used in particular ways judged to be "poetic" (the focus remaining language, however, in its one—of many—poetic function[s]). Most critics have chosen the former alternative, although a few, pushing their analyses further, have gone on to examine ramifications of the second, a domain usually considered the preserve of linguists and of certain philosophers and rhetoricians (e.g., Kenneth Burke). The identity—and function—of poetry, an age-old debate, has been sought both intrinsically and extrinsically. What science, or religion, cannot or will not do, poetry can do, say some, approvingly or disapprovingly. Others explain: Reading many poems has taught us that good or "successful" poems seem to have the following characteristics; let us list them and try to see how poems work. In any case, many criteria typical of nineteenth-century scholarship and theory have been dropped. "Race, milieu, moment," "art-for-art's-sake," the "voice of the people," biologically inspired typologies and the like, no longer interest our critics.

Some of the general New Critical principles should be reviewed before passing on to the specific question of the identity of poetry with respect to language. Nowhere is the recent critical effort—at least in its initial stages—plainer than in the influential writings of I. A. Richards, sometime Cambridge literary theorist, philosophical and psychological speculator, and poet now at Harvard University.

In many ways the early Richards is a direct heir of the Enlightenment; his rationalism, his interest in mechanistic psychology,[18] his devotion to resolutely empirical experimentation, and his taste for "objective" schemes of classification make of him, *mutatis mutandis,* a worthy successor of the *philosophes.* Richards' very universalism, his affection for various

18. This interest is evident in many of his works, but in none so significantly—at least for us—as in *Coleridge on Imagination* (London, 1934), a descriptivist reinterpretation of Coleridge's "fancy–imagination" dichotomy (especially Chapter IV) carried out in terms of recent Gestalt organicism and empirical associationism. Richards attempts to "mechanize" Coleridge, to make his synthetic system over into an analytic instrument.

"improvements" and well-constructed shortcuts (like Basic English), as well as his intense intellectual curiosity and singular freedom from prejudice, are qualities we discovered in Condillac. Entirely modern, Richards finds in man the cause and the justification of his various literary theories—theories, incidentally, that constitute only part of a total, psychologically oriented, view of man. Thus, although art cannot provide the measurable truth science does, it "organizes" and, so to speak, "registers" the most complex "impulses" of which thinking and feeling beings are capable. (Richards' early—subsequently partly disowned—writings stress the differences between the purely referential character of scientific discourse and the emotive, "mythic" nature of poetry.)[19] The greatest artists possess ex officio the "richest" impulses. Experience antedates "creation"—the experience, in poetry, is in effect translated into words in such a way as to trigger off a similarly "rich" experience in the reader. The verbal expression of the experience, the verbalized experience, is, therefore, equally expression and communication. Expression must be judged in terms of the value of the experience *as experience,* whereas the poem as verbal art must be judged otherwise, "technically," as Richards puts it. A poem may succeed verbally, yet fail experientially (i.e., be insignificant). This distinction has historical importance inasmuch as it has helped provide for the possibility, within the Anglo-American critical tradition, of dealing with highly "technical" issues. Richards' avowed "descriptivism," at least in his writings of the 1920's and 1930's, reinforced and illustrated this possibility. His reevaluation of

19. I refer mainly to Richards' important *Principles of Literary Criticism* (London, 1924–25).

the Coleridgean "fancy" and "imagination" in terms of describable function is a case in point. Since Richards, and, perhaps, Croce, many critics have learned to distinguish between such devices as purely incidental simile (Croce's *forma ornata,* Richards' transformation of "fancy") and truly operative metaphor (Croce's "expression," Coleridge's and Richards' "imagination" at work). Richards' formulation, originally free of any value judgment, has indirectly encouraged many recent studies of the metaphor both in Great Britain and in the United States. It is consequently not surprising that Richards' work has also done much to focus critical interest upon the problem of the identity of poetry.

I remarked in passing that Richards refused to concede to poetry the same cognitive status he attributes to scientific discourse; poetry must be assimilated to myth. Why, and what does this revamped Aristotelianism mean? If poetry proposes to stimulate—and thereby communicate—a "complex" bundle of "impulses" in the "correct" reader, then according to this definition the poem must possess coherent structure, a functional design permeating all levels. However, these impulses are "organized" on two planes or, better, in two steps: (1) during the creative process when the poet wrestles with his material, and (2) during the reading when the poem is experienced by the reader. The two organizations are, of course, related, but only because the poem, as object, is there and because, to a degree, experience can be shared; still they have no definable reciprocal influence. The experience touched off in the reader by the poem is necessarily unlike the author's. Structure exists, then, *in principle;* it is indispensable, but—and this is why Richards cannot find "objective" truth in poetry—in no work do the two levels or stages of structure congeal in one homogeneous, objective whole. Richards is clearly unwilling to admit that poetry is unmitigated nonsense —hence his assigning it a "meaning" different from the kind of meaning inherent in scientific discourse where an abstract, rational structure—a prefixed norm—is designed to bring together both reader and author on an established plane of cognition that Richards conventionally calls "truth" (i.e., it is measurable, verifiable, and can be repeated indefinitely). The meaning of poetry is essentially a product of the confrontation of the two structures or "contexts" provided by the poet and the reader. To be sure, this meaning is couched in a kind of language different from denotative, scientific language, a language that Richards qualifies as "mythic" or "emotive" and that the reader can accept only so long as he knows he is participating in what other critics have sometimes called a "fictional" experience. Richards develops his theory of "emotive" language along the previously established lines of his psychology: the value of emotive language lies in direct ratio to its adequacy as an "impulse organizer." Complexity, even sheer difficulty, can in themselves become values, since the greater the number of impulses organized, the "richer" the "experience" and, consequently, the better the poem. This complexity can be approached "critically"—from the standpoint of the validity of the experience—or "technically"—with regard to its "material efficiency."

In the *Principles of Literary Criticism*—as well as in the ancillary volume, *Practical Criticism* (1929)—Richards seems to define poetry by referring to its language, and to identify poetic language by, in essence, informing us that it is a kind of language proper to poetry. (Coleridge, we recall, defined "good verse [as] the most proper words in their proper places.") Poetry is discourse that behaves poetically, i.e., mythically. The argument is, to say the least, somewhat tautological, but one understands what Richards is driving at. Moreover he offers us working hypotheses that later were to be taken up, transformed, and used canonically by other critics. For our present purposes what is important is that Richards did identify poetry; not only did he establish its autonomy, he did so by relating it to a kind of discourse, more precisely to a linguistic function. Richards, too, appealed to the old rational–emotive and instrumentalist–symbolic dichotomies. He reflects a dualism that is very similar to the ones discussed in the previous sections of the present study and which, though ancient, has been revamped in our century. Contrasting science and poetry *as language* has thus also become a feature of much modern critical speculation. Richards' pioneering efforts have led to the widely held notion among literary critics that scientific discourse directs the reader's attention to some exterior element of reality whereas poetry, like a magnet, refuses to relinquish the attention that has been drawn to it. Poetry is, in part, self-centered language. Richards' fundamental attitudes resemble those we found in the theories of Edward Sapir and the Prague Circle.

Rejecting Richards' "positivistic" psychologism and his consequent refusal to accord referential value to poetry, certain critics—e.g., Cleanth Brooks—nevertheless continue to separate science and poetry; they too base a theory of poetic identity upon this distinction. In a sense, these critics narrow the scope of Richards' general assumptions and focus their sights more definitely upon literature as such. Thus, for them, poetry acquires a far more objective status than for Richards, who, as we saw, concentrated less ostensibly on the poem as a structured object than on the two structures or "contexts" of the poem-as-composed and the poem-as-read (author and reader). This new objectivity of the poem is summed up in Archibald MacLeish's famous remark that a poem is "equal to: not true" ("Ars Poetica").

The American New Critics have seldom approached poetry as "language used expressively" as have the followers of Croce and the German idealists. Their base of departure is quite different. The poem is considered first of all as a legitimate object of study in itself, related to, but also distinct from, other types of spiritual activity and discourse. It is viewed as a *monumental* thing-in-itself, as a unique but highly ordered "organism," structured according to certain principles, possessing value, and requiring both interpretation and judgment. One easily recognizes the Coleridgean heritage in these working principles.

The question of value is particularly important, since within "value" lies the ultimate justification of any poem's organic autonomy. Value is what effectively fuses Richards' "technical" and "experimental" (traditionally: form and content) sides to the poem's being. Value is also directly related to meaning. The poem's meaning depends on the interpretation made by the critic, its value is a function of the critical judgment brought to bear on the meaning as interpreted. The New Criticism's practical bent can hardly be overestimated. As a rule, the New Critics are far more interested in poetry as poems than in poems as either poetry or language viewed abstractly; hence their frequent antihistoricism: Donne, Milton, and Shelley are treated, so to speak, as contemporaries. Richards' system, then, would allow for a purer descriptivism in literary analysis than the views of the greater number of his successors, or, for that matter, than those of Hulme, Pound, and Eliot. Description for its own sake is seldom practiced by the New Critics since, for them, minute studies of any poetic feature (imagery, rhythm) must, to be ultimately valid, be inserted in specific interpretations and should lead to value judgments concerning the works analyzed. Discussion of individual ideological or formal aspects of any single work or group of works, without reference to complete wholes, can be informative and useful, and is even to be encouraged, but it cannot be confused with true literary criticism. It is secondary. Consequently, linguistic commentary, as indulged in by Brooks, Tate, Empson, Blackmur, and their peers, is either fragmentary, that is, subordinate to the context of more general analyses, or becomes a frankly secondary, essentially noncritical, by-product of their universal fascination with literature. In this respect the New Critics are most unlike their Russian formalist counterparts who emphasized literature as *Wortkunst* rather than specific examples, and who combined literary sensitivity with considerable "disinterested" linguistic sophistication. For this reason it is almost impossible to speak of any New Critical "philosophy" of language—with the exception, perhaps, of John Crowe Ransom's "ontological critic" (see *The New Criticism*). Any discussion must be limited to specific problems interpreted in terms of thematic and ideological trends.

Among the traditional linguistic disciplines the New Critics, dealing empirically with such matters as prosody and rhythm, have worked somewhat more extensively with semantics and several literary implications of structured meaning. This preoccupation is already central in Richards and, of course, in such postsymbolist poets as Pound, Eliot, Yeats, and their cohorts. In order to cope with these matters succinctly, however, it might be well to forego exhaustive recapitulation in favor of briefly reviewing at least one specifically literary problem with obvious linguistic ramifications, so as to see what the New Critics, together, have done with it in their theory. Let us take up the thorny problem of metaphor, a question intimately related to the larger concern of meaning.

Metaphor plays a fundamental role in all modernist theories of language and rhetoric. Of all the many ancient figures, metaphor—with, nowadays, perhaps metonymy—has achieved the most prominent spot in present-day "grammars" of poetry, occupying the key functional position between image (the raw material) and myth (the ultimate end) in the hierarchy of basic "iconographic" devices making up poetic language. This is doubtless due to the fact that, among the old rhetorical figures, metaphor has proved the most amenable to insertion in the new dynamic vision of language characteristic of modernism. With the disappearance of the static one-to-one *rapport* of word and object, and with the subsequent establishment of a dynamic, tripartite relationship of word, object, and self, metaphor, depending directly on the reader's grasp or perception of an unfixed, but "channeled," tenor and vehicle, has come to incarnate the problematic nature of modernist expression. Thus, according to any truly modernist literary theory, metaphor can be ideally approached from two basic angles, that is, (1) as device, i.e., as a simple function of discourse, and (2) as a reflection of the world-view expressed in the discourse, the way the given work, or literary art in general, reflects reality. Most critics combine these two approaches, but one is usually stressed over the other. The first approach tends to involve strictly analytic methods while the second corresponds frequently to a purer organic criticism, and entails eventual discussions of meaning.

In his *Traité de stylistique française* (vol. I, pp. 194 ff.) Bally classified imagerial metaphors analytically into "concrete," "affective," and "dead"—the first two are grasped by the imagination or by an "intellectual operation," whereas the last, like "clothes-tree," is a metaphorical image in name only, since it no longer really functions as such. This classification belongs to Bally's general study of French expressivity. It deals with *langue* and cannot be applied to any particular literary works, nor, for that matter, to any expression of aesthetic intent whatsoever: it uses such texts, not for their own sake, but by converting them into samples of *langue*. In Bally we have a nearly perfect example of the student conceiving metaphor as pure device, since, for him, discourse is something much more abstract than it could ever be for the New Critic. Certain Anglo-American poets and New Critics, however, have examined metaphor as a function of *poetic* discourse or, even more characteristically, with reference to given examples of poetic discourse. Thus, Ezra Pound's and T. E. Hulme's many remarks on imagery and metaphor reflect their own tastes as founders of poetic "imagism" and, by extension, their criticism of past and present kindred spirits. Hulme, for example, stresses the need for "sharp, new metaphors of fancy" in order to transform inaccurate and diffuse "plain speech" into something more precise—something unique, and therefore more real. The key to a poet's originality lies in his use of metaphors, since these metaphors translate verbally his personal vision, his distinctive "experience" (Richards).

Allen Tate has found in metaphor a distinctive trait of poetic discourse and has, in large measure, based his principal theory of "tension" upon the nature of the metaphoric device as used in poetry. Tate contrasts "literal statement" and "figurative significance" [20] (another avatar, here a reconciliation, of the science-versus-literature dichotomy), claiming that the one —presumably thanks to the ways metaphor works—does not rule out the other, but rather functions with it, dialectically. Metaphors grow, and their meanings seem to unfold within the framework of reference provided by the various stages traversed. This referential deployment, a process of motion, constitutes the main characteristic of a kind of discourse tuned inward, as it were, on its own wavelength. This discourse is typically poetic. By developing, as Tate says, "the complications of metaphor," the reader renders himself available to the complexity of meanings inherent in the sample of poetic discourse he is experiencing; he submits to its play of tensions, he penetrates its economy. This theory is in part a reworking of Richards' fundamental doctrine of "functional metaphor" (a product of "imagination," as opposed to "fancy's" ornamental simile), but, unlike Richards' notion, it deals specifically and ultimately with the identity and the value of poetry. Tate is in effect saying that by analyzing metaphors the reader can both

20. See his *On the Limits of Poetry* (New York, 1948), pp. 83 ff.

identify the text, i.e., ascertain its discoursive intent, and finally grasp its total richness, the entire gamut of meaningful reverberations of which it is the synthesis and order-principle. Yet, while dealing with meaning, he does not at this point stress the relationship of poem and reality, though this relationship is implied. The question remains basically one of device.

The emphasis many New Critics and their mentors—Eliot, Richards, William Empson, Cleanth Brooks, Tate—placed upon irony in their characterization of poetic language is also closely related to their preoccupation with metaphor. Irony, we must recall, is no longer considered a mere rhetorical device of substitution by which certain effects are achieved when one thing is said and another actually meant. It is rather, as Empson has amply specified,[21] the source of "ambiguities" thanks to which the poem becomes discourse valuable in itself and differentiated from nonpoetic discourse. Ambiguity enriches the meaning of the poem by creating deliberate ambivalences on all important levels of structure, characterization, and statement. Thus, Proust's Charlus and Dostoevsky's Karamazov are ambivalent characters; they are complex and, although not to be reduced to any one-sidedly "clear" summary, are still "truer" and deeper than, say, easily recognizable stock characters. "Ambiguous" or "ambivalent" expression should not, however, be merely confusing; only the greatest artists can consistently avoid both the overly simple and the anarchically indirect. Nevertheless, their writings prove that, within the organism of the work, a directed ambivalence reconciles what Coleridge called the "discordant" elements,

21. See especially his *Seven Types of Ambiguity* (London, 1930).

thereby increasing both the scope and the relevant depth of the work. On the linguistic level—and leaving aside for the moment all questions of a purely epistemological sort—metaphor is particularly suited to highly ironic intention since it too, as a functional device, operates by ostensible substitutions. To take a simple example, an object is designated, and thereby requalified, by a name other than the one usually employed to denote it. The new name, inserted into the context, rubs off on the object designated, and often suggests the usual name, engendering thereby a corresponding, residually significant play of verbal tension which, becoming an essentially dialectic process, adds to the meaning of the passage by supplying the possibility of ambiguity. Such metaphorical operations are dynamic; they depend completely on a series of working relationships between lexicologically separable elements that function either as a given unit or, so to speak, unifyingly, as an underlying force. Furthermore, these operations cover a considerable range of types—including, for example, complexes of purely verbal attributes, such as sound (punning, partial homophony, etc.); or features shared by the conjoined referents and/or their signs, which render the metaphor possible (perhaps the best known use of the device); or still longer-reaching associations, very common, bringing together in ironic contrast separate verses or disparate elements in fully developed paragraphs.

The New Critics—both the "analysts" and the pure "organicists"—are not known for systematic studies of these kinds of metaphorical process *as devices* (not even Tate),[22]

22. See, e.g., Philip Wheelwright, *Metaphor and Reality* (Bloomington, 1962). Metaphor and other tropes have been studied by lin-

but their emphasis upon ambiguity and irony as distinctive traits of poetic discourse has set the stage for such study. Our critics have pretended to stress what John Crowe Ransom has called the "ontology" of poetry, its identity and function—its separateness as a kind of discourse—and its relationship to reality. Discussion of the linguistic and poetic device of metaphor, although at times descriptive, has been submerged in the extralinguistic debate concerning what poetry is. The brief comparison above shows a world of difference between Bally and these critics. Yet, after reading these students of literary expression, one is tempted to suggest that important features of the general problem of irony might well be clarified, from the technical side at least, if increased and more systematic attention were brought to bear upon the workings of metaphor—and not exclusively from the viewpoint of psychology. It is admittedly a question of focus. The New Criticism's obvious interest in metaphor, apart from purely empirical considerations, is at once linked to, and a by-product of, this "school's" preoccupation with irony (interpreted psychophysiologically by the early Richards, or philosophically by Brooks). And irony, as has been intimated, is a function of the larger question of poetic ontology. Interest in metaphor has thus become a secondary, albeit indispensable, link in this chain. A change of focus, then, concentrating on the "secondary link" of metaphor and its workings, while implicitly granting the dignity

---

guists and philosophers from the formal and psychological viewpoints with greater system than is usually the case among literary scholars. See Roman Jakobson, *The Fundamentals of Language* (The Hague, 1956), pp. 76–82, and Max Black, in the *Proceedings* of the Aristotelian Society, LV (1954), 273–94.

and independence of literature, would not only contribute immensely to our knowledge of this device, but would perhaps offer valuable new perspectives for the study of the admittedly larger theoretical questions of irony and meaning. Thus, in the New Critical views, the synthetic has predominated over the analytic approach, at least in principle, but synthesis has provided a number of valuable analytic categories that should be further developed, like Tate's theories of tension. This is not only true of metaphor, but, I think, can be said equally well of prosody, rhythm, and other such matters. The New Criticism has been instrumental in imposing a modernist point of view in America; it has cleared the air and opened the way for a variety of fertile approaches to literary study.[23]

I have hardly exhausted the topic of metaphor and have barely touched on the New Critics, but it is now time to deal with a few of the "approaches to literary reality" opened up and explored by the New Criticism and other tendencies in the United States. The initial impetus of the New Criticism, we noted, was not academic, but rather given over to a creatively critical point of view designed to construct, implant, and defend the new postsymbolist modernism in the Anglo-American literary consciousness after World War I. Its apologetic rôle cannot be overestimated. Yet, for various reasons,

23. For further analysis of the New Criticism, see the following studies: S. E. Hyman's *The Armed Vision* (New York, 1948); Philip Wheelwright's *The Burning Fountain* (Bloomington, 1954); Murray Krieger's exceptionally useful *The New Apologists for Poetry* (Minneapolis, 1956); see also W. K. Wimsatt's *The Verbal Icon* (Lexington, Ky., 1954). For a sketchy, though not uninformed review of linguistics and American criticism, see F. L. Utley's "Structural Linguistics and the Literary Critic," *Journal of Aesthetics and Art Criticism,* XVIII, No. 3 (March 1960), 319–28.

the New Critics and some representative poets began to accept chairs in several colleges and universities. The "little reviews" in which they wrote took on, in several significant cases, a semiacademic tone, their books began to appear in collections published by university presses, and their pupils combined certain strictly academic pursuits with the original exegetical goals of the New Critics. After World War II most original modernist literary criticism in America (as opposed to traditional book-reviewing and a few other forms of literary commentary) was to all intents and purposes incorporated into the academic system, where it first competed against, then compromised with, and finally, in large measure, has blended into the various philological and critical trends previously there. The techniques represented by the New Criticism have transformed academic techniques and viewpoints at least as much as they have been influenced in turn by them. This blending has helped to create modern American literary scholarship or "science" at its most advanced, joining the virtues of academic scrupulousness and "disinterestedness" to the typically New Critical involvement with value and general aesthetic.

In the university the New Critical spirit was confronted with the immediate prospect of at least a horizontal widening of perspective. The critics' point of entry was normally the departments of English—in some rarer cases the newly formed departments of comparative literature or creative writing—but the university being what it is, they soon met confrères in departments of foreign languages and literatures, of history and philosophy, of art and music, of the physical and social sciences (e.g., I. A. Richards and B. F. Skinner). Colloquia—like the specialized Christian Gauss Seminars in Criticism at Princeton, the yearly meetings of the Modern Language Association—grouping colleagues from a variety of disciplines were soon formed, and they promoted much exchange of ideas and points of view. The official cosmopolitanism of the Anglo-American modernist attitude (see Edmund Wilson's influential *Axel's Castle* [1931]), effective mainly with regard to late nineteenth-century French literature and a few isolated great writers (Dante, Pascal; see Eliot's *Essays*), could not entirely efface a definite and thoroughly regrettable provincialism from which a number of American critics suffered. On the other hand, this same cosmopolitanism favored the extensive intellectual contacts the university could and did provide. Literary history, for example, became a real, debated problem in the university context. The relationship between the arts took on increased significance, both on the purely practical level and on the plane of general aesthetic theory. The universities revealed to the critics new methods and approaches to problems of language. Criticism became aware of both American and European descriptive linguistics, Ernst Cassirer's "symbolic form," German *Stilforschung,* and neopositivist theory (the "logical positivism" of Rudolf Carnap, Charles W. Morris, and others). Just as important, parallel modernist critical trends from abroad, like Russian formalism and Hispanic *estilística* (Dámaso Alonso, Amado Alonso, Alfonso Reyes) could reinforce and modify the American experience. Not only did the university provide a genuine clearing house for the importation of foreign ideas and methods into the United States, but its international contacts helped diffuse abroad the work of American critics, whose influence upon writers like Yves Bonnefoy and Jean-Pierre Richard in France, for example, has been considerable.

Of the various academic treatises dealing generally with literary theory and analysis, the most complete to date and surely the most influential has been René Wellek and Austin Warren's compact *Theory of Literature* (New York, 1949), a frequently reprinted work that is accessible to the nonspecialist, but that has no doubt exercised its greatest impact upon academic readers. Let us examine certain features of this work in some detail, considering it both as a compendium of recent attitudes toward its subject and as a program for the future. For purposes of convenience I shall concentrate on the following four angles: (1) general point of view, (2) scholarly conception, (3) status of literature and literary study, (4) rôle attributed to language and its analysis. Questions of language, as they come up, will be approached from the literary point of view espoused by Wellek and Warren.

Wellek and Warren summarize their point of view at the very outset of their book,[24] and return constantly to it throughout the volume. They immediately declare that a distinction must be made "between literature and literary study," that the latter, "if not precisely a science, is a species of knowledge or of learning" (p. 3). Both "literary criticism" and "literary history" have important tasks to perform, but these "can be accomplished only in universal terms, on the basis of a literary theory." Thus, "literary theory, an *organon* of methods, is the great need of literary scholarship today" (p. 7). Wellek

24. Page numbers—in parentheses—will refer to the 1956 Harvest Book paperback edition of the volume, a slightly revised version of the original.

and Warren hope to systematize viewpoints suggested in the rather more ambiguous pronouncements of the New Critics. Their work is organized in such a way as to sketch out a general theory of literature. It is divided into four main sections (nineteen chapters), entitled respectively "Definitions and Distinctions" (dealing with the nature and function of literature, of literary theory and study, and with several disciplinary approaches to the problem); "Preliminary Operations" (the ordering and establishment of evidence: bibliography, textual criticism, sifting, etc.); "The Extrinsic Approach to the Study of Literature" (literature and its relation to biography, psychology, society, ideas, and the other arts—paths often trodden by literary commentators present and past); and, finally, the kernel of the book, "The Intrinsic Study of Literature" (the "mode of existence" of literary works, questions of prosody, style, imagery, genres, values, and literary history).

The viewpoint of Wellek and Warren is thus essentially a matter of scope, residing at once in definitions and delimitations of material. Much deadwood has to be discarded; indeed half the volume seems to be dedicated to this task, especially "Definitions and Distinctions" and "The Extrinsic Approach to the Study of Literature." In the chapter "Literature and Society," for example, Wellek concedes that "literature is a social institution, using as its medium language, a social creation" (p. 82) and possessing, logically, a "social function." But he goes on to criticize the "narrow" and "external" inquiries frequently put concerning literature and society (Hegel, Taine, and Marx—and their lesser disciples), the ways literature has been "used as a social document" (p. 91) to the detriment of its real, literary quality: "Only if the social determination of forms could be shown conclusively," he claims, "could the question be raised whether social attitudes cannot become 'constitutive' and enter a work of art as effective parts of its artistic value" (p. 98). He is led to reaffirm his basic credo once again: Literature "has its own justification and aim." This fundamental declaration does little more than incorporate into the present context the basic New Critical affirmations concerning the dignity, independence, and inherent value of literature. However, Wellek and Warren carry these principles further along to their logical conclusion within a purely literary system, and, unlike many of their immediate predecessors, do not tarry too long over the specific philosophical justification of their stand. The climate of opinion having changed between 1930 and 1950, our authors can proceed empirically in this regard.

Through an almost typological process of elimination and definition Wellek and Warren *regularize* their conception of literature; they both enlarge and restrict the field. First the narrowing: Whether dealing with literature and society or literature and biography they admit the principle of relationships, but, as we have just seen, they are quick to point out critical abuses made in the name of these relationships. In each case they attempt to establish conditions by which biographical, social, or philosophical additives might contribute to the understanding and judgment of literature as literature. Frequently they are obliged to invert traditional rapports of cause and effect, or simply to suppress them: "It is clear that causal study can never dispose of problems of description, analysis, and evaluation of an object such as a work of literary art" (p. 61). This narrowing, however, amounts really to clarification, to a definite renewal of confidence in the strictly poetic goals of literary art. Yet our authors do not replace the codes of previous practice with any new canons. Seldom do they spell out new procedures in any specific detail. They are content to pose a number of basic conditions that (1) support and qualify their conception of literary creation, and (2) establish an essentially problematic relationship of equality and reciprocal dealings between literature as process and as product and the various "extrinsic" elements brought up. In itself this constitutes an important feature of the "widening." If literature does possess inherent dignity, if the study of literature in connection with one or more of these necessary but extrinsic elements must be carried out in *literary* terms in order to count as "study of literature" (and not as some hybrid discipline), it follows that this new coherence attributed to the *res litteraria* fills it out and increases its stature, both as an object of study and as a department of spiritual endeavor.

The introductory chapters and entire second half of *Theory of Literature* expound a somewhat more programmatic viewpoint, ranging from the general to the more specific. Literature, as considered for analysis by Wellek and Warren, will include "imaginative literature" (*Wortkunst*) and little else. In turn, literary language—since "language is the material of literature" (p. 10)—can be made into at least a partial criterion for the proper identification of literature. Here our authors return to the former New Critical distinctions between scientific and literary language, although they prove somewhat more comprehensive than their predecessors in linking the questions of language and genres. Moreover, literature is characterized by its "fictionality," at least the hardcore genres (epic, lyric, drama) are so described; its statements "are not literally true" (p. 14), although "truth" and "falsehood" seem to be inevitable factors in literary impact and influence. This is another reprise from the typical New Critical debates concerning literature and reality. Finally, the authors' insistence upon the literary work as "a highly complex organization of a stratified character with multiple meanings and relationships" (p. 16) brings in still one more angle partially explored by previous modernist Anglo-American criticism, namely, meanings and structure. As for "function," Wellek and Warren somewhat brutally clear the air. Rejecting, as absolutes, the various didactic or psychological explanations of function, they conclude, perhaps provisionally, that "poetry has many possible functions," but "its prime and chief function is fidelity to its own nature" (p. 26). Our authors consistently return to the themes of recent debates, summarize them, reject various critical idiosyncrasies of the moderns as well as many traditional views, and accept only what underlines the independence of literature and permits the theoretical establishment of analytic patterns. Their debt to the modern critical canon is very large, but this does not prevent them from scaling its representatives down to size or even going beyond it.

The scholarly conception of *Theory of Literature* offers a clue as to how Wellek and Warren envisage transforming and advancing beyond their predecessors. It is indeed an extension of their general point of view. First of all, they are somewhat shy concerning the immediate "scholarly" presentation of their volume: "selective" bibliography, incompleteness of "proof," and their desire to "go beyond 'facts.'" Nevertheless, we find a very rich bibliography, numerous references and notes, a well-constructed index—in short, the indispensable apparatus of a scholarly reference book designed, of course, to provide more than a mere compilation of data. Speaking of their collaboration, they confess sharing a belief "that 'scholarship' and 'criticism' [are] compatible" (p. vi), a point of view, incidentally, no longer requiring defense in present-day American scholarship. Yet these are mere details of craftsmanship. As suggested previously, much of the originality of this book lies in its implicit assimilation of modern critical theory into the scope of scholarly, or academic, pursuits. It is important to stress that Wellek and Warren do not by any means restrict themselves to recent Anglo-American theory, that they instead impose upon their subject a wide variety of contemporary (and earlier) views concerning both "scholarship" and "critical analysis" as applied to literature. Their scholarly attitude is not only apparent in the clarity and the material organization of their work, it resides also in the widening and confrontation of perspectives, which are in part similar to and in part different from the usual American experience, issuing from their vast acquaintance with the field both here and abroad. Thus, in a real sense—and within the context of their American situation—they not only bring the findings and mood of movements like the New Criticism to the university, they also bring the university to modern American criticism. And they do this in two fundamental ways: (1) they describe, compare, and utilize foreign theories and techniques dealing with literature, and (2) they bring other, nonliterary (or "para-literary") disciplines to bear on the study of literary phenomena. The kind of symbiosis of modernist literary analysis and academic research effected in the contemporary American university—and by now typical of it —was greatly furthered by the publication of *Theory of Literature.*

In what ways does this symbiosis, as achieved particularly in *Theory of Literature,* reflect a characteristic methodological orientation? Does it engender a special kind of academic, or other, critical "spirit"? Certain features appear to be self-evident: there is no tone of apology in Wellek and Warren, they belong to no given "school" of imaginative literature, nor, apart from favoring the study of contemporary literature in the graduate school, do they show predilection for the writings either of the past or of the present. On the other hand, they are admittedly antipositivist, at least to the degree their approach ultimately involves conscious "evaluation" of the works examined, and to the extent they shun the traditional, exclusively "extrinsic" concerns of positivist literary study. Wellek and Warren are "objective" in the style of Eliot's "objective correlative"; they cannot accept the anarchical judgments of critics reflecting a purely impressionist subjectivism, nor do they abdicate intellectual responsibility. Yet, one suspects, judgments should not be reserved for the final paragraph of the study as the traditional academic dissertation form seems to indicate; judgment and evaluation, as both writers point out, are implied even in such preliminary steps as choice of material and definition, and should be incorporated into the very stuff of description. A passage from the chapter on "Evaluation" is very significant:

"Understanding poetry" passes readily into "judging poetry," only judging it in detail and judging while analyzing, instead of making the judgment a pronouncement in the final paragraph. The one-time novelty of Eliot's essays was precisely their delivering themselves of no final summary or single judgment but judging all the way through an essay: by specific comparisons, juxtapositions of two poets with respect to some quality, as well as by occasional tentative generalization [p. 241].

Nor indeed do Wellek and Warren favor any particular genre over others. The New Critics dealt primarily with poetry (often intending that their commentary be applied to "literature" in general), but *Theory of Literature,* although incomplete in this respect, makes a decided effort to deal with the specifics of poetry, "narrative function," and genres as a whole: "The literary kind is not a mere name, for the aesthetic convention in which a work participates shapes its character" (p. 215). This admission still allows for much independent discussion of supergeneric literary devices and conditions such as "image" and "the mode of existence of a literary work of art."

These aspects of *Theory of Literature* do stress what might be called the "disciplinary" orientation of this work, its scholarly bias. Wellek and Warren prove to be consistent in their "evaluative" doctrine: there can be no complete criticism without value judgment. But once one accepts their basic premise that understanding the strictly literary elements of the work in their total organicity remains the fundamental goal of critical analysis and that such "understanding" cannot be divorced from evaluation, it appears that their "disciplinary orientation" is in effect predominantly academic, that it is governed by concern for humanistically "scientific" truth formulated, to be more precise, in "metaliterary" statements. We recall the authors' initial distinction declaring literary study to be "if not precisely a science, . . . a species of knowledge" that must be organized "rationally" if it is to be "coherent" (p. 3). Whereas modern literary criticism has championed the independence of literature as an integral branch of human activity—as legitimate in its way as science—Wellek and Warren, sharing this point of view, go further and, within the gamut of academic pursuits, proclaim the disciplinary independence of literary study. Wellek's experience with his Prague Circle associates stands him in good stead (see fn. 25). Thus, their "scholarly conception" clusters, as it were, around their particular idea of the discipline as well as around the praxis represented by their methods and procedures, as discussed above. The status of literary study—something different after all from the literary criticism reviewed above, though intimately related to it—proves to be the prime concern of our authors, even more important than the status of literature itself, in sheer volume of commentary. It is true of course that Wellek and Warren benefit fully from the *vitesse acquise* provided by previous critical speculation and experience.

It goes without saying that the independent status of literature—independent though highly problematic in actual function—determines, along with the built-in structure of academic disciplines in our day, the integral status of literary study. Much more could, and ideally should, be said about this, but limitations of space require that we look only into the question of effects. Literary study is defined first with respect to its object, the understanding, elucidation, and evaluation of dynamic structures operating within and around literary works of art. It is also defined in terms of its disciplinary orientation, i.e., the rationally coherent formulations conceived as such, with regard to the conventions of what I have described as humanistically scientific truth, and our authors, "a species of knowledge." Thus, once established, literary study must treat the status of literature itself as a legitimate problem; this Wellek and Warren do themselves. Now then, in what way do the effects of literary study contribute to a definition of the discipline? In a word, these "effects" generally confirm what we have already noticed. Literature, conceived monolithically, requires methods of study adjusted to its nature. Consequently, these methods entail first of all a fragmentation or breaking down of previously established techniques and goals of research whenever these latter are applied to literary analysis. Thus, intellectually history, commonly thought of and widely practiced in the United States as a discipline in itself or as a chapter of general history, can rightly be placed at the service of literary study only when it has been properly subordinated to the object of that study as defined above. Much commentary concerning "ideas"—their import and their sources—has been vitiated from the start by what Wellek has called "a confusion of the functions of philosophy and art, . . . a misunderstanding of the way ideas actually enter into literature" (p. 104). Poetic texts may be used documentarily for the history of ideas, but only at the cost of setting aside their "poeticalness"; and even then one wonders how liable to misinterpretation they will be under those conditions. On the other hand, no complete history of German literary romanticism would be possible, it seems, without extensive reference to Kant; but the methods designed to incorporate the study of Kant into authentic literary analysis and history will have to be sought out, methods doing violence neither to Kant's thought nor to Schiller's poetry. Roughly the same treatment is accorded to psychology, biography, sociology, and even to aesthetics. The basic question remains: How do psychological or sociological elements (i.e., elements that, when considered alone, normally are the object of these disciplines) *function* in a literary—therefore a partially foreign—context, and how can we best isolate these elements without damaging, or even destroying, the literary nature of our texts? Wellek and Warren do not take it upon themselves to answer this question in any precise instance; they are content to raise it and to declare it fundamental.

It is in the "effects of literary study"—like those just mentioned—that one grasps most clearly the problematic nature of literary analysis. (By this I do not mean to point out a weakness of such an evaluation of literary study; on the contrary recognition of its problematic nature may rather indicate an eventual source of strength.) The fact remains that quantitatively styled methods or plans of procedure are next to impossible in the kind of literary analysis proposed by Wellek and Warren; nor do methods rubber-stamping those of the scientific fields even seem desirable. Each case, determined by a given point of view chosen rationally in the hope that it will prove fruitful, requires more of one thing and less of another. Emphases shift constantly, even if some general routines seem indicated in given cases: analysis of poetry, presumably, requires a finer appreciation of sound symbolism than most novels. Moreover, as Warren and Wellek themselves show, no a priori analytic scheme will ever provide, in and of itself, anything approaching definitive statements concerning either the texts or their classification. Some may prove more exhaustive than others, but these too will be superseded one day by a change in viewpoint. Even our authors' unshakable basic principles lend themselves to a wide and varied application. *Theory of Literature*, by stressing the provisional character of "metaliterary" statement, takes stock of this dynamism and derives it from the essential nature of literary reality. At times the authors suggest that other branches of humanistic-type learning might indeed share a similar dynamism. If so, they hint, their practitioners would do well to operate accordingly, hence Wellek's longstanding admiration for Spitzerian linguistics. In any case, Wellek and Warren appear firmer in their condemnation of specific "unliterary" practices than in their recommendations concerning precise courses of action.

The fluidity of "practical" critical analysis—a fluidity derived from and reflecting the basic dynamics of the disciplinary orientation expressed in *Theory of Literature*—seems to contrast paradoxically with the decidedly objective character of our authors' scholarly point of view. The conflict, however, is more apparent than real. The uniqueness of literature is such that, when compared to other artistic or intellectual activities, it presents a somewhat hybrid complexion. Its meanings are more "referential" than those of music, its temporal patterns are utterly unlike those of painting, its logical structure seems capricious when juxtaposed against the syllogistic manner of much philosophical discourse, its language is highly personal if contrasted with the language of regularized scientific prose, and so forth. Yet literature shares traits with each of these, and still other, types of discourse. Wellek and Warren have had the merit of frankly admitting this seemingly hybrid character of literary art not only in theory but in actual practice. At the same time they do not lose sight of the special cohesion of literature, its singularity and independence. What I have called the "fluidity" of their practice represents actually a kind of suppleness that in turn permits a real unity in ultimate ends, since it is based on literature's tremendously varied reality. Consequently, the paradox is resolved in the way Wellek and Warren expand and amplify the traditional notion of scholarly objectivity to include even the provisional nature of analysis and judgment concerning literature. Its problematic quality thus becomes a constant too.

The last and most significant subdivision of the critical breakdown presented here is the role attributed to language and its analysis in *Theory of Literature*. Here, of course, as in Coleridge and the New Critics, the emphasis is synthetically literary.

In a review of *Theory of Literature* published in *Language* (1950), the linguist Kemp Malone notes that "Wellek here manages to emphasize the value of language study and condemn the 'professional linguists' in the same breath." He adds, noting Wellek and Warren's dislike of the "behaviorists," that their work nevertheless "shows an understanding of linguistic matters exceptional among present-day American specialists in literature" (p. 312). Both statements are in essence true: Wellek and Warren show little sympathy for, or interest in, the kind of linguistic interpersonalism *à outrance* characteristic of the "classic" American descriptivist school. They not only fail to see its relevance to literary study, but imply on occasion that its methods might well cause harm to the science of language in the long run: "Nearly every linguistic utterance can be studied from the point of view of its expressive value," they write, and "it seems impossible to ignore this problem as the 'behavioristic' school of linguistics in America very consciously does" (p. 167). On the other hand, they do next to nothing to point out or understand the attitudes toward literature of this school; neither Bloomfield nor, far more serious, Sapir is mentioned in their volume. One feels that rather than looking into its very real possibilities, they condemn an entire movement on the basis of its extreme positions. Other standpoints go unnoticed. One of the early contributors to *Language,* G. M. Bolling, in his "Linguistics and Philology" (1929), called for a "new philology" based on "the broadest outlook upon the purpose of our studies" (p. 32). As a rule, *Language* has been hospitable toward a wide variety of opinions (Spitzer, Messing, Leopold, Bonfante). Malone's second statement, however, is just as exact as the first. Wellek and Warren repeatedly stress the linguistic factor in literature, and on various levels too. The fact that literature is a linguistic art is its main distinctive feature; language operates as raw material and functions on all levels of literary meaning from the sound-stratum up to complex contextual relationships. An admirer of *Theory of Literature* would be hard-pressed to isolate a single area of linguistic reality about which more information would not benefit the literary scholar as well as the linguist. Moreover, our authors call frequently on a wide number of European or European-trained linguistic theorists and practitioners (Saussure, Bally, Spitzer, Vossler, Dámaso and Amado Alonso, Grammont, Jakobson) both when dealing with specifically linguistic matters and when they find themselves in need of analogies. Thus, in his key chapter, "The Mode of Existence of a Literary Work of Art," Wellek makes use of the *langue–parole* dichotomy in order to illustrate his revision of Roman Ingarden's last two strata of literary norms (*Das literarische Kunstwerk* [Halle, 1931]): the *parole–langue* "distinction corresponds to that between the individual experience of the poem and the poem as such" (p. 140). The illustration is hardly fortuitous, because Wellek employs it in order to depict and handle, in a purely literary context, what I have previously described as the "interpersonal–individual" opposition in linguistic theory of the past century and a half. Works of literature, just like language, can be approached in terms of a true, though ultimately unknowable, absolute identity (*langue,* Wellek's "structure of determination"), and they can be approached in terms of one's individual experience(s) of them. Like the study of linguistic reality, the analysis of literary works must involve both perspectives. In short, Wellek draws here an ontological parallel between literature and language, and has even gone so far as to recognize—up to a point—a consequently strong methodological similarity between a certain kind of linguistic science and literary study. The parallelism is developed further—though not very clearly—when Wellek compares literary "units of meaning" and their organization with the grouping into meaningful patterns of phonemes and morphemes.[25]

25. "Certainly I perform . . . the reading; but number presentation or recognition of a norm is not the same as the number or norm itself. The pronouncement of the sound *h* is not the phoneme *h*" (p. 142). Wellek's adaptation of the phonological (phonemic) principle reflects his mid–1930's association with a group of lin-

Language seen as "cultural heritage" and as expression offers partial grounds for a definition of literature. Wellek takes up the New Critical (and Aristotelian) dichotomy of scientific versus literary language (the latter is apparently interpreted as linguistic modes), but adds a third mode, "the everyday." "Scientific language" aspires toward "such a system of signs as mathematics or symbolic logic" (p. 11); it turns out to be a highly specialized mode of expression. "Quantitative," "pragmatic," and "referential" criteria must be used to distinguish between "everyday" and "literary" language: literary language exploits "the resources of language . . . much more deliberately and systematically" than everyday speech (quantitative), it is predominantly aesthetically oriented (pragmatic), and its statements point to a particular, fictionalized truth of convention (referential) (pp. 12–14). Lan-

---

guists and literary theorists I have mentioned only in passing, the so-called Prague Circle. Indeed, his lengthy essay "The Theory of Literary History," published in the *Travaux du Cercle linguistique de Prague,* VI (1936), 173–91, already prefigures his (and Warren's) later bestseller. ("The sounds read from these letters . . . are different 'realisations,' but are no work of art in themselves. They are 'performances' just as the performances of a piece of music" [p. 178].) Like his Prague school colleagues, Wellek is careful to isolate the concepts of literary language and poetic speech. Thus, he adopts in 1936 the Prague school notion of "structure" (versus the Russian formalist and German "form"), defining it as "a concept including both content and form as they are organized for aesthetic purposes," and the literary work of art "as a whole dynamic system of signs or structure of signs serving a specific aesthetic purpose." He favors collaboration with linguistics since "the development of linguistics in the direction of a functional conception makes this collaboration possible, for the first time" (p. 177). Yet Wellek's stress of "values," already present in his discussion of Roman Ingarden (pp. 178 ff.), prefigures his later inclusion of value judgment as a fundamental part of literary criticism.

guage used this way is likely to be literary. The distinctions correspond almost exactly to those of the Prague *Thèses*.

Wellek and Warren also discuss (literary) language as device—in terms of what might be called general devices and stylistic, or "specific," devices. By "general" devices I mean those uses either determined by the language in which the work is written or the general aspects of devices possessing also a personal, stylistic side (metaphor, for example, can be looked upon as a general or as a stylistic device). By "stylistic" devices I refer to particular instances and their functions in given works. *Theory of Literature* contains three chapters dedicated to these questions: "Euphony, Rhythm, and Meter" (chap. xiii), "Style and Stylistics" (chap. xiv), and "Image, Metaphor, Symbol, Myth" (chap. xv). They constitute the heart of Section IV, "The Intrinsic Study of Literature." These chapters reaffirm the authors' belief that a "thorough grounding in general linguistics" is a necessary prerequisite to stylistics (p. 166); without such a background the stylistician risks succumbing to mere "impressionism." The function of linguistics seems to be to ensure an objective frame of reference for the discussion of these traits as they emerge in literary compositions: "one of [stylistics'] central concerns is the contrast of the language system of a literary work of art with the general usage of the time." Wellek thus stresses the parallelism of method ("system") he would observe in the study of literary language as it has been followed in linguistics. Simple ad hoc commentary is insufficient. (Let us note in passing that *linguistics,* as used by Wellek, means some kind of generalized methodology, an almost abstract science of language, especially as practiced by the Geneva and Prague schools and by the idealists; this conception has certain evident disadvantages, compensated for however by the over-all picture of linguistic science it provides, a healthy ecumenical spirit.)

The "sound level" of literary works—the level par excellence of euphony, rhythm, and meter—can be approached as "performance" or as "pattern." Ideally both must be considered, since, placed at the service of the principle of artistic integrity, the one makes little sense without the other. And discussion of sound levels must eventually be interpreted in terms of "some general conception of its meaning or at least its emotional tone," an interpretation necessarily requiring statements that transcend pure description, since it ties in with critical evaluation. Problems of "sound level" break down into two types (and several subdivisions, as shown in the title of Wellek's chapter): general statements of a theoretical nature, like those of Wellek in this instance, and remarks applicable to specific texts. Actually these two types must be examined in conjunction with one another. Thus, the Russian formalist theory, cited by Wellek, according to which rhythmic feet have no existence independent of the whole verse of which they are a part, constitutes a general theory of the rhythmic device known as meter, but in order to be of use it must be applied to the analysis of specific works. In these matters theory must act as a guiding principle in practice. When analysis is placed at the service of the theory, when it affirms and qualifies it, we may speak of emphasis upon general device, a legitimate concern of poetics and literary theory. By the same token, emphasis may be brought to bear upon the individual work, either with respect to patterns or performances (or both), and the theoretical classification can function in an explicative and evaluative rôle. In literary theory and practical criticism, point of view occupies a position analogous to its place in linguistics; without point of view research cannot be oriented. But in literary study point of view is somewhat less gratuitous than it appears to be in linguistics, since, even in the most "scientific" criticism, it must eventually lead to possibilities of evaluation.

This chapter contains, however, no precise information concerning the relationship of linguistics to such "sound level" research. Obviously, linguistics plays its greater rôle on the theoretical plane. Apart from the previously noted methodological parallelism, linguistics and sound analysis appear to meet in several areas: (1) Linguistic science provides the surest source of information concerning the sound system (phonemes, accentual patterns, quantity) of the language in which the text is written, frequently using poetry as a source of documentation, especially in diachronic study; (2) Comparative linguistic analysis is indispensable for any general theory of meter or rhythm transcending given language systems; (3) The experimental nature of much linguistic research has helped break the stranglehold the classical tradition had placed upon metrical studies, and its objectivity has promoted greater freedom from prejudice in the evaluation of certain past and present phonetic experiments in literature (e.g., quantitative verse in English). Nevertheless, one regrets that *Theory of Literature* does not point out closer and more precise disciplinary affinities between general linguistic science and literary study with respect to the analysis of the sound stratum. One is left with the impression that a climate of necessary rapport and reciprocal influence has been established—already a great deal, of course, and symptomatic of new trends in American literary scholarship—but that a great deal more must be done to set the relationship on a clear footing, based on mutual needs and assistance.

In "Style and Stylistics" Wellek returns to the problem from another angle. He tries to show how linguistic study can *become* literary ("only when it serves the study of literature, when it aims at investigating the aesthetic effects of language —in short, when it becomes stylistics" [p. 166]);[26] by *aesthetic effects* he presumably means, as I have mentioned, language utilized as literary devices (viewed generally or stylistically). Expressivity, Bally's almost psychological criterion, is not sufficient. Much stylistic commentary, declares Wellek, has been at best "haphazard," relying heavily on the outworn categories of ancient rhetoric. Two methods seem valid: "the first is to proceed by a systematic analysis of [the work's] linguistic system and to interpret its features, in terms of the aesthetic purpose of the work, as 'total meaning' . . . [and] a second, not contradictory, approach is to study the sum of individual traits by which this system differs from comparable systems" (p. 169). In the first case, the needed referent would

26. In his fine essay on "Verbal Style" in *The Verbal Icon* (pp. 201–17), W. K. Wimsatt presents a similar point of view with interesting practical modalities: "A study of verbal style . . . ought to cut in between a Platonic or Crocean monism, where meaning either as inspired dialectic or as intuition–expression is simply and severely one meaning, and the various forms of practical affective rhetoric, Aristotelian or modern, where stylistic meaning bears to substantial meaning a relation of *how* to *what* or of *means* to *end.* The term *verbal style,* if it is to have any clear use, must be supposed to refer to some verbal quality which is somehow structurally united to or fused with *what* is being said by words, but is also somehow to be distinguished from *what* is being said . . ." (pp. 201–202).

be the "total meaning," requiring thereby a circular movement from feature and device to entire effect, and back—a
very delicate maneuver reminiscent of Spitzer's "philological
circle," with its positive merit and its hazards. In the second
case the referent must be the rather nebulous norm of the
"comparable" system (one wonders how it is "comparable").
Wellek seems to recognize the difficulties since he deems
"preferable . . . the attempt to describe a style completely
and systematically, according to linguistic principles," quoting
attempts made by Viktor Vinogradov and Amado Alonso, but
without going into more detail about them. This chapter is
less than satisfactory, since, by stressing once again his literary
bias, Wellek creates a false problem and seems to have
reached a methodological impasse. Linguistics cannot be re-
tailored into literary criticism; put that way, the problem can
even degenerate into paradoxical wordplay. The literary analyst may well utilize—like a dictionary—the findings, and
even certain methods, of linguists. But it remains to be seen
whether, and in what ways, an important part of the critic's
task might be best resolved by using—and respecting—purely
linguistic techniques. This seems to be one of the directions
taken by Wellek.

Common sense indicates that Wellek's insistence upon
"meaning"—an emphasis recalling the German idealists
more readily than the "information"-centered American linguists—should however not be interpreted as an insurmount-
able barrier between linguistic science and the new literary
science. *Theory of Literature,* through its objective spirit and
its generous recognition of the value of linguistics, goes more
than half way to meet the linguists' position. (And, happily,
some linguists in America today show less recalcitrance to-

ward literature than in the past.) But the aesthetic direction of Wellek and Warren, when contrasted with the descriptivist interpersonalism of much contemporary linguistic theory, creates a seemingly untraversable chasm between linguistics and literary criticism. On the one hand, *Theory of Literature* has done much to reconcile literary and linguistic study; on the other, it appears to crystallize their differences. Moreover, until very recently, linguists in the United States have shown extreme caution in dealing with problems of meaning; semantics has been the poor relation of linguistic research. One wonders then if the chasm might be bridged, at least temporarily and, so to speak, experimentally, if both linguistic interpersonalism and the branch of literary criticism especially dedicated to the study of language as expressive device (general and stylistic) were partially subsumed into the higher category of sign theory. Some work has been done along these lines, particularly by Prague school theorists (Mukařovský, Jakobson) and by the neopositivist philosophers (Carnap, Morris, and others), and there remain the impressive beginnings of the semiotic theorist Charles Peirce. Among contemporary linguists we can quote the semantic essays of Uriel Weinreich, concerned with setting up embryonic analytic categories, though unfortunately these essays display a decidedly antiliterary bias, and the new semantics of Katz and Fodor. A fertile point of departure could well be offered by lexicology, a field stimulating new interest these days,[27] espe-

27. See Fred W. Householder and Sol Saporta, eds., *Problems in Lexicography,* Indiana University Research Center in Anthropology, Folklore, and Linguistics, Publication 21 (*IJAL,* 1962), especially the contributions by Malkiel, Weinreich, Conklin, and Gleason.

cially in view of Wellek's reminder that the student of literature will "need linguistics of a specific kind—first of all,
lexicology, the study of meaning and its changes [sic]" (p.
165). At any rate, it seems clearer nowadays that language, as
used in literature, cannot be approached exclusively either
from the purely literary or aesthetically oriented viewpoint or,
for that matter, from the strictly interpersonal angle of descriptivist structuralism—with an opportune backwash from
each falling back on the other. Both attitudes remain perfectly
legitimate in terms of their own goals, but, as we have seen,
exclusive concern with one or the other leaves too many obvious questions unanswered. No great cultural language can
ever be properly described until the linguist learns to deal, in
linguistically relevant ways, with its literature, nor can any
verbal work of art be adequately analyzed until its sign-
structure is pertinently studied. A possible starting point
would be to divide, for purposes of analysis, literary "language" into two functions: a "rhetorical" and "stylistic" function or point of view that would permit the student to approach the text in terms of specifically aesthetic devices (as
summarized by Wellek and Warren), and a general "linguistic" function (semiotic) that would allow the text *in all its
complexity* to be incorporated into a body of material, techniques, and methods leading to a deeper understanding of sign
mechanisms. A given device, like metaphor or symbol, would
thus be analyzable both generally and specifically ("stylistically") in terms of aesthetic meaning and value as well as in
terms of language and sign. Focus and techniques would involve a dualism of approach preserving the "literariness" as
well as the properly linguistic in the text or texts. In the long

run such a dualism would help provide needed referents of analysis on both sides. This of course would not outlaw the type of linguistic analysis that at present makes use of the materials provided by literary works while deliberately ignoring questions of literary value (e.g., historical phonetics and morphology). This is why initial experimentation with lexicological material might be most suitable, since the lexicon is clearly less than amenable to traditional interpersonality. In a sense, the modernist trends polarized in Condillac and Coleridge should be synthesized to the degree that such synthesis is possible—at least in the important borderline fields where synthesis seems both feasible and desirable. As I have had occasion to remark, they cannot be properly "homogenized." A unified theory of language ought to be more than a pious hope, but if progress is to be made toward such a goal, it should be attempted on favorable grounds.

But our position as students of language and literature should be made clear from the start. Such a modernist theory of language, although in the long run it may prove to be more *fundamentally* illuminating about the workings of literary signs than much "stylistic" study as practiced to date, must constitute an end in itself. The language of literature, as defined by Wellek and Warren, remains distinct from, as well as related to, the "language" of linguistics, and by and large that is as it should be. In recent pronouncements Wellek has reiterated this stand in accents as energetic as those of Bloomfield defending the autonomy of linguistics thirty years earlier: "Literary analysis begins where linguistic analysis stops. . . . A literary stylistics will concentrate on the aesthetic purpose of every linguistic device, the way it serves a totality, and will beware of the atomism and isolation which is the pitfall of much stylistic analysis." [28] However, I am suggesting a rounding-off, a completion, of what linguistics and literary study have to tell us about language, as well as what the one can do for the other, respecting withal its own integrity as a discipline. I am speculating about the possibility of a new modernist trivium. Let me add that not the least attractive trend of contemporary American literary scholarship is its apparent willingness to listen to such suggestions. Much of the merit for this new receptivity to ideas emanating from colleagues in linguistics and philosophy is due to the structure of the university in the United States. The linguistic consciousness of the New Critics played an important part too. But the significance, in this respect, of the pioneering theoretical *summa* of Wellek and Warren can scarcely be overestimated. It would be a pity not to seek new solutions for the many problems they raised with such cogency.

The Linguistic Point of View

Scholars primarily concerned with the relationship of linguistic and literary study have been very rare in the United States. Over the past twenty years or so, linguists who have dealt with literary questions—apart from the textual critics, or philologists, whose work has maintained a steady rhythm throughout the period—have tended to specialize in areas somewhat peripheral to the activities represented by the hard

28. See René Wellek's "Closing Statement from the Viewpoint of Literary Criticism," in *Style in Language,* ed. T. A. Sebeok (New York, 1960) pp. 417 f.

core group of "American linguistics." However, during the 1960's, the crisis involving linguistic research in this country —its methodology, its philosophical assumptions, its goals, and its techniques—has by and large favored increased speculation in domains formerly considered either uninteresting or, by some, not pertinent to the linguist. Taken as a whole, linguistics in America has reverted from the extreme, monolithic position favored by Bloomfield and his disciples to a new "open-endedness" reminiscent of Edward Sapir.

This is not the place to describe the exciting turmoil of contemporary linguistic research in America. But before reviewing the work done by certain American linguists on literary problems—work best described as "activity" rather than as the product of well-defined "approaches" or "schools"—some brief mention should be made of the dominant outlooks in linguistics over the past two decades in this country and their implications for our topic.

I have already dealt with the stress on interpersonality— the "language" of the "average native speaker"—in American structural linguistics as well as with certain formal emphases and disciplinary quirks, e.g., the very circumscribed nature of the "language" of Bloomfieldian taxonomic linguistics. If literary criticism and scholarship have tended to distinguish between the properly literary or poetic components of verbal composition and, by extension, of critical analysis, taxonomic linguists have been no less careful to root out "non-" or "extra"-linguistic features present in expression and communication. Thus, such linguists generally avoid dealing with "psychological responses," except as they can be correlated behavioristically to specific "linguistic stimuli." Moreover, the kind of tight classificatory grammar taxonomic linguistics strives to construct qualifies as "extragrammatical" many of the utterances on which literature, as such, depends. Furthermore, in Bloomfield's view grammar handles constructs only as far as the "sentence level" (*Language,* pp. 170 ff.). Longer utterances, with which literary study perforce must deal, are organized by other than the means recognized as "grammatical"— hence "linguistic"—by Bloomfield's theory. Finally, unlike Prague or Geneva structuralism, which, we saw, applied its techniques to literary analysis, Bloomfieldian practice has traditionally been less interested in vertically deployed paradigms than in horizontal syntagmas. European "structure" is more globally conceived than its American counterpart and is usually presented in terms of a much more highly developed psychological theory. The "mentalist–mechanist" debate is a more authentically late American phenomenon—from 1930 to 1950—than a European one; one need only compare Bloomfield with Sapir and Saussure on this count to see the difference. Less concerned with immediate syntagmatic realities, European structuralism has understandably felt more at home with those literary traits that it would analyze vertically, or paradigmatically, since the underlying "mentalism" did apply in both cases. Consequently, American investigators familiar with the work of their European colleagues—especially Slavists, Romance specialists, and Germanists—were more likely to study literary problems in what, for them, were authentically *linguistic* frameworks than those who did not undergo this influence.

Over the past decade and a half, certain specifically American approaches to grammar and syntax, growing out of

Bloomfield's *Language* yet reacting against several of its emphases and, above all, concerned with broadly conceived linguistic structures, have concentrated on units encompassing several sentences. One thinks of Zellig Harris' "discourse analysis," with its stress upon formal, nonsemantic, unifying structures (*Language,* 1952), and, more recently, of Samuel R. Levin's specific adaptation of these, and related, principles ("coupling") in his stimulating *Linguistic Structures in Poetry* (The Hague, 1962). Later research in distributional structure and meaning (see Zellig Harris, *Word,* 1954) has sought to go still further beyond Bloomfield's "sentence," and has, in turn, led to Noam Chomsky's transformation grammar, and so to theories, in many respects, quite opposed to taxonomic linguistics.

The polemics surrounding the publication of Chomsky's theories of generative grammar (*Syntactic Structures* [The Hague, 1957], *Aspects of the Theory of Syntax* [Cambridge, Mass., 1965]) and the work, in semantic theory, of Jerrold J. Katz and Jerry Fodor not only serve to indicate the intrinsic worth of the theories presented but also the latent dissatisfaction many scholars felt with respect to the voluntary limitations Bloomfield and his disciples had placed upon linguistic research. By the late 1950's, when generative grammar came to be known, a number of American linguists—chiefly those associated with the linguistic circle of New York and the journal *Word*—had familiarized themselves with the Prague school orientation and, consequently, were prepared to accept a more broadly based theory of language than that underlying the purely domestic taxonomic approach. This is not to say that linguistic research in this country has overnight renounced its former goals and embraced those of the MIT transformationalists. On the contrary, as suggested previously, the situation has merely become more fluid. Experimentation has become the order of the day.

Only some tentative application to literature has been made of the new generative grammar. In addition to S. R. Levin's above-named *Linguistic Structures in Poetry,* one may cite the same author's "Poetry and Grammaticalness" (*Proceedings of the Ninth International Congress of Linguists,* reprinted in *Essays on the Language of Literature,* edited by Seymour Chatman and S. R. Levin [Boston, 1967]), Richard Ohmann's "Generative Grammars and the Concept of Literary Style," (*Word,* December 1964) and "Literature as Sentences" (*College English,* January 1966, reprinted in *Essays on the Language of Literature*), and Sol Saporta's "Linguistics and the Study of Poetic Language" (discussed below). By elaborating generative rules of linguistic production governing the relationship of "deep" to "surface" structure—and the "translation" of the former into the conventions of the latter—transformation theory in fact establishes a dynamic syntactic norm–deviation dichotomy. This dichotomy, when cogently applied, might offer objective characterizations of "poetic language" as "distinct" from "normal usage," and, ideally, a methodological framework for the reconciliation, within a single, all-encompassing theory of language, of the polarity. Since it operates mainly with sentence production and, of course, ascribes psychological reality to sentences in order to relate their grammatical structure, as human beings do, to semantic wholes ("content structures" that correspond, presumably, to universal "patterns of the mind"), generative grammar purports to offer ways out from certain impasses built into the taxonomic view of the sentence. (One recalls Abelard's *sermones* and Descartes' concern with the forms of language and mental process.) As Eric P. Hamp tentatively put it: "In this form of analysis the analyst asks not What does this form stand next to? but rather To what distributionally different expressions is this form grammatically equivalent" ("General Linguistics—the United States in the Fifties," *Trends in European and American Linguistics, 1930–1960* [Utrecht, 1961] p. 172).

Ohmann's "Literature as Sentences" characterizes the sentence as "the primary unit of understanding" (*Essays,* p. 231). The "surface structure" of the sentence "overlays" a "deep structure," but the latter informs this surface structure. Analyzing a clause from Joyce's "Araby," Ohmann shows how the reader must grasp "the relations marked in the deep structure," and how "the sentence . . . activates a variety of semantic processes and modes of comprehension, yet in brief compass and in a surface *form* that radically permutes *content*" (p. 233). Deviations and dislocations occur, but, as Ohmann indicates, these tend to indicate "more fully the build of the work." In essence Ohmann describes, with symbolic notation, the act of reading, i.e., what goes on in the reader's mind as he deciphers the discourse before him, and, in consequence, is able to reconcile form and content as simply the "distinction between the surface structures and the deep structures of sentences" (p. 238). The literary work as such is fully respected, but given the orientation of generative grammar, according to Ohmann, analysis of its operations contributes significantly not only to our understanding of style, rhetoric, and literary structure, but also—presumably—to our understanding of linguistic operations as well. The methodology involved thus permits, indeed encourages, use of wide varieties of "discourse." All language is grist for its mill.

In contrast, a rather more Bloomfieldian notion of grammatical equivalence stands behind Mac Hammond's recent "Poetic Syntax," an essay presented at the International Conference of Work-in-Progress Devoted to Problems of Poetics (Warsaw, August 18–27, 1960) and printed in *Poetics/Poetyka* (The Hague, 1961). Hammond utilizes "grammatical equivalence" as a formal device for identifying poetry; he draws up an opposition rather than a set of procedures or transforms. Thus, he says, "syntax is poetic when grammatically equivalent constituents in connected speech are juxtaposed by coordination or parataxis, or are otherwise prominently accumulated" (p. 482). He goes on to "limit the term 'poetic syntax' to *noticeable* instances of grammatical repetition," i.e., a pattern of repetition whose meaning "in any particular poem will reside in the nature of the construct itself and not in the [extralinguistic mimetic] analogies its linguistic properties suggest." Though his techniques are radically different, Hammond's conclusions offer a sample of the kind of dynamic description, focused on identifying poetic language, that one might eventually expect from adepts of generative grammar. This understanding of "grammatical meaning," though unlike that of the transformationalists, allows him to formulate the relationship between "form" and "content" in just as problematic a way as Ohmann. All that lacks is the transformationalist notion of "degrees" and the sense of *process*.

Charles C. Fries has suggested in the above-mentioned *Trends* that "Bloomfield's stress upon the nature of scientific descriptive statements . . . turned American linguistics into a 'way of stating' rather than a 'set of statements' " ("The Bloomfield School," p. 211). This characteristic "way of stating," evident in Bloomfield, Harris, Chomsky, as well as in Ohmann and Hammond, implies both a terminological quest and, of course, the establishment of a distinct subject-matter. The latter is, in a sense, tailored to fit the kind of metalinguistic statements American linguists, whatever their ideological allegiance, wish to make. Thus, contrasting the new American interest "in the connexions between formal linguistic and literary study" as manifested in recent times, Hamp (op. cit., pp. 173 f.) has declared that "this time, unlike the focus some decades ago of the Prague group on the broader aspects of formal literary analysis, interest has tended to concentrate on an analysis of linguistic markers of style and on the question of basing literary studies on textual data expressed in terms of sound linguistic analysis." Everything hinges on what is meant by "sound linguistic analysis," of course, but so far, by and large, no general linguistic theory in America has been implemented in such a way as to deal systematically with the language of literature. "Poeticalness" remains a concept analogous to "grammaticalness." An extreme example can be found, not surprisingly, in Robert Abernathy's information-theoretical "Mathematical Linguistics and Poetics" (*Poetics/Poetyka,* pp. 563 ff.). Declaring that "linguistics stands in much the same relationship to poetics as does, say, organic chemistry to zoology—the former studies the 'raw material' of life, the latter the forms of life itself," Abernathy depicts poetry as "the transmission of a large amount of information via a low-capacity channel," and tentatively classifies, in mathematical terms, rates of information with respect to expectations (and critical attitudes). He hints at the possibility of isolating "in precise mathematical formulation" certain phenomena of "poetic languages and utterances" (p. 569).

The lack, so far, of a true all-embracing theory of language, or "linguistics," in which literary and linguistic study would have well-defined rôles has not, however, stifled experimentation along such lines. On the contrary, what I have called the crisis of linguistic research has stimulated such experimentation, often with interesting results. One fact must be borne in mind, however, namely, that the relation of linguistic to literary study is primarily a matter of *activity*, not of systematic effort. Cross-disciplinary collaboration has increased and has involved both literary scholars and linguists, but it has remained essentially circumstantial and fragmentary. The present study has attempted to show why this has been the case. Before going on to offer alternatives, it would be well to examine, in some detail, precise instances of such cross-disciplinary activity. For the purposes of the discussion, I shall concentrate—but not exclusively—on *Style in Language* (New York, 1960), a compendium of papers presented by critics, linguists, anthropologists, psychologists, and philosophers, during a symposium organized by the Social Science Research Council, at Indiana University, in the spring of 1958.[29]

In keeping with Hamp's above-quoted commentary and as

29. This discussion will draw on portions of my review-article, published in *Romance Philology*, XV (May 1962); I have found helpful the review-articles by Michael Riffaterre, *Word*, XVII (December 1961), and Yakov Malkiel, *International Journal of American Linguistics*, XXVIII (October 1962).

its title implies, *Style in Language* endeavors to clarify a problem most linguists and literary critics have felt constitutes the most fertile area of collaboration, i.e., *style.* Wellek and Warren had already defined linguistics in the service of literary study as "stylistics," and Bally before them had spoken of "style analysis" (as opposed to "stylistics") as a literary discipline. In his *An Introduction to Linguistic Structures: From Sound to Sentence in English* (New York, 1958), A. A. Hill takes off from Bloomfield's argument and defines style and its study as what includes "all those relations among linguistic entities which are statable . . . in terms of wider spans than those which fall within the limits of the sentence" (p. 406). Yet *style* is a most imprecise term. A mere glance at *Style in Language* offers ample evidence of this imprecision, since the reader is led from R. M. Dorson's empirical "Oral Styles of American Folk Narrators" and D. H. Hymes' statistically oriented "Phonological Aspects of Style: Some English Sonnets" to theoretical pronouncements concerning the relationship of linguistics and literary material on various levels of complexity (Saporta, Richards, Jakobson). For some contributors style consists essentially in deviations from norms, though Hymes, for example, quotes the anthropologist A. L. Kroeber to the effect that "style may be not deviation from but achievement of a norm" (p. 109). The views expressed by some psychologists (Osgood) and linguists (Saporta) engender sharp criticism on the part of the literary critics (Wellek, Hollander). Much of this diversity is due to the variety of academic disciplines represented and to the seeming polarity of the "interpersonal" linguists and "individualist" literary critics. Some critics seem to stress what the other fellows' discipline might do for their own, and some appear to point out ways their discipline might assist the others. There is a great deal of disciplinary partisanship, and, curiously enough, the linguists seem to feel that "style" sums up what is literary in linguistic expression, whereas the literary analysts define *style* methodologically as what is specifically linguistic in literature. To add to the confusion, a certain number of trends important in modern stylistic analysis are inexplicably absent from the proceedings of this Conference (notably *Stilforschung,* which has been well represented in the United States by the late Leo Spitzer, Helmut Hatzfeld, and others).[30]

Most interesting for us at this point is the fact that, among the linguists themselves, the term *style* undergoes a number of very different applications. The linguists' position can appear monolithic only when contrasted with one of the other disciplines represented. Even then, a linguist like Jakobson remains closer in a number of important ways to critic–scholars of literature like Richards or Wellek than to some other declared linguists. We must take stock of these nuances before summing up the general linguistic point of view. These differences and similarities are not always a matter of mere emphasis or even of method. They sometimes correspond to entirely different orientations.

An important trend represented in *Style in Language* is the one that systematically divides language into two main sub-

30. See, in this regard, Helmut Hatzfeld's *A Critical Bibliography of the New Stylistics* . . . , *1900–1952* (Chapel Hill, 1953), and the recent, up-dated (with Yves LeHir) *Essai de bibliographie critique de stylistique française et romane* (Paris, 1962).

types (like Bally's famous *logical* and *affective*) and places literature, not always but frequently, under one of the two headings. This position is, in a sense, modernistically "classical," confirming by and large the previously noted distinction between the "language" of literature and the "language" of linguistics. For most of the scholars working with such a dichotomy, style is exclusively a function of literature. This trend is perhaps strongest in C. F. Voegelin's "Casual and Noncasual Utterances Within Unified Structure" (pp. 57–68). Voegelin separates within language utterances of "casual" and "noncasual" type; normative grammar has traditionally been written on the basis of noncasual utterances whereas the descriptive grammars of modern linguistics tend to be based exclusively on casual utterances. Purest noncasual speech would be the specialized "language" of mathematics, although literature, to a large extent, is a repository of such utterances. Casual speech is more or less what Wellek, in *Theory of Literature,* referred to as "everyday" language, whereas noncasual utterances would correspond to his "scientific" and "literary" languages. (Voegelin insists, however, that literature is not always equivalent to noncasual.) Unlike certain predecessors, Voegelin makes no effort to determine the relationship between the two types of speech; he is not interested in maintaining his distinction beyond a certain level. He seems, moreover, to praise linguists "who . . . now show some incipient inclination to investigate poetry, too, and other noncasual utterances in a given language" (p. 57). He shows specific interest in the possibilities of a new theory of unified linguistic structure or "new hypotheses concerned with the interdependence of diverse structures within one language." His dualism—an essentially binary vision of linguistic reality—is thus placed at the service of an analytic, though monolithic, view of language. The angle of approach, however, remains typically "linguistic" in that his method involves listing and classifying usage "deviant" from casual standards; and "casual" seems to be very close to "interpersonal." Voegelin recognizes that the structure "carved out of the common speech of the language" might well be a fiction, but he declares such a conception "operationally useful," especially inasmuch as "no single linguistic definition adequately serves to distinguish casual from noncasual utterances in languages generally" (p. 60). Such distinctions are both helped along and confirmed by "cultural recognition," i.e., by partially extralinguistic reactions on the part of "the person-in-the-culture" (pp. 60 ff.), as Voegelin points out with respect to usages prevalent among the Hopi Indians.

Voegelin's system is not designed specifically to permit analysis of stylistic traits either literary or expressive; it is rather offered as a palliative to grammars that, to quote Sapir's phrase, "leak"—its function is remedial. Complete descriptions must cover the entire maze of dovetailing categories that permeate the many levels of usage. The "massively resistant class grammar," goal and ideal of Bloomfieldian linguistic research (p. 67), may isolate the kernel of language, but it cannot represent the whole; witness the impasse that lexicological research has reached in a system according to which "irregularities," as Bloomfield recommended, are to be consigned *in toto* to the dictionary. Until a new vision of the language whole is formulated, grammars will continue to leak, i.e., remain incomplete or otherwise imperfect—this seems to be

Voegelin's main point. He expresses the malaise felt by many linguists of our time.

As suggested in earlier sections of this essay, the structuralists' overriding concern with linguistic interpersonalism (juxtaposed against possible overemphasis of the individual in much linguistico-literary commentary) created the mentality that governs the binary distinction utilized and redefined by Voegelin in his interesting and symptomatic essay. To the extent that Voegelin endeavors to reunite a linguistic science fragmented in the recent past by two opposed analytic tendencies, and given the fact that his initiative stems from the "linguistic" side of the polarity, his technique consists essentially in gluing the two pieces together again. He operates with the same assumptions governing the original division; the most he can do is weld the two halves, since each half retains substantially the same identity it had when the original split was effected. Considering then, in Voegelin's terms, that a grammar that does not leak is equivalent to the lost unity restored, we must ask how successful this procedure can be.

The main objection must be raised against the maintenance of the casual-vs.-noncasual polarity. This distinction seems at best valid as an analytic device to be used for purposes of restriction in either one sense or the other. Also it might well be useful as a way of presenting the problem within the context of much taxonomically oriented linguistic research. But it is difficult to see how noncasual utterances can be structured in terms of their own resources, or, if so doing is beside the point, why bother about the opposition at all? On the theoretical level several contradictions emerge: *Casual* and *noncasual* are essentialist terms meant, unfortunately, to deal less with real norms than with functions; functions have little or nothing to do with this kind of norm. Words and constructions seldom can be made to correspond to such norms *in all functions,* so we are once again back to Bloomfield's dictionary of "irregularities," only this time the irregularities will be of two types. Nowhere do we learn how the interworkings of casual and noncasual—this is the real issue—will be described (a problem of central importance in literary analysis, for example). Voegelin's note of divergencies between casual and noncasual norms in Turkish sentence structure, as well as his other illustrations, do happen to fit his scheme, but what about, say, proverbs in Spanish, many of which present samples of archaic or otherwise unusual speech when isolated out of context? Yet, as proverbs, they enjoy a relatively high incidence of probability in a number of diverse contexts. The casual–noncasual opposition makes a *critical* point insofar as it stresses, negatively, the inadequacy of "the usual grammar based on casual utterances," but it raises grave doubts as to whether the kind of dualism upon which it is based is capable of solving the larger issue of "unified structure" and its description.

Voegelin does not identify literature and noncasual speech; he is not concerned with literature as such, although a number of his examples seem chosen from expression others might well consider literary. But were we to adopt his scheme and try to apply it (in two ways) to language used in literature and to literary language, we should find that, by virtue of its high degree of intentionality, the language of literature would more often than not cluster around the noncasual pole—at least when considered as a species of language. (Jakobson, rejecting this classification entirely, wisely reminds us that all language, apparently casual or not, is "purposeful" [*Style in Language,* p. 351], but we are merely associating purpose in a special way with aesthetic intent as defined by modern literary criticism.) Yet literature makes use of "casual" speech too, sometimes jealously guarding its casual nature in the most noncasual of contexts. In his review of *Style in Language* (*Word,* December 1961) Michael Riffaterre suggests that such literary use of both casual and noncasual speech should be envisaged in "la *représentation* de l'usage 'spontané,' et celle de l'usage 'réfléchi' " (p. 332). Riffaterre's conception adds another dimension to the picture, since "representation" implies that literary language is by definition something distinct from nonliterary language, that it is subject to conditions other than those that govern discourse in general. Here he shows substantial agreement with the literary scholars who, like Wellek and Warren, are preoccupied above all with literature's special status. This viewpoint remains entirely legitimate, but it necessarily transforms somewhat the issue raised by Voegelin's dichotomy. Possibly, "noncasual" could be usefully employed, as Voegelin has expressly designed this concept, that is, as an abstract category grouping linguistic usages amenable to structural or, at least, generic classification but departing from the conditions normally operative in casual speech, accentuating some and downplaying others, and doing so with a certain consistency (cf. Hammond's study, quoted above). In literary language—i.e., considered as a linguistic subspecies, as a whole—"noncasual" usages would involve mainly certain conventions and processes that seem to enjoy a quasi-existence of their own and that can be profitably isolated in study: rhyme, metrical patterns, certain recurring images (the "rose" in the Renaissance lyric, and so forth). Interpreted this way, the "noncasual" becomes a step along the way leading to the eventual integration of literary language into the general theory of verbal signs discussed earlier; it may be identified with what I have called the study of general linguistic functions specifically operative in literary discourse. As an abstract category suitable especially for the description of static conditions, the noncasual remains incapable of engendering definitive statements concerning all aspects of these linguistic functions. Nor can it help with respect to literary qualities, since these are subject to value judgments. As an abstraction it shares the limitations of abstract formulations, but it may well aid in the gathering of valuable information concerning literary operations of at least intermediate, if not ultimate, importance. Furthermore, it offers research possibilities somewhat more congenial to certain analysts than the pure "criticism" represented by *Theory of Literature.*

At most, then, we must conclude that exclusivist dualisms of Voegelin's "casual–noncasual" type can be of limited usefulness in the application of linguistic techniques to literature. When applied totally, as by A. A. Hill in his ambitious "Program for the Definition of Literature," [31] they can turn out to be dangerous. Hill proposes to establish an English literary corpus based on the kind of utterances that "all known societies . . . have regarded as of sufficient importance to preserve permanently." Within this corpus the student must seek out "formal characteristics which can be used as a diagnostic

31. University of Texas *Studies in English,* XXXVII (1958), pp. 46–52. Published in *Style in Language* as an abstract, pp. 94–95.

for definition." The process, however, requires elimination from within the corpus of "those utterances which do not differ from casual utterances." According to this approach, verbal idiosyncracies with a high level of permanence would be equivalent to literature (or would at least provide the foundation for a definition of literature, which distorts almost as much). No literary critic would admit that such a procedure could possibly advance our comprehension of literature, nor can I see how it could further our understanding of linguistic structures. Hill ascribes far too much importance to static absolutes to be useful to anyone; on the contrary, he even appears to deny the existence of purely literary structures on the aesthetic plane—agreeing, curiously enough, with certain positions of Croce, who, denying the possibility of long poems, once described the *Divine Comedy* as a series of beautiful poems interpolated into long stretches of outmoded, prosy, didactic discourse.

Another typical binary system advanced by some linguist contributors to *Style in Language,* this time one ostensibly designed to fit literature into a general linguistic scheme, is summed up in Sol Saporta's "The Application of Linguistics to the Study of Poetic Language" (pp. 82–93). Saporta treats the problem of style in a manner more in keeping with the volume's declared purpose than either Hill or Voegelin. He speaks of the language of poetry as opposed to the language of prose ("or colloquial language, or casual language," p. 82); he also contrasts "language" (which is "within the proper domain of linguistics," i.e., what I have called the " 'language' of linguistics") with "art" (music, painting), and considers poetry as sharing characteristics with both domains. However, as a self-conscious linguist, Saporta remains faithful to the descriptivist tradition, claiming that he must approach poetry as language, knowing all the time that it is in some ways distinct from "language" ("not all language is poetry," p. 83). The contradiction, of which Saporta is fully aware, is obvious. He hopes to resolve it by borrowing Chomsky's notion of "degrees of grammaticalness"; poetry will be described as language, but the linguistic traits that differentiate it so clearly from the language of linguistics are to be described in terms of a hierarchical scale of "grammaticalness" or "ungrammaticalness." In short, Saporta's basic assumptions are founded on a polarity resembling Voegelin's, but, squarely facing the issue of poetry (as Voegelin did not), he endeavors to construct criteria capable of depicting the web of relationships tying the two poles of his system. This system is consequently—at least potentially—dynamic. It is fundamentally abstract and exclusivist (no value judgments are permitted lest some non-science creep in), but it is made to concentrate on a series of partially working relationships. The intuition seems very promising. However, we are more than surprised to learn that the purpose of all this is merely "to identify poetry" for the linguist; poetry is made to stand, with respect to highly "grammatical" discourse, in a position analogous to "unassimilated loan words or slips of the tongue" (p. 85). Literature, then, as such, has no intrinsic interest for Saporta; he is merely trying to advance a particular brand of "linguistic" analysis.

Style—and literature or poetry, which, as Saporta uses the terms, seem to be highly "stylized" discourse—consists essentially in deviations from norms. Here "norm" is equivalent to (perfect) grammaticalness, that is, easily generated sentences.

There are two principal types of deviation (pp. 91 f.), namely, (1) the presence of "agrammatical or ungrammatical sequences" in the message (i.e., features "that do not occur elsewhere" in the language), and (2) the presence of restrictions, like meter, not required by extraliterary "general grammar." Saporta stresses "syntactic statements" over semantic ones, since syntax is largely a matter of distribution, that is, an essentially mechanical function. Questions of *poetic* meaning, considered fundamental by literary critics, play no real part in Saporta's system. All the literary analyst can hope to glean from this system is "that a typology based on the kinds of deviations [it generates] will yield clusters that correspond to [or perhaps significantly modify] such notions as sonnets, epic poems, etc." (p. 93). On the practical level, then, we see that not only does Saporta's original polarity remain, it leaves the encounter fortified. Saporta is finally less interested in the working relationships he first proposed to examine than in the ways they can be made to strengthen the basic differences between the two poles. Curiously enough, his system is apparently far less contrastive in essence than the casual–noncasual distinction of Voegelin appears to be, yet, although he admits that "poetry [be defined] as a subclass of language" (p. 84), he goes on to reinforce the traditional view of linguists "that a grammatical description need not accommodate poetic messages." Whereas Voegelin's "unified structure" leaves some room for advance in the delicate business of linguistics and literary criticism, Saporta returns to the old demarcation lines and winds up defending the status quo.

Another approach utilizing the norm–deviant dichotomy, although not represented in *Style in Language,* deserves mention at this point, since it offers a fertile point of departure for a more conscious reconciliation of linguistics and literary analysis within a general and specific theory of *style* (stylistics). I refer to Michael Riffaterre's discussion of style as expressed in several theoretical articles and a significant book-length study.[32] According to Riffaterre, style is a function of the given text, or context, to be examined. It is also a function of the reader. Riffaterre borrows a key principle of modernist literary criticism when he makes his system depend upon a re-creative collaboration of both "author" and "reader" (*encoder* and *decoder*) who together make the text (*message*) what it is. One is reminded not only of the transformationalists' dynamism but also of I. A. Richards' doctrine of "correct" (though possibly variant) readings versus misreadings (*Style in Language,* pp. 241–52), since Riffaterre defends the principle of (flexible) "correct" readings determined by the text as it operates upon the reader. But how are "correct" readings achieved? Riffaterre finds that much pure literary criticism is based on sheer intuition—intuition that can easily change from moment to moment according to the mood of the reader, and that, subject to psychological interpretation, can cause the method of literary analysis to run two grave risks: (1) switch its attention from the text to the subjective state of the reader, and (2) degenerate into methodless impressionism. Riffaterre introduces his "linguistic" point of view in

32. Apart from his review-article of *Style in Language,* we should note: *Le Style des "Pléiades" de Gobineau; Essai d'application d'une méthode stylistique* (Geneva-Paris, 1957); "Criteria for Style Analysis," *Word,* XV (April 1959); "Stylistic Context," *Word,* XVI (August 1960), and various review-articles appearing in *Word, Romanic Review,* and *Romance Philology.*

order to minimize the effects of gratuitous intuition. The attentive reader—linguist must consciously allow himself to be governed by the *facts* of the text; his job requires that he describe the formal characteristics of each segment of discourse that has provoked a reaction (normally a value judgment) on the part of the reader.[33] If, at any precise point, the linguist discovers a structural particularity, he must conclude that the reader's reaction was "motivated" by the structural feature isolated. If, on the other hand, no structural peculiarity supporting the value judgment is discovered, the linguist concludes that the motivation was provoked by other than authentic linguistic causes. The "structural features" thus form the goal of linguistic analysis as applied to literature; they are to be envisaged as so many "keys" inserted into the text by the "author" who, consequently, "controls" the decoding of his text and thereby solicits the reader's "collaboration."

Stylistic contexts, in Riffaterre's view, vary according to the texts. He rejects the traditional norm—deviation dichotomy that considers the "language" of the writer, taken as a rather abstract whole, as a "deviation" from the even more abstract "general language" (the simplistic application of Saussure's *langue—parole* opposition). Each text constitutes its own stylistic norm: "The stylistic context is a linguistic *pattern suddenly broken by an element which was unpredictable,* and the contrast resulting from this interference is the stylistic stimulus" ("Criteria for Style Analysis") that prompts the afore-

33. See Riffaterre's "Vers la Définition linguistique du style" (review-article of *Style in Language,* in *Word,* XVII, especially pp. 320 ff.). I translate or paraphrase a number of Riffaterre's statements at this point.

mentioned value judgment. The twist given by Riffaterre to the norm–deviant pair is very significant and, I think, indicative of the general direction taken by much recent—post-Prague school—research in both literary and linguistic analysis, namely, a kind of "functionalism." Both "norm" and "deviation," for Riffaterre, correspond to functional, not a priori abstract, categories. The "norm" behaves as such only when contrasted with a "deviation" that is itself a deviation *because* of the norm. Thus, any linguistic device is potentially effective stylistically—none are per se stylistically operative. Moreover, "norm" and "deviation" operate in dialectical relationship to one another; they are resolved into the context and belong to the "meaning" of the text. To offer an example, the sudden use of an imperfect subjunctive verb in a colloquial French text can constitute a "deviation" in terms of the colloquial contextual "norm," but when its effect—irony, humor, grotesque—is understood with respect to the tensions, the checks-and-balances, of the context, it ceases to be a "deviation." On the level of meaning it is reincorporated into the meaning or system of values represented by the text. The principle of norm–deviation is no more than an analytic device; by no means does it constitute a definitive point of arrival.

At the risk of some oversimplification it might be said that Riffaterre's originality, with respect to other theories so far looked into, lies in the way he reconciles linguistic and literary analysis by appealing to a system neatly subdivided into two levels. First, the level of impression and analytic description, depending on the norm–deviation pair and engineered to deal specifically with textual complexities. This level is the more properly "linguistic" one, since, although the process is set off by a critical value judgment, it is characterized by as great an objectivity as possible and is concerned with language operating as *device*. We are reminded of Bally, who described literary stylistics as "the observation of the means of style," and who, in his general stylistics of linguistic expressivity, invariably based his study upon comparison of "ordinary language" (i.e., ideal, or neutral, nonexpressive discourse) with discourse carrying expressive weight. Riffaterre's "ordinary language" is, of course, his contextual norm; both function in exactly the same way. (Nor is the difference great between Bally's "affective" point of departure and Riffaterre's initial "stylistic effect"; Bally, a pioneer in the field, stresses somewhat more the psychological side of the question, whereas Riffaterre takes that matter for granted.) Moreover, Bally's criterion of usage, as opposed to abstract grammatical rule, already points the way to Riffaterre's textual realism. Riffaterre complements Bally's original system, applying his most fundamental doctrines to literature and frankly admitting his interest, not in expression for its own sake, but rather in the use the author makes of the means of expression. Although Riffaterre's attachment to literature—a terrain of notoriously shifting sands—cannot permit the ultimate generality for which Bally strove in his results, he remains faithful to interpersonality. This is evident in his manifest desire to "objectivize" as far as possible the description of the grounds upon which the whole edifice of stylistic effects is built. For him, interpersonality would be a function of the collectivity of readers. In a sense, he operates in each case with an "ideally encoded message"—Richards' implicit "correct readings"—and must assume that, in spite of "variant readings," his findings will point to the ideal message, or closely approximate it.

If Riffaterre can be classified—at least provisionally—as a kind of Bally in reverse, the reason should be sought in his unequivocal intention of placing linguistic analysis at the service of literature. Here we touch upon the second level of his analytic procedure or, more exactly, upon the synthesizing process in which the "deviation," once described, is reintegrated into the "norm" on the level of meaning. Quoting, in his review-article, Wellek's statement that "a work of literature is, by its very nature, a totality of values which do not merely adhere to the structure but constitute its very nature" (*Style in Language,* p. 419), Riffaterre claims, with considerable justification, that his method satisfies these conditions: the stylistic effect is not judged in isolation from the value structure of the work; on the contrary, it departs from an original value judgment and is eventually reincorporated into a general artistic judgment concerning the work. What I have called Riffaterre's two procedural levels of style and of meaning, he himself names, respectively, *analyse stylistique* and *critique métastylistique.* Wellek's "literary stylistics" (which he opposes to Bally's "general stylistics"), concentrating on "the aesthetic purpose of every linguistic device" (p. 418), corresponds in essence to what Riffaterre accomplishes, although Riffaterre objects somewhat to the arbitrary subdivisionary status assigned by Wellek. Wellek's distinction is still valid in that it serves to distinguish between the very different goals sought by Bally and the literary stylisticians.

Riffaterre's literary bias is certain, as is the linguistic character of his method. What remains harder to grasp, perhaps, is the linguistic intent, if any, his method and purposes might have. Is he content with merely placing the tools of linguistic analysis at the service of literary study or does he expect that linguistics itself—the science of language—will also benefit from his endeavor? A number of possibilities emerge. First, the foregoing discussion of Riffaterre's adaptation of the norm–deviation dichotomy shows that he has rejected the concept of "literary language," at least as it has been traditionally used by linguists and literary historians alike. This implies (1) that style is a function of aesthetic intent in the realm of *Wortkunst,* and (2) that language as a whole—not any subdivision thereof—is amenable to stylistic employment. Furthermore, since style is defined as the formal structure of literature accessible to the linguist, it follows that, in literature, one can find uses to which language is put that are perhaps not to be found elsewhere—or that are not to be found to the same degree either quantitatively or qualitatively. To my knowledge, Riffaterre does not elaborate upon this point in any significant detail. It seems taken for granted also. But his resolute incorporation of literature into the general linguistic field does widen the sphere of activity normally considered pertinent to linguistics, and that in itself constitutes an immediate benefit. Perhaps even more significant, however, is the possible practical result, for linguistics, of competent stylistic study. As defined by Riffaterre, style can be considered as a focal point marking the conversion of any specific linguistic trait—phonetic, morphological, syntactic, lexicological—into a given, and significant, effect. Thus, whereas much descriptivist linguistic analysis tends inevitably toward compartmentalization —even a full-scale morphophonemic analysis involves minute specialization when compared with the totality of linguistic possibilities—style study, directed and organized according to aesthetic aims, offers a microcosm displaying an immensely wide range of purely linguistic features. A single sonnet can, and indeed in practice frequently must, entail commentary of great linguistic scope, depending on the complexity and variety of resources used. In a sense, stylistic analysis can ideally function as a kind of test laboratory for diversified linguistic theory and practice. Moreover, it can prove useful in pointing out wider relationships between disciplines; Riffaterre himself exemplifies the general compatibility existing between Geneva and Prague school linguistic structuralism and modern structuralist literary criticism as represented in the United States by Wellek and Warren and their New Critical antecedents.

Unfortunately, space does not permit further discussion of the remaining theoretical papers in *Style in Language* that treat the general problem of language and literature from the standpoint of dualisms such as the ones we have observed in Voegelin, Hill, Saporta, and also in Riffaterre (who, we recall, is not represented in the volume). By and large, however, the remarkable vitality of the various dualist approaches in contemporary linguistico-literary analysis, as well as the main directions these approaches have taken, have been underscored. Of the four viewpoints considered it appears that Voegelin's and Riffaterre's—though in very different ways—stand some chance of paving the way for significant advances in the field. Both offer schemes that can be built upon. One wonders, for example, how their exclusively synchronic slant might be modified to accommodate a diachronic view as well. Most important, both Voegelin and Riffaterre tend to increase the scope of linguistics as a discipline, and for this one should be grateful.

Other contributors to *Style in Language* testify to the considerable activity of certain branches of linguistico-literary research in the United States. The section on metrics stands out particularly. The conference's linguistic spokesman, Fred W. Householder, stated that a fairly general agreement between linguists and literary critics on "all essential points" (p. 346) was shown in the papers by John Lotz ("Metric Typology"), Seymour Chatman ("Comparing Metrical Styles"), John Hollander ("The Metrical Emblem"), W. K. Wimsatt and Monroe C. Beardsley ("The Concept of Meter: An Exercise in Abstraction")—Benjamin Hrushovski's "On Free Rhythms in Modern Poetry" was considered a possible exception.

Lotz's contribution (pp. 135–48) is exemplary in several respects: it is unabashedly "linguistic" in approach—Householder considers it "as being one of the best and clearest introductions to general metrics I have ever seen" (p. 346)—and it strives to set up a typology; typological classifications constitute one of the principal concerns of contemporary linguistics in the United States. Furthermore, Lotz, an American with extensive European training, personifies the previously noted blending of the two modern structuralist tendencies in the field of metrics. Contacts between American and European linguistic research have multiplied since World War II and, by now, have indelibly marked both camps.

Lotz is not concerned with style, nor does his work imply immediate critical evaluation; he is as resolutely descriptive as the phonological schools whose methods he utilizes in the context of metrics. *Meter* is defined at the outset as a "most deliberately formulated, and experimentally varied, use of language" (p. 135); it is "numerically regulated" (hence very amenable to quantitative analysis). Lotz depends heavily on Prague school theory: thus *verse* and *prose* are considered "polar opposites," as a "marked–unmarked" pair (p. 137). Since, according to Lotz, "verse is a purely formal notion" referring to "the language signal alone without reference to function," [34] he concludes that "metrics is entirely within the competence of linguistics"—a justifiable conclusion only if one were to consider metrics, at least temporarily, as a semi-independent descriptive science. Lotz does precisely this, so he is in a position to point out those aspects of language that are relevant to meter; he does so brilliantly, formulating the *"principle of metric relevancy* in analogy with the principle of relevancy in phonological and grammatical analysis" (pp. 137–38). His entire typology is based on this principle (ignoring deliberately the ways "the language material used in verse might differ from the 'normal' use of the language"). He divides the linguistic study of meter into two sections: "(A) study of the linguistic constituents and (B) study of the metric superstructure." The former, not surprisingly, is further subdivided into *phonological* and *syntactic* constituents. Among the phonological constituents *syllabification,* being universal, is clearly the most important; *pitch, intensity,* and *duration* are significant in some systems. Yet metrics, we learn, never utilizes "all the phonemic features available for verse" (p. 139); normally, there is a correlation between "metrically relevant features" and "phonemically distinctive

---

34. "Function" is best described here as "overall function," since Lotz himself points out another kind of function (p. 146): "The increasing number of [two contiguous light syllables] symbolizes clearly the growing tension and the fright of the child in Goethe's 'Erlkönig.'" This is an evident example of metrical function with reference to the specific semantic exigencies of the poem in question.

features," though the "subphonemic distinction" between the syllabic and nonsyllabic allophones is also metrically relevant. Syntactically, *sentence* and *word* seem to be consistently relevant, and *cola* frequently so. Other phonological and syntactic elements (assonance, rhyme, refrain, etc.) serve to emphasize the metric structure, but they are not of primary importance; they also function in prose. Lotz applies these criteria to existing metric structures and concludes that "we have basically two pure types of meter" (p. 140): *pure syllabic meter* (entirely based on "the number of syllables within the syntactic frames"; Mordvinian verse) and *syllabico-prosodic* meter, which breaks down into three subclasses: *durational* (classical Greek and Latin), *dynamic* (syllabic counting plus contrast of heavier and lighter syllabic pulses, as in English and German), and *tonal* (distinctive contrasts of pitch; classical Chinese). There are also a number of "intermediate types" (French, Byzantine Greek). Lotz points out what seems to be a universal trait of metrics, namely, that metrically "the phonological elements are grouped into two base classes, never into more" (p. 140); he shows that in English there are obviously more than two stress levels, just as in classical Chinese there "were nine (or six) phonemic tones," but that the opposition remains binary in both cases (English: heavy versus light; classical Chinese: even versus noneven tones).

Lotz presents an extremely elegant graphic typological scheme (p. 142) on the basis of these essential characteristics, claiming (pp. 141–43) that other criteria could have been used, but with considerably greater risk. Brief sample analyses of each type follow. In the section on the "dynamic type" we find that, among the linguistic constituents, phonologically, the syllabic base classes are heavy and light. This system allows great freedom in the assignment of syllabics since the same morpheme "can be assigned to different base classes" (p. 145). Syntactically, words, cola, and sentences are possible. As for metric structure, seldom are more than two light or heavy bases allowed "in immediate succession." Metric levels include *lines, strophes,* and *cycles.* There are two types of lines according to positional distribution of lights and heavies: *isosyllabic* and *isodynamic.* "Lines in the same poem often show a difference in the number of added light syllables at the end of the line, most often zero versus one (*catalex*)." Finally, a brief metrical description is provided of some lines from "The Ancient Mariner"; this is accomplished by marking off and enumerating the number of "contiguous light, syllabics" in each line and by indicating their presence or absence at both the beginning and end of the line. Thus (p. 146):

*I*t is *a*n anc*i*ent Mar*i*ner   I   I   I   I   O

Although incomplete, this summary of Lotz's "Metrical Typology" emphasizes the kind of regularity typological study can achieve, a regularity valuable for its own sake, but also of wider interest, since it tends to summarize previous theory and clear the terrain for future speculation. A properly handled typology, presenting an objective and highly organized scheme of research in a given field, can heavily influence subsequent practice, even in areas somewhat tangential to the one covered by the typology. Thus, for example, Riffaterre, commenting on Lotz's contribution, is led to remark that Lotz's defining the regularity of different meters "implies a typology of the contrasts possible with respect to each one" (see Riffaterre's review-article), which, of course, would be significant for his general theory of style. And I have already pointed to

Lotz's conception of the purely linguistic function of metrical schemes (citing advertising jingles and the example of versified legal codes, he denies that verse serves an exclusively aesthetic function; see Jakobson's comment, p. 359). This notion of function is hardly compatible with most views entertained by literary critics, who would be more likely to emphasize function in terms of symbolic values (e.g., Lotz's example of Goethe's "Erlkönig," as quoted in footnote 34). Clearly, the term *function* stands in need of some revision if the two points of view are eventually to come together again, as they should, since no real difference separates them on this issue.

Lotz's application of phonological principles to metrical theory offers an authentic instance of transference of one basic kind of linguistic methodology in a field other than the one for which it was ostensibly designed. His phonological principle of "metrical relevance" provides the cornerstone for his entire system. Not only elegant but genuinely effective in the circumstances—without it Lotz could have done little—this principle seems applicable in other contexts too, e.g., in the delicate matter of sound symbolism or perhaps in synesthesia. Besides, Lotz is not dealing in this article with a problem traditionally classified as a purely linguistic one. He utilizes a linguistic approach in the analysis of borderline material. He recognizes that literary critics "often understand more about relevant features of verse and language than many linguists do" (p. 137, n. 5), implying their greater professional interest in these questions. Metrics is less an inherent *feature* of language than a conventional *use* to which language is put. By the same token, meter, in poetry, is a convention rather than an inherent feature. Success or failure of poems does not depend on the presence or absence of meter; it is entirely the way meter is used in the poem that counts. In short, metrics is to general linguistics roughly what it is to literary theory and criticism, as well as being a clear link between the two. This, in part, explains Lotz's undeniable success from the viewpoints of both linguistics and literary study, and can only encourage similar—and equally circumspect—experiments (typological or other) in analogously ambivalent areas.[35]

A number of contemporary American linguists and literary scholars have found various linguistic techniques and procedures either indispensable or very congenial to their literary studies. Although they have explored these techniques perhaps not quite so systematically as Lotz (who restricts himself to meter), they have frequently gone beyond the limits recommended by *Theory of Literature.* In a sense, linguistics plays a part, with respect to these analysts, analogous to a doctrine like Freudianism in the studies of certain psychological critics, that is, as an extremely important analytic tool. The goal, however, remains the formal and semantic explication and classification of literature, not primarily the study of language. Among the contributors to *Style in Language,* D. H. Hymes ("Phonological Aspects of Style: Some English Sonnets," pp. 109–31) represents this tendency. Borrowing and amplifying techniques previously elaborated, especially by J.

---

35. I do not mean to imply that any linguistic approach to metrics must meet with unqualified approval on the part of literary critics. In their essay and in their ad hoc remarks, both in *Style in Language* (pp. 194 ff. and 200 ff.), W. K. Wimsatt and Monroe Beardsley convincingly criticize the controversial theories advanced by G. L. Trager and H. L. Smith in *Outline of English Structure* (Washington, 1957). It so happens that Lotz's techniques are "relevant."

J. Lynch ("The Tonality of Lyric Poetry: An Experiment in Method," *Word,* December 1953, 211–24), and—to a lesser degree—by Pierre Guiraud (*Langage et versification d'après l'œuvre de Paul Valéry* [Paris 1953]), Hymes applies methods of rigorous phonetic description and statistical analysis in order to approach the problem of sound symbolism in twenty sonnets by Wordsworth and Keats. Lynch had intended to use data provided by linguistic science in order to "propose a method of [linguistic] analysis that [would] . . . not only contribute to the understanding of specific poems, but also suggest other ways of bridging the gap between linguistics and literary studies." He analyzes phonetic data with a view of discovering "the total effect of a poem's euphony or tonality or musicality" (Wellek's "orchestration"). He therefore takes into account the metrical stress, the "stress" of the "prose" or "thought" statement, and the "prominence due to repetitive utterance"; he relates all this to the "metaphorical structure of the sonnet, and then to its prose statement." Hymes goes even further than Lynch, since, as he puts it, "the total organization may operate on levels both above and below that of the phoneme" (p. 130). Quoting Wimsatt and Hatzfeld to the effect that "complexity" and "unity" are two essential criteria of poetic value, Hymes claims his method can suitably indicate the ways in which the individual poem is "complex" and "unified." However, he does not pretend that "the results of this approach are . . . themselves a criterion of value."

In their respective final statements Householder and Wellek seem to disagree on the value of Hymes's technique. Householder concludes that, in its present form, "it is a waste of time," because the statistical relationship between phonemic frequencies was artificially overweighted in favor of conclusions that could have been reached by simpler means (343 ff.). Wellek, on the other hand, finds that Hymes "has re-examined the problem [of sound symbolism] sensitively," and, though disagreeing with certain conclusions, praises his gift of using statistics "to some purpose" by showing "that there are 'summative' words in these sonnets" (pp. 412–13). Householder rejects the method; Wellek seems cautiously to accept the method on the basis of some of its results.

Josephine Miles, a scholar (and poet) not represented in *Style in Language,* has used paralinguistic and statistical techniques in a number of literary studies (e.g., *Eras and Modes in English Poetry* [Berkeley, 1957]—see also *PMLA, LXX* [September 1955]—and *Renaissance, Eighteenth-Century, and Modern Language in English Poetry: A Tabular View* [Berkeley, 1960]). These deal mainly with poetic diction, but recently Miss Miles has attempted grammatically oriented generic studies of the epic, differentiating between various modes (e.g., Tasso, the *Song of Roland*) by means of careful, objective analysis of distributional patterns—number of verbs with respect to nouns and adjectives, and so forth. Her work does not seem to reflect any systematic linguistic "philosophy"; it proceeds empirically, but it definitely constitutes a part of the general linguistic–literary trend I have been discussing. She relates grammatical features predominant in the works of given periods to broader questions of "poetic history." In "Parts of Speech in Periods of Poetry" (*PMLA, LXXIII* [1958]), the late linguist–anthropologist A. L. Kroeber attempted "to carry further and perhaps to sharpen her approach" to the problem of correlating stylistic epochs and quantitatively describable verbal features present in literary compositions. Like Lynch and Hymes, Miss Miles deals somewhat incidentally with "style" as such; she subsumes stylistic matters into historical or cultural constructs. Her latest work, however, is more stylistically oriented (*Style and Proportion: the Language of Prose and Poetry* [Boston, 1967]).

Once again limitations of time and space forbid going into greater detail concerning this important, and typical, "miscellaneous" tendency of linguistic and literary scholarship. I have tried to do some justice to the variety of viewpoints discussed so far, but it is now necessary to inquire of *Style in Language* what provisional systematizations seem possible. A summary is in order. Each of the systems implicit in the theories of Voegelin, Saporta, and Riffaterre, as well as the systematic tailoring of phonological speculation to the needs of metrical description in the typology of Lotz, is characterized by the partiality of its goals. Saporta wishes to "define" literary qualities for very particular reasons; Riffaterre seeks to establish an independent science of style (cf. Wellek's "literary stylistics"); and, of course, Lotz confines himself to meter alone. Voegelin presents the broadest perspectives of the four, but his point of view remains anchored in traditional American descriptivist theory and does not cope especially with either style or literature. On the other hand, Roman Jakobson's lengthy "Concluding Statement: Linguistics and Poetics" (in the section of *Style in Language* entitled "From the Viewpoint of Linguistics," pp. 350–77) surely provides the best angle from which to summarize and complete the present section of this study. Jakobson assumes the rôle of a linguistic scientist, yet since his early days among the Russian formalists and Prague school structuralists, he has maintained a long-standing and steady interest in literary matters. Moreover, having lived in the

United States for many years and participated fully—by both teaching and writing—in linguistic research as practiced here, he can now be considered an American scholar. As a widely traveled European immigrant to this country, he remains steeped in modernist traditions of poetics and linguistic study as developed in eastern, central, and western Europe, thus typifying the intense cosmopolitanism that has come to characterize so much American intellectual life, especially since World War II. Jakobson's example proves that "national scholarship" cannot be adequately appraised without direct reference to its international context. These facts, plus the extraordinary intrinsic interest of Jakobson's "Linguistics and Poetics," make this programmatic contribution an almost ideal basis for this summary.

Jakobson brings his whole varied experience and wide reading to bear upon his analysis, which Yakov Malkiel frankly praised as almost a "jewel" (op. cit., p. 281); he utilizes Karl Bühler's *Sprachtheorie,* V. I. Propp's structuralist approach to fairytale analysis, the Russian formalists (Osip Brik), John Crowe Ransom and the New Criticism, C. S. Peirce's "semiotic," Gerard Manley Hopkins' poetics, Claude Lévi-Strauss' anthropology, A. A. Potebnja's "protoformalism," and his own linguistic thought as expressed in such key works and articles as *Fundamentals of Language* (1956, with Morris Halle; see particularly chap. v, "The Metaphoric and Metonymic Poles"), "Über den Versbau der serbokroatischen Volksepen" (1933), and "Randbemerkungen zur Prosa des Dichters Pasternak" (1935). His remarks are based on a few central descriptions and assumptions. "Poetics deals primarily with the question, *What makes a verbal message a work of art?*" (*Style in Language,* p. 350). Poetics is also concerned "with problems of verbal structure"; it forms a part of the "whole theory of signs, that is, [of] general semiotics" (p. 351). Criticism and study of literature must not be confused: "The label 'literary critic' applied to an investigator of literature is as erroneous as 'grammatical (or lexical) critic' would be applied to a linguist" (p. 352). Jakobson's bias is therefore "scientific" and "academic," but, unlike Wellek and Warren, his final goal is not restricted to literature as such, but rather to verbal signs and to sign operations as a whole ("The linguistic scrutiny of poetry cannot limit itself to the poetic function" [p. 357]). He nevertheless recognizes, as we shall see, the *particular character* of literature. He remains a linguist, yet he refuses to concede that his position as a linguist restricts him to nonliterary matters: *"Linguista sum: linguistici nihil a me alienum puto"* (p. 377). This ability to rise above "linguistic" and "poetic" sectarianism seems to be a trait of much central and eastern European thought—e.g., among the Prague group and in the works of Karl Vossler.[36] It invariably in-

---

36. Jakobson shares other traits of Vossler's kind of modernism, as evidenced in the following statement: "Poeticalness is not a supplementation of discourse with rhetorical adornment [Croce's *forma ornata* again] but a total re-evaluation of the discourse and of all its components" (p. 377). His techniques of analysis show the Prague school orientation to which, of course, he too contributed a great deal. Thus, in "Sur la Langue poétique," a section of the anonymous forementioned "Thèses," in *Travaux du Cercle linguistique de Prague,* I (1929), we find Jakobson's "poetic function": "Il résulte de la théorie disant que le langage poétique tend à mettre en relief la valeur autonome du signe, que tous les plans d'un système linguistique, qui n'ont dans le langage de communication ["interpersonal" speech] qu'un rôle de service, prennent, dans le langage poétique, des valeurs autonomes plus ou moins considérables" (p. 18). Both *Literaturwissenschaft* (as opposed to pure "criticism")

volves attachment to a category superior to interpersonality and individualism: for Vossler, "general linguistic 'science'" focusing on "expression," for Jakobson, "verbal" and "general sign theory." Language is a unified whole of disparate-seeming elements—Jakobson's point of departure is thus Voegelin's ideal point of arrival—and the poetic must be considered a part of this whole.

Jakobson approaches the problems of language and poetics from the angle of functions, not from static categories. He adopts the following scheme of *factors* of verbal communication:

CONTEXT

ADDRESSER   MESSAGE   ADDRESSEE
                      CONTACT

CODE

Each factor entails a corresponding *function* and/or *Einstellung* of functions:

---

and linguistic poetics constituted two disciplinary focuses utilized by Prague school practitioners; Mukařovský's "La Phonologie et la poétique," in *Travaux*, IV (1931), 278–88, is two-pronged in this way. On the one hand phonological theory is "essential for the analysis of the phonic side of the literary work of art" (and literary works in general); on the other hand profit from such study can be gained by linguistics too: "Une langue fonctionnelle [poetry] ayant pour but la désautomatisation des moyens d'expression, une langue où tout élément linguistique, même celui qu'habituellement on remarque le moins, peut prendre la valeur d'un procédé nettement téléologique, doit fournir des matériaux inappréciables à toute analyse phénoménologique du langage" (p. 288).

REFERENTIAL

EMOTIVE   POETIC   CONATIVE

PHATIC

METALINGUAL

This depiction of factors and functions, showing emphases and subcategories, permits a combined analytic and synthetic presentation of the elements of communication and their interaction. Factors and functions correspond, in a sense, to the old form–content dichotomy, but instead of stressing the opposition between them, Jakobson is able to emphasize their essential unity. The emotive function concentrates on the speaker's attitude toward what is said, the conative focuses on the addressee (vocative, imperative), the phatic deals with the contact (does the channel of communication work properly?), the metalingual examines the code used. Here is the way the poetic function is determined:

> Recall the two basic modes of arrangement used in verbal behavior, *selection* and *combination*. If "child" is the topic of the message, the speaker selects one among the extant, more or less similar, nouns like *child, kid, youngster, tot,* all of them equivalent in a certain respect, and then, to comment on this topic, he may select one of the semantically cognate verbs—*sleeps, dozes, nods, naps.* Both chosen words combine in the speech chain. The selection is produced on the base of equivalence, similarity and dissimilarity, synonymity and antonymity, while the combination, the build up of the sequence, is based on contiguity. *The poetic function projects the principle of equivalence from the axis of selection into the axis of combination* [p. 358].

232

Thus, in one sense, poetics emerges "as that part of linguistics which treats the poetic function in its relationship to the other functions of language." But, in "the wider sense of the word," poetics "deals with the poetic function not only in poetry, where this function is superimposed upon the other functions of language, but also outside of poetry, when some other function is superimposed upon the poetic function" (p. 359). As a category, "poetry" possesses, for Jakobson, some kind of arbitrary status derived from its own ostensible nature; his ultimate "definition" of poetry is not clear. However, through "poetics" poetry exists on two analytic planes—independently, i.e., as literature, and as incorporated into general language. The semiotic question appears again later when Jakobson illustrates sign-operations with an example borrowed from Russian folk poetry. Taking the line that, translated, reads: "A fierce horse was coming at a gallop to the court," he analyzes an ambiguous "semantic connection" brought off through a metonymic device:

A comparison between the appearing bridegroom and the galloping horse suggests itself, but at the same time the halt of the horse at the court actually anticipates the approach of the hero to the house. Thus before introducing the rider and the manor of his fiancée, the song evokes the contiguous, *metonymical* images of the horse and of the courtyard: possession instead of possessor, and outdoors instead of inside. . . . the "fierce horse," emerging in the preceding line at a similar metrical and syntactic place as the "brave fellow" [in a previously quoted line: "A brave fellow was going to the porch"], figures simultaneously as a likeness to and as a representative possession of this fellow . . . [p. 370].

233

These metonymical structures point out an essentially poetic equivalence (along "the axis of combination"). Jakobson's dualist manner (function/factor) of dealing with the case stresses his capacity and willingness to cope with the *formal complexity* of linguistic expression, but the results, as tabulated, remain clear and speak for themselves. Other examples follow. Jakobson discusses a purely phonetic value: "In a sequence, where similarity is superimposed on contiguity, two similar phonemic sequences near to each other are prone to assume a paranomastic function" (p. 371). Jakobson goes on to illustrate this axiom in a brilliant analysis of a few lines from Poe's "The Raven" (the lines beginning: "And the Raven, never flitting, still is sitting, *still* is sitting," etc.). He shows that "the relevance of the sound–meaning nexus is a simple corollary of the superposition of similarity upon contiguity" (p. 372). Both "meaning" and "sound"—normally distinguished as two separate levels and studied either independently or as complete entities in relation to one another— are here subsumed into the higher, though common, category of verbal signs. Within the sign-structure of the poem their semiotic reciprocity can be seen clearly (hence Jakobson's insistence, in this instance, upon the extraphonetic and extrasemantic terms *contiguity* and *similarity*).

A word now concerning the disciplinary orientation given these theories. At the beginning of his essay Jakobson answers those who would not include poetics "as an integral part of linguistics." The transposition of poetical works into another art medium (film, ballet) merely proves that poetry, like other verbal discourse, can be subsumed into general semiotic operations and studied by means of sign theory. The relationship between poetry and reality—a constant theme of modernist criticism—is a problem concerning "not only verbal art but actually all kinds of discourse," and ultimately the question must "exceed the bounds of poetics and linguistics in general." Jakobson seems to reject the common New Critical belief that poetry enjoys a special relationship to reality; of course, he does not operate with the science–poetry polarity the New Critics did, so that, in a sense, he and they do not speak of quite the same things. As for "evaluation," central even to the "literary scholarship" of Wellek and Warren, Jakobson contrasts "normative" evaluative criticism with literary science (poetics), rejecting, for his purpose, the application to literary science of evaluative modes just as he rejects the imposition of normative grammar upon pure linguistic theory and description. The point seems well taken, at least to the extent that, by substituting "knowing more" for "knowing absolutely," Jakobson is able to open up many avenues of approach, many new fascinating subjects, hitherto recalcitrant to the systematic critical analysis that leads to eventual value judgments. Moreover, Jakobson rightly stresses the transient character of literary fashion and critical modes—without denying their necessity. Nonetheless, it seems that any reconciliation of literary and linguistic study that results in the incorporation of the former into linguistics (however broadly based the brand of linguistics may be) must entail the suppression of concern for value. (We have already seen that the kind of linguistics acceptable to Wellek and Warren is a very reduced species.) Finally, Jakobson warns against the "illicit" restrictions to which the field of linguistics has been subjected by theoretical *parti pris* and "bigoted linguists." He proves to be realistic in his own approach, showing that the "over-all code" is actually made up of a "system of interconnected sub-

THE STUDY OF LANGUAGE AND LITERATURE

codes" (p. 352), and implying that misdirected exclusivity has no claim, in linguistics, on the last word about anything. (Martin Joos's rejection of emotive "secondary factors" in speech, we learn, "is a radical experiment in reduction—*reductio ad absurdum*" [p. 353]).

These remarks, plus those dealing with the linguistic factors and functions, show that in reality Jakobson is advocating as thorough an overhaul of linguistic as of literary perspectives. From the point of view of many linguists participating in the 1958 conference at Bloomington, Jakobson is surely as "radical" as he seems to be for some literary critics. Much of his commentary constitutes an oblique—and sometimes direct —criticism leveled at certain trends, some of them fossilized, in traditional American descriptivism. Yet finally, his innovations are a good deal less than they seem; he summarizes what has been done by himself and many others, and frequently— perhaps this is his greatest originality—he is satisfied merely to point out the disciplinary relevance of this past work, the possibilities it uncovers. His long discussion of Gerard Manley Hopkins' brilliant insights into the linguistic structures of poetry ("the science of poetic language" [p. 358]), and his enthusiastic acceptance of certain affirmations made by critics like John Crowe Ransom and William Empson, seemed designed to emphasize what modernist linguists and literary commentators possess in common. Hopkins' theory of poetic parallelism leads Jakobson to declare that "equivalence in sound, projected into the sequence as its constitutive principle, inevitably involves semantic equivalence, and on any linguistic level any constituent of such a sequence prompts one of the two correlative experiences which Hopkins neatly defines 'as comparison for likeness' sake' and 'comparison for unlikeness' sake' " (pp. 368 f.). Jakobson adopts this formulation and applies it to the analysis of several features of Russian wedding songs (see above); his analysis is purely linguistic, proving the essential identity of spirit in his and Hopkins' approach. Somewhat later, he takes up the fundamental New Critical notion of ambiguity—Empson's "The machinations of ambiguity are among the very roots of poetry" (*Seven Types of Ambiguity*)—and declares it to be "an intrinsic, inalienable character of any self-focused message, briefly a corollary feature of poetry" (pp. 370 f.). This is explained in terms of his scheme of functions as follows: "The supremacy of poetic function over referential function does not obliterate the reference but makes it ambiguous." Examples illustrate this principle, which successfully incorporates Empson's theory into Jakobson's linguistic framework. Moreover, literary critics can follow his observations and see how linguistic analysis can deepen and complement their own insights. Thus Jakobson reiterates his previously published remarks concerning metaphor and metonymy. Metaphor—as earlier shown in the section dealing with the New Criticism—has consistently attracted students of literary figures; their attraction to the study of metaphor is a function of their interest in verse and poetry, and it has entailed neglect of "realistic literature, intimately tied with the metonymic principle, [which] still defies interpretation." Jakobson claims that "the same linguistic methodology, which poetics uses when analyzing the metaphorical style of romantic poetry, is entirely applicable to the metonymical texture of realistic prose" (p. 375). Linguistic objectivity would seem to compensate in part for the somewhat deformative tendency of taste-inspired criticism.

In effect Jakobson's "Linguistics and Poetics" shifts back

and forth from one disciplinary admonishment and recommendation to another. Thus he appears to be addressing the linguists in particular when he insists that in poetry "the internal form of a name, that is, the semantic load of its constituents, regains its pertinence" (p. 376). Poets and men of letters would be quick to exploit—and some linguists perhaps, as such, just as quick to dismiss—the fact that the word *cocktails* regains its primitive kinship "with plumage" in these lines from Mac Hammond, "The ghost of a Bronx pink lady / With orange blossoms afloat in her hair," and in "O, Bloody Mary, / The cocktails have crowed not the cocks!" Jakobson concludes "that a linguist deaf to the poetic function of language and a literary scholar indifferent to linguistic problems and unconversant with linguistic methods are equally flagrant anachronisms" (p. 377).

Jakobson's proposals concerning linguistics and literature are thus more sweeping in their effects than those so far examined in this chapter. In a sense, they *include* the other propositions whenever these have tended to widen the perspectives of linguistics as practiced today (those of Voegelin and Lotz, for example) and whenever they favor the reconciliation of literary and linguistic studies. On the other hand, they reject the proposals—like Saporta's—that arbitrarily restrict the fields of both literature and linguistics. Riffaterre's comments are interesting in this "professional" context. In his review-article Riffaterre agrees in substance with Jakobson's theories, preferring, however, *style* or *stylistics* to Jakobson's *poetic*. If, he argues, the poetic function is oriented toward the message as sign, if its purpose is to direct decoding operations, he would propose substituting his own term *stylistic function,* since *poetic function* is difficult to use without "premature value judgments." He is right as far as he goes, i.e., in that he remains within the boundaries of his method, but one suspects he goes both too far and not far enough. Riffaterre's entire *system* is a stylistic one, he reconciles linguistics and literary study by "creating" a new discipline designed to accomplish certain precise purposes. To the extent that his stylistics, as a system, is monolithic (no matter how precisely delimited), a thing-in-itself, it perforce differs from the "integrated" poetics of Jakobson, a part of a larger whole. Conversely, Riffaterre's stylistics is a very circumscribed affair, whereas, being an integral part of a wider theory, Jakobson's poetics necessarily reflects that whole. In spite of apparent similarities, which Riffaterre clearly indicates, his stylistics and Jakobson's poetics are two very different things; the quarrel is not one of empty names. Qualitatively the two scholars speak a similar language, quantitatively (e.g., in scope) they are miles apart.

Jakobson's "linguistics" is a global affair. It appears to encompass the greater number of linguistic theories so far examined—Saussure, Bally, Vossler, Bloomfield, *Style in Language* —and, to a significant degree, to advance beyond them. The reason lies in his pervasive dynamism. Linguistic dynamics has played a characteristically important part in all modernist theories, but in Jakobson a dynamic—one might say, phenomenological—point of view dominates everything else— and with remarkably little risk of overdilution (less, certainly, than Vossler's monolithic theory and practice). His "themes" —whether poetic imagery, phonemic theory, or translation[37]

37. For a fascinating statement of his ideas concerning translation—a subject far from irrelevant to this essay, since Jakobson views translation as the fundamental semiotic process—see his "On Linguistic Aspects of Translation" in the important *On Translation,* ed. Reuben Brower (Cambridge, Mass., 1959), pp. 232–39.

—are ultimately mere illustrations of the dynamic patterns of language; they are rarely to be considered, in themselves, as independent "objects of investigation." Now then, this represents one logical conclusion of the general modernist view. We have seen that, since Condillac, one of the principal tenets of linguistic modernism is that any linguistic element can be literary, that is, put to literary use. The ancient hierarchy of styles no longer functions, except perhaps distinctively in terms of more or less established genres. We have furthermore observed that the newly traditional interpersonal–individual polarity, applied in different ways by many scholars in order to distinguish between the language of linguistics and the language of literature, has never been accorded status as an absolute by the greatest linguistic theorists of the past, that it has in reality been a matter of emphasis. And even recent literary scholarship, exemplified in Wellek and Warren, has refused to maintain the polarity absolutely. Many contemporary scholars seem to eliminate the problem entirely by operating with categories neither static nor absolute but rather directed toward the solution of specific problem types. For Riffaterre, literature, seen as context and style, and initially determined by value judgments, turns out to be a *use* to which language is put and, as such, can be approached linguistically. For Jakobson verbal art remains verbal—he agrees with Ransom that "poetry is a kind of language" (p. 377) and it is significant that he seldom refers to *literature* as a category, preferring *poetic function* or *poetry*—hence it lends itself to the analysis any kind of verbal discourse must undergo, and it is no more dependent on critical statements of value than linguistic descriptions are.

This discussion has by no means exhausted the "linguistic point(s) of view" in the scholarly activities dedicated to problems of language and literature. I have barely mentioned some of the literary implications of transformation grammar; I have not examined the long series of stylistic dissertations prepared at the Catholic University of America under the direction of Hatzfeld; I have failed to bring up a number of isolated studies and joint productions that, like *On Translation,* show many valid and interesting avenues of approach. I have avoided specific topics and some relevant general ones—like the larger question of linguistics, psychology, and anthropology, which is important in the United States (witness the work of Boas, Sapir, and Kroeber), or the problem of specific fields (Romance, Germanic, Slavic, etc.) and their characteristic contributions. I have been unable to isolate a single, unified American point of view concerning linguistics and the study of literature; the truth is that there is none—at least no single viewpoint so widespread even as idealism in prewar Germany. Nevertheless, I have tried to show that American linguistic scholarship is witnessing a rebirth of interest in literature and literary operations. The fact that I have had to take stock of a wide diversity of opinions is itself noteworthy; diversity, clash of ideas, experimentation—these are the marks of a vigorous discipline. Too much uniformity leads to stale conventionality. By letting a few representative scholars speak for themselves we have observed that a number of trends—some of them highly original and, I think, significant —have gained support and, in a few cases, have begun to bear fruit. I have tried to show their genesis and their general direction. What then is the upshot of all this? First, that linguistic theory and practice in the United States—in spite of certain handicaps and *idées reçues*—has made an effort not only to take cognizance of, but also to renew its approach to, literary material. Sometimes timidly, sometimes boldly, it has proved willing to begin anew a dialogue interrupted years ago. (Herein lies the considerable interest of the format of symposia like *Style in Language* and collections like *Essays on the Language of Literature.*) Linguistics has shown itself even capable of revising essential procedures in order to fortify its position in this dialogue. Nobody can accuse Voegelin, Lotz, Riffaterre, or Jakobson of betraying linguistic values in the statements that have been reviewed here. Most important, we have seen that open contact with the complex world of language represented by literature has, in several instances, led to profitable speculation concerning a unified theory of language. These signs point to the vitality of linguistics as practiced today in the United States, a vitality fully as great as in the heroic days of the founding of the Linguistic Society of America but potentially even less inbred, permitting both self-criticism and revision. At the same time, suggestions from specialists in other fields—literature, philosophy—seem to be welcome and even, within limits, heeded. For the health of linguistic science and of literary scholarship, it is to be hoped that these contacts will be pursued with an even greater intensity in the future.

❧ III ❧

CONCLUSIONS

It is time to review the implications of what we have so far observed and to assess constructively the tendencies we have examined. In keeping with the purposes of the Ford–Princeton Humanities series I shall confine my remarks to the relations between linguistic and literary study in America. What concrete suggestions may be offered? What seems to be the future of the collaboration of these disciplines in this country? Rather than "answer" these questions exhaustively, I shall merely sketch out certain possibilities.

Accomplishments

The preceding survey has shown that, in the United States, modern linguistics and literary scholarship are equally well entrenched as university subjects, but that neither has been definitively described with respect to purpose, scope, or methods. In all likelihood such description would be pointless or even damaging. Thus the fundamental character of each discipline seems to have been determined with some consistency, but the question of essential relationships remains open. Whatever their precise orientation, literary scholarship and linguistic science always imply both a *method* and a *subject matter;* the overlap between them has consistently required interdisciplinary cooperation. For example, at present a number of scholars appear to favor the establishment of a "literary science" based on a revised descriptive linguistics and structuralist literary analysis. This "science" would be divorced from exclusive concern with pure grammar and would avoid aesthetic value judgments. Jakobson holds that such a literary science, in conjunction with a liberalized linguistic theory, would offer rich areas of collaboration to both linguistics and literary study, and might profitably renew aspects of language study now in some danger of stagnation.

Scholars who have proved to be amenable to suggestions of systematic collaboration between linguistics and literary criticism usually fall into two main groups—those who believe in "centralization" and those whose approach is "decentralized." The former group favors the possibility of bringing together traditional American linguistics and modern criticism within a scope wider than either one alone; this group—and Jakobson is its spokesman—seeks a general theory of sign operations that would reflect technical possibilities and usage. The study of the "languages" of linguistics and of literature is recognized as complementary rather than opposed. The second —decentralizing—trend emphasizes partial reconciliations on given levels. Certain scholars object to the monolithic nature of much linguistic and literary research, claiming, for example, that rigorously structuralist techniques suitable, say, for morphophonemic or formal poetic analysis do not apply so well to etymology, stylistics, or semantics, and that these nevertheless remain legitimate fields of inquiry. On this decentralized level more or less ad hoc cooperation between linguistics and literary analysis has proved to be fruitful. Yet, in fact, decentralization and centralization do not constitute irreconcilably opposing tendencies; they offer two modes of approach to the same basic problem.

On the surface, then, the relations between linguistic study and literary criticism appear to be anarchic. The reasons for this apparent "anarchy" are clear; they reflect the history of the two disciplines within the broadly viewed evolution of modernist linguistic doctrine. Thus, I tried to describe the two modern theories of expression–communication, the one inclined synthetically and aesthetically, as suggested by Coleridge, and the other inclined analytically and linguistically, as represented by Condillac. In time the *mode of approach* came to take precedence over the initial unity. The frequent methodological distinctions between "interpersonality" and the "individual" provoked temporary disciplinary splits that in turn threatened the principle of unified views. The split in America was most evident in the antiliterary bias of Bloomfield's descriptivism as contrasted with the similarly structural-ist—but proliterary and aesthetic—tendency of the New Criticism and allied academic scholarship. Likewise, in Europe, the positivist–idealist dichotomy (Saussure and Bally as against Vossler and Spitzer) indicated that principle seemed to conquer reality there as well, even though, as Malkiel has wisely pointed out in his *IJAL* review of *Style in Language,* "the presently critical gap between these domains is simply a temporary maximum distance peculiar to a certain evolutionary phase" (p. 286). However, the divorce was never so complete in Europe as here, and, since World War II, the distinguished work of Stephen Ullmann (*Style in the French Novel* [Cambridge, 1957]) and of many other younger scholars (Zumthor, Bousoño, Barthes, Fónagy) proves that activity to do away with the "gap" has not diminished in the Old World. Meanwhile in the United States almost from the start, certain New Critics felt the need to deal with "linguistic questions"; a number of significant studies of prosody, metaphor, and style appeared before World War II. This trend was strengthened and systematized by the new academic literary scholars and encouraged by many specialists just arrived from Europe. Concomitantly, linguists, who worked in "borderline" or slightly unfashionable fields, were forced to attenuate and modify certain practices current in "pure" linguistic description. The needs of Romance scholars are such that they cannot long afford to ignore the literary dialect the way their colleagues interested in indigenous American tongues can and must. Consequently, at present the old question of disciplinary unity or of intermeshing is once again before us. Characteristically, linguists concerned with "cultural anthropology" and, especially, with English, a "prestige" tongue, are in the forefront of those native Americans who have been most willing to deal with literature.

The disciplinary fragmentation of the past half-century, especially acute in the 1930's and 1940's, has thus been largely a result of methodological focus and goals. But the very instability and relativism characteristic of modern thought in general constitute the background of this fragmentation. The terms *language* and *literature* are in a state of crisis: each mode of approach tends to define them as it wills. Vossler's *linguistic* would hardly be called so by a contributor to *Language* or *IJAL,* nor would Taine's *literary history* be easily recognized as entirely legitimate by a follower of Wellek. This terminological crisis is likely to continue, since, in the contemporary context, the value accorded terms depends almost entirely on the function they fulfill within the disciplinary focus. Thus, I have spoken here mainly of the kind of "literary criticism" frequently referred to as "poetics," a common East European term, though Wellek, in "The Main Trends of Twentieth-Century Criticism" (*Yale Review,* Autumn 1961, pp. 102–18), isolates a number of essentially nonlinguistic-critical approaches (psychoanalytic, Marxist, organicist, formalist, etc.). Few words, as we have seen, have been more subject to multiple interpretation than the term *style;* the disciplinary chasms were painfully evident in the Indiana Conference.

A most dangerous tendency today—found in the several brands of "literary criticism" and descriptive "linguistics"—consists in annexing a portion, and no more, of the rival discipline. Wellek praises Spitzer's acknowledged willingness to subordinate linguistic goals to those of proper literary elucidation (*explication de textes*). If extended, such an approach could lead to making of that brand of linguistic research (*Stilforschung*) a kind of "literary" linguistics. Conversely, representatives of the Bloomfield tradition have shown willingness to deal with literary texts and their many ramifications only after eliminating much of what, in reality, would make a given discourse "literary." Contextual generation of meanings, unless specifically correlated to grammatical or, perhaps, grammatico-syntactical features, is considered to be an "extralinguistic" process, and therefore ignored. Abernathy's double analogy between, on the one hand, linguistics and organic chemistry and, on the other, poetics and zoology poignantly illustrates this attitude. In short, disciplinary "integrity" remains the ideal, whereas the *realia* that, in the case of poetic usage, cut across such boundaries, are frequently lost in the shuffle. (Sadder still, of course, is the obscurantist attitude of aesthetes who protect spiritual values by cultivating their impressions and by refusing on principle any organized, scientific formulations whatsoever.) Poetics or literary criticism should not open its doors to linguistic methods and goals only to close them again after assimilating what could be annexed without fear of "contamination." Nor should linguistics attempt to preserve its scientific status by serenely closing its eyes to whole areas of language reality. Contacts between the two approaches must be cultivated with a view to transforming both, probably on levels higher than each, in hardcore form, is accustomed to operate.

The "anarchy" prevailing in contemporary linguistic and literary research is nevertheless more apparent than real. Despite divergencies in outlook, the spirit of unity lies at the very heart of our modern theories of language and expression. One should realize that, by now, "linguistics" and "literary criticism" are both best defined as "modes of approach." This *fact* characterizes all styles of investigation and has come to outweigh in importance what these "modes of approach" were originally intended to imply. Realities of language may indeed be profitably viewed through disciplinary prisms, but nobody seriously considers the results of such an examination as an absolute expression of that reality. It is the purposefulness and relevance of the viewing that count. A number of scholars have realized this important point. Their work—and I have tried to point to specific examples in recent scholarship —proves that the quantity and the quality of such experimentation in America since World War II have been impressive. At this juncture I should like to ask—and tentatively answer —this question: To what extent and by what means may the relations between literary and linguistic study be further systematized in order to reflect still more accurately the intellectual requirements of our time?

Structure

During the twentieth century, structuralist formulations common to literary study and linguistic analysis have provided grounds on which practitioners of these activities could meet without losing their separate disciplinary identity. Interdisciplinary concepts like that of "style" have also brought scholars together. When taken in the essentially synchronic, Prague school sense, with connotations at once psychological and "objectively" graphic, the notion of "structure" has encouraged representations that effectively communicate one's understanding of linguistic and literary operations. "Structure" also provides categories that, on certain levels, comprise relationships between such operations. There have been "closed" as well as "open-ended" structuralisms, as we saw. Structural configurations remain gratuitous, however. In reality they inhere neither in novels nor in languages. They translate the scholar's "interpretation" of the "language" or the "novel" and, in a sense, are designed to depict graphically the relevance of the interpretation. Yet structuralist thought is invariably linked to wider ideological assumptions.

The effects of structuralism have been very beneficial. The Prague school doctrines of "poetic" and "literary" language, for example, have hardly been exhausted by scholars concerned with questions of literary form and expression. Structuralism offered the first comprehensive and pertinent framework for expressing objectively—in "patterns"—human activity concerned with "signs" for their own sake. It was—and is—the active branch of the semiotic it purports to formulate.

Yet one need merely contrast the "structuralism" of a Wellek with that of a Jakobson to point out the vulnerability of their approaches. Wellek admits that literary works are structures of linguistic signs—as does Jakobson—but Wellek, understandably, is unwilling to deny even temporarily his aesthetic formalism. Wellek's "literary work" is conceived monumentally, as a thing-in-itself, in an a priori formalistic way. His structuralism is placed at the service of a "literature" abstracted out of time and space. The concept of "literature" is retained, but the preservation is arbitrary. Jakobson, of course, is less concerned with the notion of literature as such, but, as Wellek points out in *Style in Language,* his linguistic point of view threatens to dissolve literature into the broader, but equally *abstract,* theory of signs. What is properly "literary" is shunted aside by linguists who operate, *as linguists,* with literary discourse. Furthermore, the constructs with which structuralism usually works are of the broadest sort and often are methodologically incompatible with the details that constitute much of the charm, and value, of literature.

During the nineteenth century, we recall, students of both language and literature dealt with essentially historical concepts. History was usually interpreted as a chain of causes and effects, and often, under the influence of the biological sciences, in a deterministic way. Twentieth-century structuralism constitutes a reaction against such historicism and the "abuses" committed in its name. (Claude Lévi-Strauss' refutation of Lévy-Bruhl is a classic example of such a reaction.) The earliest proponents of what would eventually become structuralism, however, endeavored to reconcile their new "psychological" orientation with the best of the earlier historicisms. Thus, Sapir, in this country, reinterpreted language phenomena in terms of structures—his "phonetic system," for example, is virtually a later generation's "phonemic inventory." But Sapir also took stock of "drift," that is, of linguistic structures *evolving,* not suddenly "readjusting," over time. The temporal dimension of "becoming" was retained. Furthermore, Sapir, as we saw, employed the notion of "culture" in order to reconcile the individual creator and the society in which he lived, their "language" and his use of it. "Culture," in Sapir's sense, offered a means of relating, dialectically, poetic creativity and linguistic form, in history—either diachronically or synchronically.

Later structuralists abandoned history or rather reduced historical concepts to the state of pure analytic categories. There is nothing really historical about Prague school diachronic phonology, for example, unless one accepts the fact that linguistic systems exist in a very abstract "becoming." Sound changes occur and are "handled" by the system which "immediately" adjusts itself accordingly. History becomes a lifeless metaphor. It has been so utterly taken for granted that "historical" phenomena are dealt with entirely in terms of analytic categories dependent not on a genuine historical viewpoint but rather on attitudes proper to the discipline itself. Analogously, New Criticism also disavowed "history." Dante, Donne, Pascal, and Milton are authentic "contemporaries." Culture is abstracted out of the historical dimension.

Nevertheless, the proliferation of "viewpoints"—some quite arbitrary—in both linguistics and literary criticism has led, as I remarked earlier, to a new sense of purposefulness in research. What counts is the activity expended in scholarly work and its "relevance." Structuralist formulations place a premium on interpretation; the nature of the "reality" studied is itself transformed by such interpretation. One must judge whether the transformation is useful or not. The activity is thus evaluated for its own sake and in terms of its capacity for generating constructive enthusiasm and similar activity in other persons. The scholarly attitude latent in what I have called structuralism reflects a very liberally conceived freedom; one has faith in enlightened opinion rather than in a priori system. This is pure modernism, if one will, the logical conclusion of a way of thinking whose roots go back to the Renaissance. Thus, it seems that, at this point in time, the genuine efficacy of a general theory of language in the Platonic, Aristotelian, or even Cartesian sense can no longer be counted on. Yet elements of what might be called the Platonic, the Aristotelian, or the Cartesian traditions constantly reappear in the coherent *attitudes*—not systems—that summarize modern thought on language.

Let me illustrate this point. Jerrold J. Katz's recent *The Philosophy of Language* (New York, 1966) rejects the purely empirical, behavioristic view of language acquisition, and the taxonomic (Bloomfieldian) structuralism that accompanies it. Katz defends the generative grammar of Chomsky, a new "structuralism" based, we recall, on rationalist theory of conceptualization—innate ideas. He declares that "the genetic endowment of a human being qua human being is the only invariant feature of language acquisition contexts which can causally account for nonverbal infants achieving a successful internalization of languages having the universal properties described in the theory of language" (p. 273). Cartesian doctrine "works." What about the question of a priori knowledge? Discussing this question, Katz hits on the essence of structuralist freedom: its "objectivity" and the nature of the "informed opinion" on which its statements are based: "That any particular one of the principles in the theory of language is a priori is, then, a consequence of the empirical success of the explanation of language acquisition which employs it *and so accords it the status of an innate principle*" (p. 282, italics mine). Evidence contradicting the innate principle, as stated, merely leads to the formulation of a better "innate principle." What is important here, then, is the *activity* Katz associates with "philosophy." Rejecting one brand of structuralism thus provides a way of remaining faithful to the spirit animating earlier structuralist research, that is, to relevance and the best informed opinion.

Now then, in connection with what I have said regarding Wellek's aesthetic and recalling Sapir's more broadly based evaluation of literature and language, one wonders whether the "dignity" of literature might not be better and more pertinently served by replacing the arbitrary identification of literature with aesthetic by a more stringently defined concept of culture. The "freeing of poetry" from dependence on language—i.e., the old rhetoric—is simply no longer applicable today, as Wellek himself, in criticizing Coleridge, half admits. Hegel's distinction between the "accidental externality" (*accidentellere Aeusserlichkeit*) of language and the "inner representation" that is the soul of poetry, whatever its validity, runs totally counter to the means we have of approaching poetry— means that must themselves involve language. I do not intend to imply that Jakobson's technical structuralism—his semiotic —is sufficiently broad to embrace literature adequately; its use, as he himself realized, is primarily scientific, or provisional. It offers remarkably useful techniques of analysis, suitable for the gathering and classification of information concerning—in Prague Circle terms—"poetic" and "literary" language. But much of what literature is escapes such analysis, as Wellek correctly states. "Culture," however, in Sapir's sense, is a more dynamic concept and is, I think, essentially more relevant to literature than either "semiotic" or "aesthetic." It allows for the reincorporation of authentic history into the discussion of literature. This, of course, is the sense of literary tradition in Western civilization. To take two extreme examples, both Dante and Rousseau in their works participate in a context that is more adequately described as cultural than philosophical, and, formally, their works are essentially literary. Yet one is quite justified in speaking of Rousseau in aesthetic terms, whereas such is hardly the case with Dante.

Culture

In Chapter One of this study I discussed at some length both Dante and Rousseau, in particular their stress of the symbolic functions of language, the one within the old traditionalism of medieval Europe, the other within the "historical" context of the Enlightenment. Each wrote about language and each saw clearly the importance of articulating a coherent view of language in terms of the possibilities open to him. Both illustrate the Western tendency to associate a theory of language with broad intellectual constructs—a world-view, a "philosophy," a coherent sense of reality. Yet our review—in Chapter Two—of the disciplinary activities that grew out of modernist thought and that deal with language and literature showed, in this country and abroad, the emergence of a tendency to consider linguistic theory as the cornerstone on which to base the active participation in reality that modern intellectual creativity in all humanistic domains seems to demand. Linguistic theory provides objective corollaries for that creativity, since, in effect, it can be construed as *constituting* the theory of creativity. The following passage from J. J. Katz's *The Philosophy of Language* illustrates this tendency. (Other texts could have been used, but this one is as clear as any):

> The theory of language is a statement of linguistic universals, i.e., of features that all natural languages have in common. It formulates the principles that determine the necessary form and content of natural languages and defines the notion 'natural language.' From the viewpoint of linguistics, the theoretical constructions in a theory of language are devised to provide the apparatus for representing features that are invariant from natural language to natural language. From the viewpoint of my approach to the philosophy of language, on the other hand, these theoretical constructions provide the apparatus for constructing solutions to philosophical problems. Accordingly, unlike the linguist who asks only whether these constructions are adequate to

serve the scientific function for which they were intended, the philosopher of language must also ask whether they meet the conditions for solutions to philosophical problems. Hence, if there are theoretical constructions in the theory of language that do meet the conditions for the solution to some philosophical problem, and if their empirical support in terms of linguistic evidence is strong enough, then these constructions must be an acceptable solution to the philosophical problem [pp. x f.].

One recognizes in these words certain fundamental problems that have repeatedly cropped up in our previous discussions. Katz is committed to "objective truth"—e.g., "solutions" of philosophical difficulties—but his commitment is matched by the awareness that his—and others'—activity in such matters is primary. The framing of solutions is symbolic of his activity and so must be judged in terms of their disciplinary relevance, i.e., their results with respect to the "philosophical" activity of others. Though entitled *The Philosophy of Language* Katz's work is first and foremost a "philosophy of philosophy." Consequently, his stress on language and linguistics is doubly significant. First, linguistic "production" is linked to human creativity, and second, the study of language provides the paradigm for all formal inquiry into the nature and purpose of such creativity. Aristotelian "analysis" is thus subsumed into, and governed by, Platonic "symbolism," but the latter is nevertheless "controlled" by the former, since, I repeat, Katz's discipline is "philosophy." As we saw, Katz proposed a "structure" of language acquisition which, in his view, accounted more adequately than other proposals for the nature of this phenomenon. His structure posits the existence of innate ideas—or rather depicts a mechanism depending on such ideas—and, as he points out, this structure leads to empirical success in coping with myriad questions—hence its "validity."

It is no exaggeration to say that the proliferation of modern "approaches" to reality has generated, in our day, a new sign-oriented culture. Katz's "disciplinary relevance" has important cultural ramifications. Whatever the outlook implied and whatever the nature of the activity, contemporary intellectual endeavor focuses upon signs and their ordering. Instead of the received grammatical tradition operative in the Middle Ages, however, our cultural ambiance requires actively *created* grammars, i.e., principles of order analogous, for the purposes of empirical analysis, to those we "discover" in language. These "grammars" vary from the specialized nomenclatures and syntaxes of the several sciences to the private rhetorics of poets and certain philosophers. The kind of truth available to a philosopher like Katz differs from that available to a poet like Wallace Stevens only in the degrees of analysis and synthesis appropriate to the discourse within which each works. By understanding their respective "grammars" one grasps the identity—or lack of identity—of their intuitions. Profound differences are a matter of assumptions rooted either in conviction or in history. The *fact* of grammar underlies all discourse, we know, but our techniques for dealing with the actualization—the hows and whys—of these principles in usage have remained rudimentary.

Dante identified the principles that support his poetry with the Illustrious Vulgar. One is tempted to revise structuralist theory and to conclude that, though all sign systems possess a certain degree of "literature," it is convenient, from the viewpoint of analysis, to associate "literature" with discourse that calls attention to the ways general grammatical possibilities are worked out in combination. In the long run, I believe, Wellek's criterion of "fictionality" (*Theory of Literature*) is less satisfactory than this one, since it does not provide for the incontrovertible fact that Rousseau's *Confessions* or *Discours sur l'inégalité* are, in this sense, just as "fictional" as his *Nouvelle Héloïse.* Our concept, the pure linguist might object, enlarges excessively the notion of "grammar." This objection must be met by citing once again the nature of the modern approach to literature—what is common to all modern approaches to literature and, for that matter, to reality—namely, that in the grammatical order of language one discovers analogs of order that permit our dealing pertinently with literature. It will not do to confuse the issue, however. Literature is "of" and "in" language in a far deeper sense than, for example, sculpture is in stone. The student of literature must operate with sign relationships that are themselves based not only on linguistic "raw material" (English, French, Latin) but also include other components: generic structures, social and psychological contexts, values, etc. The heat of Rousseau's convictions and the profundity of Dante's religious faith constitute important factors of their writings, because these writers worked them into the fabric of their art. Conversely, Aristotle's religious convictions are a matter of little concern to the logician who takes no interest in Aristotle's work *as literature.* The *Divine Comedy* poeticizes Dante's experience and the spoken language of his time. What commands our attention is precisely the poetic process, how the grammaticalization is achieved, how it functions, and what relevance may be ascribed to it.

Just as no "complete" description of any natural language will ever be composed, so, in a similar framework, no "total criticism" of Dante is possible. But one hopes for relevant descriptions of linguistic process, and analogously one should hope for pertinent literary analysis. The language of literary criticism must be sufficiently powerful to formulate analytic categories that convey adequately the grammatical relationships symbolizing, in texts, the poet's creativity, i.e., his *use* of language. It is in his use of language—the concrete texts— that the poetic process finally occurs.

Literature, I have suggested, participates more directly in Western culture than any other form of discourse; this has been traditionally so and, I think, remains so today. (A scientific experiment or a syllogism may be extrapolated out of time and space with less damage than a poem, play, or novel.) The reason lies in what constitutes literature, namely, its calling the reader's attention to its own organization. Literary discourse is thus by nature linguistically symbolic. When it is made to yield to an analytic control based on other forms of discourse, it merely serves "philosophy," "science," or "history," and it suffers accordingly. We observed that Dante was himself clearly aware of the symbolic nature of poetry. Consequently, the variety of forms, of aspirations, and of experiences that constitute culture appear, in literary discourse, in their purest form. Our basic myths and deepest social and ethical attitudes, with all their contradictions, constitute the very stuff of literature. This is why, despite the "self-centeredness" of literary discourse, we willingly associate the literary with the real. Until the eighteenth century, the close relationship of literature and culture was usually taken for granted, but with the advent of modernity this relationship too became problematic. It is only recently that it has become imperative to restate the relationship cogently. In my opinion, a general reformulation of the dialectic between literary expression and cultural value leading to meaningful analysis may be based on linguistic categories.

In such a reformulation "language" ostensibly plays two distinct parts. Linguistic usage—discourse—in literary forms incarnates cultural process; linguistic "form," that is, language grasped by means of formal analysis, provides the necessary categories on which to base one's approach. The student must be thoroughly grounded in the techniques of formal analysis not, however, merely in order to "apply" them, but rather in order to grasp fully the *possibilities* they contain. No "school" of linguistic research is in and of itself sufficient. On the other hand, the modern experience of linguistic investigation, in all its dazzling variety, offers truly relevant points of departure. Not least among the advantages is the one stressed by a number of the scholars whose work I referred to above, that by definition linguistic research—activity—is cumulative. The principle of collective study is built into its techniques. Yet the stress upon usage as such remains basic. To penetrate the symbolic constructs that constitute the essence of literature it is not enough to describe, no matter how elegantly, purely formal patterns. If, as Jakobson reminds us, all discourse is purposeful, it is above all the symbolic purpose of the literary text that claims the student's attention, the dynamic operations governed by the play of provisionally isolable "components" that, in given contexts, may include such varied matters as rhyme, theme, characters, situations, images, and the like. The list is endless. Prior judgments are virtually useless, since, until one knows what one is about, what may seem transparent in a given literary work actually may turn out to be a matter of great complexity. Conversely, what seems at first glance to be hermetic may, in reality, constitute a means of achieving clarity.

I have insisted on "culture" as process, because, quite obviously, a static view of culture is of little use. We remember the case of Rousseau. His lexical and syntactic innovations, when compared to a statically viewed "French language," are quite restricted. However, given the expressive goals of the *philosophes* of his day, Rousseau, in contrast, is revolutionary. His usage is totally innovatory; he mythologizes, in aesthetic terms, the analytic categories of Enlightenment thought and discourse. But, when dealing with processes, it is clear that exhaustive discussions are out of the question. Thus, whereas it is theoretically possible to list all the neologisms introduced into eighteenth-century French usage, it is quite impossible— and pointless—even to suggest all the cultural implications present in a given literary work. (Just as no phonetician would dream of describing "all" the phonic shadings of the English phoneme /i/ as actually pronounced.) One selects one's corpus—the text or texts, or the problem—and one works with it; one's activity is then to be judged according to its *degree of relevance.* Close examination, say, of the tense structure in a medieval Romance poem may lead to statements deepening our understanding of verbal constructions, of narrative techniques, and of the sense of reality that poem depicts, in very concrete terms (e.g., Stephen Gilman's *Tiempo y formas temporales en el "Poema del Cid"* [Madrid, 1961]). Similarly, when brought to bear in cogent ways upon certain texts, the analysis of a mythic construct—like that of *l'amour-passion* in Denis de Rougemont's *L'Amour et l'occident* (1939)—may well illuminate relevant features of the texts and their language. The ultimate exhaustiveness of such studies will be determined by the light they shed on the nature and quantity of the expressive possibilities open to the culture—or cultures—that may be involved.

Linguistics and Literary Theory

In the middle section of Chapter Two of this report, I suggested that perhaps we may be justified in looking into the possibilities of a new trivium—a new theory of language, including a grammar, a rhetoric, and a dialectic suitable to our age. The detailed elaboration of such a theory obviously lies beyond the scope of this volume. However, the thesis of this review has been that the history of our attitudes toward language—of our most fundamental linguistic assumptions—does not tolerate, for long, the fragmented concepts that at times have emerged. Furthermore, as one takes stock of recent developments in literary theory, philosophy, and linguistics, even in America, where specialization is usually a matter of course, one is struck by an identity of values, techniques, and aspirations. We have noticed the fundamental importance of grammatical research in all fields concerned with signs; we have seen an increased willingness on the part of scholars to pay closer attention to real usage, to language in all its vitality; finally, I have tried to hint at the necessarily close relationship between philosophical assumptions and both linguistic science and literary theory—a relationship that scholars of widely differing intellectual persuasions are more and more apt to admit today.

If, as I have inferred, the broadest context for discussion of the operations most intimately connected with such a unified view of language is that of cultural process, it follows that, so far as literary criticism and linguistics are concerned, the most fertile area of cooperation must, at least initially, be that offered by history. The revitalization of linguistic and literary history has become imperative in our day. The very concept of cultural process entails the notion of history. Our interests have progressed beyond the practical philological questions that legitimately claimed the lion's share of nineteenth-century research in the field, and, for that matter, so have our techniques and our ways of looking at things. However, surely, we must sharpen our tools and our vision by submitting them to the exacting task of interpreting meaningfully the dynamic and real dialectic between linguistic usage at its most interesting, or purest, and the possibilities open to that usage. We certainly stand to learn a considerable amount about "creativity" by looking closely and appropriately at "creation." That—it seems to me—is the irreducible truth of the humanist's position. The workings of creativity may be delineated in the constitution of an Old Spanish "word family" as pertinently as in the complexities of a Baroque lyric; in both cases language is directly involved and the same analytic principles apply. At this point, I hope, I should not have to dwell on the numerous and marvelous implications that naturally derive from such study.

More difficult perhaps, but none the less challenging, is the very difficult problem of assembling the results of individual investigations into larger, but meaningful, historical constructs. The dangers of abstraction and distortion are great. There are no built-in safeguards. The theory of "literary" and "linguistic" history must therefore itself be formulated as work along these lines is accomplished or as what already has been done is rendered explicitly illustrative of the kind of cooperation I have discussed. Meanwhile "essays" in the field are very much to the point.

Let me conclude these somewhat scattered remarks by stating that I am fully aware of the insufficient "coverage" I have given to the many topics treated here. Though I have tried to provide a historical sketch, I have done so in order to point out certain theoretical ramifications of the tendencies and modes discussed. I am also aware that many of my colleagues —linguists and literary scholars—do not share my optimism, nor, in some cases, my enthusiasm. Quite possibly, many will feel obliged to reject my conclusions and, perhaps, the premises—historical and other—on which they are based. That is how it should be. Only when discussion occurs may deficient thinking be remedied and more adequate perspectives formulated. Indeed, one may be thankful that the intellectual climate now prevailing in the United States favors the free discussion of ideas concerning language and literature and is willing to take such discussion seriously.

INDEX

I wish to record my gratitude to Mr. Drake G. Cook (Princeton, '69) for his invaluable assistance in compiling this Index.